Six Men Who Built the Modern Auto Industry

Six Men Who Built the Modern Auto Industry

Richard A. Johnson

MOTORBOOKS

First published in 2005 by Motorbooks, an imprint of MBI Publishing Company, Galtier Plaza, Suite 200, 380 Jackson Street, St. Paul, MN 55101-3885 USA

Motorbooks titles are also available at discounts in bulk quantity for industrial or sales-promotional use. For details write to Special Sales Manager at MBI Publishing Company, Galtier Plaza, Suite 200, 380 Jackson Street, St. Paul, MN 55101-3885 USA.

ISBN 0-7603-1958-8

Editorial: Rob Golding, Scott Pearson, Mark Yost
Designer: LeAnn Kuhlmann

Printed in the United States of America

Front Cover: The six men—Henry Ford II *Ford Motor Company Limited*, Soichiro Honda *Honda Motor Company*, Lee Iacocca *Lee Iacocca*, Eberhard von Kuenheim *BMW AG*, Bob Lutz *Bob Lutz*, and Ferdinand Piëch *Ferdinand Piëch collection.*

Contents

CHAPTER ONE

The Starting Pistol

L ee Iacocca didn't slam the door as he stormed out of Henry Ford II's office on July 13, 1978, after being fired as president of Ford Motor Company. But there still was a big bang so forceful that it shaped the global automotive industry for the next quarter century.

Within just a few months, Iacocca would go head-to-head with the 61-year-old Ford—as head of Chrysler Corporation. In time, Iacocca would lure dozens of Ford executives to the crosstown rival and instill in the No. 3 automaker Ford's lofty business culture. Among those Iacocca would steal from Ford was an ex–U.S. Marine fighter pilot named Bob Lutz, a Swiss-American whom Ford had hired away from BMW in 1974.

Ten years later, a miracle would occur at Chrysler. All of the wisdom of the post-war automotive industry would come together in the person of Lutz. He had absorbed all of the auto industry's post-World War II lessons and combined them perfectly into the culture and products of one company.

In the early 1970s, Lutz had learned about brand management from Eberhard von Kuenheim at BMW. Indeed, von Kuenheim was the man who mastered the art of prosperity at an auto company. And though many saw him as a servant of BMW's controlling family, he was very much his own man when it came to managing BMW's phenomenally successful enterprise.

Rounding out his resume, Lutz learned product packaging and high-stakes marketing from Iacocca. At Ford, Henry II's "Whiz Kids" analysts had taught Lutz the equally important lessons of cost discipline.

When Lutz arrived at Chrysler, he also drew upon the well-established genius of Soichiro Honda, studying and copying the best of Honda Motor Company's product development processes, which had been revolutionary in more ways than one. In the 1950s and 1960s, Japan's culture was one of consensus and homogeneity. Furthermore, it wasn't the most likely place to look for an industry maverick. But Soichiro Honda was a unique individual—not just in his vigorous and eccentric personal life, but in the way he took the largest motorcycle business in the world and turned it into one of the most innovative carmakers.

Ferdinand Piëch was a twentieth-century version of the great nineteenth-century mechanical minds that founded the automobile industry. As a young man, the socially awkward German was the technical inspiration at Porsche. Ford, Iacocca, and Lutz had all marveled at Piëch's work. Not coincidentally, Piëch also turned to Honda when masterminding the rebirth of Audi.

How do you put a personal stamp on a $1 trillion industry that produces 60 million vehicles annually and employs over four million people around the world? It takes thousands of engineers, designers, and product planners to develop each new model. Thousands more are needed to bring a new vehicle to market. While each person makes a qualitative contribution to the entire process, each is also capable of screwing it up. The complexity is endless—the risks and rewards almost unfathomable.

This is the story of a half-dozen extraordinary men who—against all odds—transformed the seemingly immutable automotive world. What makes their success even more remarkable is that while individual entrepreneurs, designers, and engineers could change the course of an industry in the first half of the twentieth century, it was a much more daunting task in the second half. The automotive industry had become a mature, entrenched business with the fundamental technology and basic vehicle concepts well established. Not only was it harder to change, but the risks of failure were greater than ever before. In this environment it took a new kind of genius to effect fundamental change.

So how did Soichiro Honda, Henry Ford II, Lee Iacocca, Eberhard von Kuenheim, Robert Lutz, and Ferdinand Piëch cast such long shadows? With brains, bravery, charisma, luck, vision, a gift of prophecy, and an inspired choice of colleagues. Add one more important ingredient for success: giant egos. A massive sense of self is the price of admission to the master class, and they all had it.

When the time came for them to acknowledge that they had made their mark and that it was time to go—some of them got it wrong. Henry Ford II misjudged the threat from the Japanese and allowed innovative vehicles conceived at Ford to be built elsewhere—probably costing the No. 2 automaker its last chance to catch General Motors. Iacocca, the hero of Chrysler, allowed himself to be talked into a misguided attempt at a hostile takeover by a corporate raider—after taking his pension from the company. Von Kuenheim pushed through BMW's ill-advised acquisition of Rover in 1994, then meddled with Bernd Pischetsrieder's management of the British company. After retiring as CEO of Volkswagen, Piëch was accused of interfering with his successor.

In retrospect, all six men were too human and all too capable of making big mistakes. But they had breathed life into an industry that in many ways had grown stale. So complete was their involvement, so convinced were they of their own self-importance, that it was difficult for them to let go.

And their impact on the industry was so great that there is no end to stories of how their moves affected the careers of others. For instance, Bob Lutz's aerodynamic 1982 Ford Sierra was so revolutionary that it shook up the entire European auto industry, including rival General Motors Europe. In response, GM chose a radical design for its next big-volume model—the 1985 Opel Kadett. The small Opel's shapely exterior set it far apart from the competition and put GM on a higher product plane. The move also put GM on a growth curve that reached its peak in the late 1980s and early 1990s. Furthermore, the resounding success of the Opal Kadett elevated several American executives who just happened to be assigned to GM Europe and who would—in their own way—make their own mark. Among this group was GM Europe President Jack Smith, his chief financial officer, Rick Wagoner, and Smith's successor as head of GM Europe, Bob Eaton. Perhaps an even greater testament to Lutz's impact on the industry is the fact that following his move to the United States soon after the Sierra debuted, Ford of Europe reversed course on innovative design and was more conservative through the remainder of the 1980s.

Smith and Wagoner, of course, went to the very top of GM, with Wagoner eventually succeeding Smith as chairman and CEO. To bring the whole saga full circle, in 2001 Wagoner lured a 69-year-old Lutz out of retirement and brought him to GM. In between, Eaton was Lutz's boss at Chrysler. All the result of Lutz's 1982 Ford Sierra redesign.

Of course, other events have helped to shape the auto industry over the past 30 years. But the one constant has been the presence of one of these six men.

THE YEAR 1971 was a watershed year for the modern automobile industry. America was facing a kaleidoscope of government-mandated vehicle safety and emissions requirements that would soon spread across the globe. Within two years, fuel prices would skyrocket, and the look, feel, and price of automobiles would change forever. Every manufacturer would have to rethink the vehicles and engines they produced and sold. Only the cleverest would survive.

But more than economic and regulatory forces were at work in 1971. An extraordinary coincidence occurred, in which these six men arrived simultaneously in positions of dominance at a time when external forces were demanding internal change.

Had other leaders emerged, the car business might have become a jumble of weak producers controlled by price-cutting retailers. Or it may have evolved along the lines of the personal-computer industry, a cartel of two or three manufacturers that dominate simply through production and distribution efficiency. No one knows. But one thing's for certain: the auto industry would likely be vastly different today if it were not for these six key men. Without Henry Ford II, Ford Motor Company would have been squashed by General Motors, leaving behind an American automobile industry even fatter and more complacent than it was when European—and later, Japanese importers— entered the U.S. market.

Chrysler would have vanished in the early 1980s without Lee Iacocca. Or it would have disappeared in the early 1990s if not for Lutz.

Without Eberhard von Kuenheim, BMW would have surrendered its independence, and the industry would have been bereft of its most daring idioms for driving dynamics, electronics, and brand appeal.

Without Ferdinand Piëch, Porsche would have been swallowed up at its weakest moment—in the early 1990s. Without Soichiro Honda, the Japanese automotive industry would have been vastly different from the one we know today.

While each played their own unique role, it's clear that Soichiro Honda was the intellectual and spiritual godfather of the group. Honda Motor Company had built cars for less than a decade, but by 1971 it was selling tens of thousands of four-wheel vehicles outside Japan. Three years before, Honda invaded Volkswagen's German market with his N600, a small car with an engine only a third the size of the Beetle's.

The little Honda was shown at the Paris, London, and Los Angeles auto shows and generated almost as much talk as Honda's motorcycles had in years past. At the Paris show, even the most protectionist statesmen stopped to see it.

"Oh, the new Honda," said President Charles de Gaulle.

Back at Honda's technical center in Wako, Japan, history was being made. In early 1971, a small task force set up two years earlier to research and develop a low-emissions engine was beginning to produce results. The team of eight brilliant young engineers had come from Honda's fledgling Formula One team, and several of them would later become Honda's top executives. They developed a low-emissions powerplant called the "compound vortex controlled combustion (CVCC) engine." By the following spring, the team had a prototype ready for testing by the U.S. Environmental Protection Agency. The CVCC met the United States' stringent new anti-pollution standards two years before they became law and 10 years before any other manufacturer could do the same.

The first payoff was at home. As fuel prices soared, Japanese domestic car sales plunged 40 percent in the first quarter of 1974. Yet because of the CVCC, Honda's sales increased 76 percent over the previous year.

As a result of his innovative thinking, Soichiro Honda's engine indirectly brought about Lee Iacocca's downfall as president of Ford Motor Co. In 1975, Iacocca spent a festive two days as Soichiro's personal guest in Tokyo. Iacocca was in a terrific mood as the men shared gifts, sake, and stories. Honda even put on a fireworks display for the Ford president. Iacocca was delighted. While in Tokyo, he'd swung the deal that he was sure would give Ford a crucial advantage over General Motors in the small-car wars that had come to Detroit in the wake of the first OPEC oil crisis.

His mood would be shattered a few days later at Ford's "Glass House" headquarters in Dearborn, Michigan. Iacocca strode into

Henry Ford II's office to lay out his plan to buy 300,000 units of the CVCC engine for installation in Ford's Fiesta. It was a lifesaver, Iacocca said. But Ford stopped Iacocca in mid-sentence: "No car with my name on the hood will ever have a Jap engine," he bellowed.

Iacocca was dumbstruck. He knew this was the beginning of the end for him at Ford. Yet he had been inspired by Honda's maverick ways. Iacocca saw that Honda was the antithesis in a country where hierarchy was holy, education sacrosanct, and respect for authority paramount. Although Honda had little formal education, he had an uncanny knack for being able to draw brilliant young disciples from Japan's less prestigious colleges and set them to work on impossible tasks—and they would succeed.

Honda also fought Japan's zaibatsu corporate networks even though it cost him the support of the country's traditional bankers, who several times threatened to kill his business. Like Ford, Honda came of age during World War II. He saw death and destruction on a scale that the serious young executives who followed never experienced. And as much as Honda was a tireless worker, he was also a tireless drinker and womanizer for much of his life. To Honda, pleasure was as important as work, and that spirit influenced his products.

Henry Ford II turned 54 in the autumn of 1971, a time when he began shifting his attention outside the United States. Four years earlier, Ford had ordered the integration of the company's once scattered and openly competitive European operations. Now he was in search of European companies to buy. He had all but wrapped up a deal to acquire Ferrari in 1963 when Fiat used its influence with Enzo Ferrari to kill it. Fiat eventually bought control of the sports car company itself. Ford still ached for a famous European brand with a racing heritage. He wanted to make tiny Porsche a jewel in his Ford empire, but young Ferdinand Piëch, then running his family's sports car company's racing department, was dead set against it. Piëch's 917 was already beating Ford's GT40 on the track. Why did Porsche need Ford? Ford had once courted Soichiro Honda's fledgling motorcycle and car company, too. But mostly he wanted BMW. In 1971, Henry Ford made the first of what would be many offers—usually casual, always courteous, but very serious. He would never miss an opportunity to declare his interest to von Kuenheim and BMW's owner, Herbert Quandt. After Quandt died, Ford made his polite pleas to Quandt's widow, Johanna. The Quandts and von Kuenheim always turned him down. It became a kind of joke whenever Ford paid a courtesy call on the Quandts.

"Now, Henry I know why you are here," Johanna Quandt scolded Ford when he arrived at her estate in Bad Homburg.

Lee Iacocca was 46 in 1971 and was consolidating his power as the president of Ford—a job he had taken over less than a year earlier. Iacocca had spent his entire career in the United States and was still learning about the company's European empire. In the summer of 1971, he appointed a trusted top lieutenant, Harold "Hal" Sperlich, to oversee Ford in Europe and was himself traveling to the continent more often—usually with Henry Ford II. Iacocca was at the peak of his power at Ford, fully trusted by "the Deuce" (Henry Ford II), who was making his own personal transformation—divorcing his wife and building a European playboy lifestyle, like his friend Gianni Agnelli at Fiat. As Ford stepped back, Iacocca rushed in. In the process, Iacocca seemed to invent modern business charisma. He represented the drive of post-war America and was anxious to reap the fruits of the new prosperity. Iacocca represented the brassy confidence of the nation.

He willed his way to a seat alongside Henry Ford II and built, in time, a horde of followers inside Ford. When Henry turned against him, Iacocca could at least threaten the family's hold on its own company. But he was much more than a corporate infighter. As a young man in the 1950s, he had invented entirely new ways to sell cars. Over a 29-year period that began in 1964 and ended in 1993, Iacocca put more new categories of passenger vehicles on the road than anyone before him—from the Mustang to the minivan.

While all this was going on in Dearborn, Eberhard von Kuenheim, 43, was busy mapping out the future of BMW. A little-known machine-tool executive, he was named chairman of BMW's management board in 1970 by financier Herbert Quandt, BMW's controlling shareholder. Quandt installed him over the popular and talented head of sales and marketing, Paul Hahnemann. The appointment stunned company insiders and worried BMW's growing legions of fans. Hahnemann called von Kuenheim's appointment "the most expensive apprentice-ship in the world." But by the summer of 1971, von Kuenheim was in the process of ousting Hahnemann and enticing a tough, impressive 39-year-old sales-and-marketing executive from General Motors' Adam Opel subsidiary to replace him. That man was Bob Lutz.

Along the way, von Kuenheim took one of Europe's weakest car companies and transformed it into one of the world's strongest by the turn of the century. Indeed, no car brand traveled further in public esteem than did BMW under von Kuenheim. He ignored the German seniority system, put young men in top jobs, and built the first luxury youth brand in the industry. No executive ever trained so many future leaders of car companies. As a result, no single man could claim greater influence on the industry at the dawn of the twenty-first century. He believed deeply in the value of electronics in cars, and he believed in manufacturing flexibility as the way to remain small but independent. The industry's most successful firms at the turn of the century would follow von Kuenheim's example.

Soichiro Honda met von Kuenheim in 1971. Their two companies had mirrored each other's progress during the 1960s, each building on their success as motorcycle manufacturers to emerge as producers of passenger cars. In a way, they were both 10-year-old companies. Honda the motorcycle manufacturer began building minicars in 1961. BMW had built its first automobile in 1928, but only became competitive again in 1961 after Quandt rescued the company from bankruptcy, re-energized it, and introduced its model 1500 automobile.

By the mid-1980s, BMW and Honda had become the two most cherished mid-market brands in the car business. Each was the model for the other. Von Kuenheim would often say that Honda was the company he admired most and the only one he could see BMW aligning with. Indeed, the only company BMW ever bought—Britain's Rover Group—had become a Honda dependency by the time the German company acquired control of it in 1993.

Late in 1971, von Kuenheim finally hired Lutz away from General Motors. This was a shock for Opel, which had plans for the young man. Opel's Rekord B was being launched in Nice, France. On the first day of the presentation, reporters filed into the hall. A nervous-looking Opel President Alex Cunningham—later GM's vice chairman—took a seat next to veteran Austrian reporter Georg Auer.

"I hope this presentation will work," he whispered. "This morning, Bob Lutz pushed a letter under my hotel room door. It said: 'Sorry, I had to leave early for Munich. Tomorrow I start my job as BMW's sales vice president.'"

Cunningham had to get the president of Opel Italy to do the presentation. Lutz had been unhappy with the way GM executives in Detroit had treated Opel. He felt the German brand was being starved of the investment and technology it needed to compete with the growing performance levels of German cars.

Meanwhile, Lutz had admired BMW from his perch in Rüsselsheim. Once in Munich, he set about building an image to fit the company's nimble and zippy sport sedans. While von Kuenheim gets the majority of the credit for taking BMW from good to great, it's no coincidence that Lutz was also present at the transformation. Moreover, Lutz set BMW on its decisive path to success in the United States.

One of Lutz's first moves was to kill a plan to "modernize" the company's blue-and-white propeller logo. And he was soon sketching a new car that would become the legendary 6 Series coupe. Had von Kuenheim not hired Lutz in 1971, word of BMW would not have spread as far or as fast. And had Lutz not been exposed to the power and passion in Munich, he would have certainly made less impact at Ford, Chrysler, and, ultimately, General Motors. Indeed, at the end of his career, Lutz would finally get around to teaching the lessons of BMW to GM. He would wean GM from a long period of using ex–diet soda and shampoo marketers to fine-tune the brand appeal of its auto-mobiles. Lutz had not only absorbed von Kuenheim's brand expertise, he also understood Henry Ford II's financial discipline and Iacocca's marketing savvy.

Among the industry leaders, Bob Lutz was the greatest car enthusiast since Soichiro Honda. But he was a great organizer too. Lutz's platform teams at Chrysler combined engineering, design, production, account-ing, and marketing, and took a concept from a blank sheet of paper through the assembly line. This process sped new-model development and improved efficiency.

Much of Chrysler's success came from the fact that under Iacocca and Lutz, the company had studied, dissected, and adopted Honda's ultra-efficient system for producing automobiles. Lutz asked a French engineer named François Castaing to set up the Honda-style teams. He then asked a former Ford finance executive named Tom Sidlik, a mem-ber of Castaing's staff, to implement a cost-control system for Chrysler based on the Ford Whiz Kids' "red book" (so named because of its red three-ring binders). So successful were the cars that poured out of the system that Chrysler became the hottest carmaker in the world.

In 1971, 34-year-old Ferdinand Piëch was looking for a job. Though Piëch was a dazzling technician who had rejuvenated Porsche's racing program, he had just been ordered out of the family business. As Piëch, his siblings, and their cousins squabbled over control of the sports car company, the heads of the clan, Ferry Porsche and Piëch's mother, Louise, abruptly decided that no family member could hold an execu-tive position. (Soichiro Honda had made a similar sensible decision in the 1960s, which was a model for the Porsche and Piëch families.)

In early 1971, Ferdinand Piëch had become technical director of the company, and now he was out. He had expected to spend his entire career in the family firm, but now found himself at a crossroads.

Joachim Zahn, the head of Mercedes-Benz, invited Piëch to Stuttgart to discuss a consulting job. Piëch suggested designing a five-cylinder diesel engine. After he had met the six-month deadline for this project, Zahn asked Piëch to succeed Hans Scherenberg as Mercedes' development chief. When Zahn added that there was no big budget for research and development, Piëch promptly responded: "Then I am the wrong man."

As he cast about, Piëch was anxious to work on something other than performance and racing cars. Gerhard Richard Gumpert, VW's powerful distributor in Italy, organized a brief stay for Piëch at Italdesign, the fledgling independent design studio headed by brilliant stylist Giorgetto Giugiaro. When Piëch came to Italdesign in Turin, the company had just finished developing the first-generation Golf and the gorgeous Scirocco coupe. Piëch spent his time at Italdesign making technical drawings of various mechanical layouts. Every time Giugiaro entered his office, Piëch sprang to attention—like a soldier in front of his general. Giugiaro felt that Piëch's response wasn't called for. For one thing, Piëch was a year older than Giugiaro. Every time the designer said something to Piëch, he wrote it down several times, "until I've fully learned it," Piëch would say.

Piëch moved to Audi-NSU in August 1972 and managed the special projects department. Three years later, in 1975, he was named Audi's head of research and development.

When Piëch joined Audi, it appeared to be just another famous pre-war automotive brand that would not live to see the end of the century. He brought with him a technical fanaticism that was his strength, but which also led him astray.

Piëch was the most magnetic, not to say obsessive, of the six giants. His eccentricity chased away more talented engineers and managers than all the others combined. He questioned every idea ever presented to him. He employed fear and menace as tools—often to his own detriment. Yet he collected as many acolytes as Soichiro Honda.

The room at the top of the modern auto industry is small. The six could not help crashing into one another on a regular basis, and the results were sometimes explosive. They hired, fired, and inspired one another. At times they could all be completely ruthless in the way they treated one another. Ford sponsored Iacocca then sacked him; Lutz managed to penetrate the inner chambers of Ford, Chrysler, GM, and BMW; and Iacocca passed over Lutz as his successor. Also along the way were the expressions of mutual admiration that took the form of offers of merger or acquisition.

At the start of the 1970s, the international auto industry had more questions than answers to multiplying economic and legislative challenges. As the decade came to a close, and as Henry Ford's door swung shut behind the indignant Iacocca, the leadership that would provide answers was in place.

CHAPTER TWO

Henry Ford Moves Out the Mob

By the summer of 1943, Franklin D. Roosevelt and his top officials on the War Production Board had grown impatient with the Ford Motor Company. The problem was the company's inept operation of the B-24 bomber plant in Willow Run, Michigan, a massive factory that only a few months before had been hailed as the foremost symbol of America's Arsenal of Democracy. In September of 1942, Roosevelt had visited the plant—the biggest bomber factory in the world—in an effort to boost Allied morale.

But Willow Run had turned into a national disgrace. It was producing a tiny fraction of the planes it had promised, while other aircraft factories, including those run by General Motors and Chrysler, were churning out war planes at the rate of one an hour. Willow Run was an embarrassment for both Ford and for the United States government. The main problem was that 80-year-old Henry Ford—disabled by two strokes and mentally adrift—was still calling the shots at the company he had founded 40 years earlier. And Willow Run highlighted a much deeper crisis at the Ford Motor Company. Henry Ford's son Edsel, the company's president, had died of stomach cancer earlier that summer, and the founder had reinstated himself as president. The

Roosevelt administration decided there was only one real solution to this desperate problem—Navy Ensign Henry Ford II, the founder's unimposing 25-year-old grandson, who was biding his time at the Great Lakes Naval Training Station near Chicago, awaiting orders for sea duty.

The administration arranged for young Henry to leave the navy and return home. In July, Navy Secretary Frank Knox sent the ensign a letter that read: "You are hereby released from the Navy to get you back to work at the Ford Motor Company." Henry Ford II arrived in Dearborn on August 10 to involve himself in a company that employed 130,000 people in the United States, including 75,000 at the River Rouge plant in Dearborn. But before he could take control, he would have to fight the battle of his life against the dark forces that had taken his family's firm hostage. The final engagement would not take place for two more years, but when it did, young Henry Ford would be ready. His personal D-day was September 21, 1945, when he became president and chief executive officer and began to expel the odious men who had a stranglehold on the company.

Young Henry's first act as president was to fire the man who had protected him as a child, the bow-tied Harry Bennett. Purging the sinister henchman of the aging and out-of-touch Henry Ford I was the harsh entry examination for the young, inexperienced industrialist. Bennett was a pugnacious former boxer and ex-sailor who had seized control of Ford Motor as though it were a borough of New York City and he was the local crime boss. Henry II's rapid consolidation of power in the fall of 1945 was more like an FBI sting operation than a reshuffling of corporate personnel. For months, Henry II had planned the strike. The objective was nothing less than casting out the confederation of thugs, hoodlums, and fixers who—under Bennett's direction—had eaten away at the foundation of a once great automobile manufacturer. It was as though the old man, in keeping with the general petulance he felt about modern times, had decided the firm would not outlive him. He was killing the company as surely as he had brought it to life. But there was no way that Henry II would allow this to happen, and his mission was to revive and rebuild it. It's hard to recall a more heroic act by an overindulged member of third-generation industrial royalty.

The lightning strike by the 27-year-old scion empowered him for a lifetime and gave the Deuce an authority with his family that enabled him to face down Lee Iacocca 33 years later, as well as anyone else who dared oppose him. To the members of the Ford family's third generation, Henry II was as much of a legend as Henry I—and was owed just as much for having saved the company from certain ruin.

For 40 years, Henry Ford II would be the voice of the American auto industry, far better known to the public at large than the gray men who ran General Motors. The origin of his power was his destruction of the old Ford Motor Company and the rebirth of a new one. Harry Bennett ran the 3,000-man Ford "Service Department," a security force that had for many years terrorized Ford employees. It caused hardened factory workers to eat lunch in stony silence for fear that if they were caught gossiping or complaining they would be reported and punished.

To staff the Service Department, Bennett had rounded up ex-criminals and rough-hewn former athletes and various other desperados. Finding refuge in a giant corporation, the drifters were given the task of busting unions and keeping factory workers in line.

Bennett's spies were everywhere. They infiltrated every nook and cranny of the company. During Bennett's years in power, throughout the 1930s and early 1940s, Ford employees avoided being seen in groups or even speaking to one another. Engineers ate lunch at their drafting tables. "It was a brutal operation," Clinton York, a former assembly-line worker at the River Rouge plant in Dearborn, Michigan, told the trade magazine *Automotive News* many years later. "The foremen were sinister. They were always present, and if they saw you going to the restroom, they'd stop you and tell you to return to work." The young Lee Iacocca got a taste of Bennett's world after joining Ford in 1946. Fresh out of Princeton and working as a trainee at the giant Rouge plant, Iacocca wore a badge that read "Administration." To the assembly-line workers, the badge meant he was part of the spy network. Bennett was gone by the time Iacocca arrived, and most of his horde had been dispersed. But some of them slipped back into the ranks. Assembly-line workers still feared the leg-breakers who might lurk in the company's shadows.

For over 20 years, Harry Bennett had been Henry Ford's right-hand man, and for much of that time, Bennett greeted the aging founder each morning and drove him from his mansion, Fair Lane, in Dearborn, Michigan, to the Ford administration building nearby. Along the way, Bennett offered feel-good news from the empire, listened to the old man's ravings and wild opinions rooted in the nineteenth century, and carried out Ford's orders, no matter how preposterous they may have been. He fed the old man's delusions and paranoia—telling the doddering Henry Ford what he wanted to hear. He catered to the boss's rigid anti-Semitism, once attempting to prove that Jews were responsible for the assassination of Abraham Lincoln. When not humoring the chairman, Bennett brutalized executives who fell out of Henry Ford's favor, including the founder's own son—Henry II's father, Edsel Ford. Edsel's widow, Eleanor, believed Harry Bennett had hounded her husband to death through years of harassment and psychological abuse that was approved and even promoted by Henry Ford himself.

Bennett was a brute of a man who kept caged lions in his Ann Arbor, Michigan, mansion and sometimes brought them to work. Guns were his constant playthings. Once, to make a point, he shot a cigar out of a man's mouth. Another time, he blasted a visitor's hat while he held it. Bennett's power derived from Henry Ford's hatred of the industry's growing labor movement—and the founder's delight at the little man's toughness and can-do attitude. But as the Service Department grew in power, it began to sap the strength of the company, undermining Ford's ability to compete with General Motors and other American auto companies. And it was turning the Willow Run bomber plant into a laughing stock.

Still, Henry Ford II's ascension was no foregone conclusion. His father had once complained that nothing could be done about Bennett, and Bennett hardly took Henry II seriously when the young man returned from the navy in 1943. Edsel's son had shown only a rudimentary interest in the family firm after having lived one of the most privileged boyhoods in American history. He seemed in no hurry to make his mark and appeared almost devoid of personal drive. Everything he had done prior to joining the company was tinged with mediocrity. He loafed through Yale and got by in the navy.

"Lard Ass"—the nickname he picked up in prep school and never really shook—was even tossed out of Yale for turning in a paper written by someone else. During a short stint working at the company between college and the navy, Henry II was utterly unimpressive—a good-humored lad who made terrific small talk and put people at ease, but had no obvious aura of command or sense of purpose, or even much interest in the business of automobiles. He seemed no more than a playboy prince-in-waiting.

Like his exact contemporary, John F. Kennedy, Henry II sensed that serious responsibility would be thrust upon him soon enough. He was out to enjoy life before bearing the burden of the company. His upbringing was unlike that of scions of other powerful industrial families of the era. His father was no imperious leader, but a thoughtful, even fragile, man. Edsel Ford did not drill a pseudo-military psyche into Henry Ford II or fuel his competitive fires as Joe Kennedy had done with his boys. The result was that Henry Ford II appeared to be nothing more than a slowly maturing aristocrat inclined to self-gratification rather than self-glorification.

And the image of a slowly maturing aristocrat would in some ways haunt Henry Ford II later in life—after he had fired Lee Iacocca, married for a third time, was arrested for drunk driving, and was sued by a group of stockholders for alleged extravagances. Part of the problem was that, both as a young man and as an old one, he looked the part of the spoiled brat. Henry II had none of JFK's lean attractiveness; he was a large man, stooped and fleshy. He looked weak and spoke with a whiny Midwest accent.

Life magazine observed in 1943 that Henry II had shown "no pronounced aptitude" and showed little chance of "finding himself" any time soon. The second Henry Ford was being profoundly underestimated all around, even by his own family. Yet what was perceived as weakness was a source of strength. To be sure, the world was handed to him on a silver platter. The size of his personal wealth was hard to fathom. It came not only from the Ford side of the family, but from his mother's family, too. If the Ford Motor Company had disappeared one day and its wealth evaporated, Henry Ford II would still have been one of the richest young men in America. He needed the car business less than the car business needed him. The immense financial security left him with little personal ambition, but he was nonetheless a driven young man who was obsessed with his responsibility to his family and to Ford Motor Company.

Six days after Edsel Ford's death, Henry Ford met with Henry II and his brother Benson, 23. The two young men spoke for the 41.9 percent of shares that had been held by their father. Old Henry informed the young men that he would take over as president himself, which was tantamount to giving the job to Harry Bennett. Edsel had held the title since 1919, but wielded no power. Henry was 79 and had suffered strokes in 1938 and 1941, but was worried that his grandchildren weren't experienced enough to take over the company should he die. The decision to retake the president's job stunned Henry I's longtime production chief, Charles Sorensen. The legendary "Cast Iron Charlie" knew better than anyone that the old man was not up to running the company and that as he continued to decline Bennett would gain even more influence. The decision also worried Detroit industrialists who feared Ford would go bankrupt and destroy the local economy. And it had a sobering effect on the Roosevelt administration. Official Washington was anxious about the sad state of affairs at Willow Run. The president pushed for Henry's release from the navy so that he could return to Dearborn and take charge of the company.

Not much could be expected of Henry Ford II in August 1943, the first time he walked through the doors of the Ford Motor Company in an official capacity. Soon after Edsel's death, Henry had pored over his father's personal papers with Ernest Kanzler, Edsel's brother-in-law and a Ford executive. They were looking for any document that might guarantee Henry II's ascension to the company's presidency. They found nothing. At the same time that old Henry took over as president, he elevated Bennett to the board of directors and gave him a title that better reflected his power in the company—director of administration. Bennett's power was unchallenged, and there seemed no way the young ensign could navigate the choppy political waters of the Ford Motor Company.

While Bennett saw little threat in young Henry, he was taking no chances. He convinced old Henry to authorize a codicil to his will that called for the company to be managed by a trust for 10 years after Henry Ford's death. When Henry II learned of the codicil in January 1944, he threatened to leave the company, sell his stock, and campaign for Ford's dealerships to break their ties with the company. John Bugas, Ford's director of industrial relations and one of Henry's few allies, talked him out of it. The codicil turned out to be worthless, either because Henry I never signed it, or due to the fact that he had rendered the document meaningless by carrying it around in his pocket and scribbling Bible passages on it.

Meanwhile, Henry II had moved into his father Edsel's old office and began the slow work of establishing his own power base amid Bennett's forces. He had been written off as a loafer, but he had in fact studiously prepared to take up the fight at Ford. When in Michigan during his college years, he would often slip into the Rouge plant unannounced to scrutinize its operations. He frequently grilled Ford executives about company affairs. Henry would ultimately surprise and delight his family by showing a degree of fortitude never seen in his father. In the process, he engendered a fear among the rest of the clan that he would use throughout his life. Henry "had the drive that Edsel lacked," said John Davis, the legendary Ford sales manager of the 1930s and early 1940s. The outcome of his battle with Harry Bennett would mean everything. The future of Ford was in doubt. If Henry II failed, the company could not continue as an independent company. Already there was talk in Washington of nationalizing Ford and putting it under the control of Studebaker.

And now Henry II was getting a firsthand look at the rot that had set in. While at the naval training station, he had asked for regular reports on Ford's operations from Sorensen's assistant, Russell Gnau. But he was stunned by the disorder he found when he began working at Ford. Many years later, he told *Look* magazine that cost controls were virtually nonexistent. He learned that the accounts department weighed its invoices to calculate costs. "Can you believe it?" he asked the interviewer.

The second Henry Ford was also wily enough to exploit the low expectations that surrounded him. His father had been bright and imaginative, but weak-willed. Henry Ford II allowed himself to be viewed as a meek fledgling, more like his late father than his grandfather. It was easy for Bennett and his men to believe that young Henry was another Edsel and was perhaps even more faint-hearted.

But Henry II was cagey—and he knew his enemy. The young man got his first taste of Harry Bennett as a boy, in the late 1920s. He had been intimidated and bullied by the very Ford Service Men who were meant to protect him. Bennett's men would spy on the boy's comings and goings and report back to his grandfather. Henry II would later call

Bennett, "the dirtiest, lousiest, son of a bitch I ever met in my life." As he got to know the company, Henry shamefacedly told everyone he met, "I've got a lot to learn." One thing he had already come to grips with was that "The Ford Administration" was tearing the company asunder. And morale had sunk to a miserable low.

In his 1938 book *The Story of the CIO,* labor leader Benjamin Stolberg described "about 800 underworld characters in the Ford Service organization. They are the Storm Troops. They make no pretense of working, but are merely 'keeping order' in the plant community through terror. Around this nucleus are, however, between 8,000 and 9,000 authentic workers, a great many of them spies and stool pigeons. Because of this highly organized terror and spy system, the fear in the plant is something indescribable."

Henry could see the fear in the eyes of employees and hear it in their voices during his first few months, but few complained directly to him. Who knew what side he was really on? Many expected him to rely on Harry Bennett to help him learn the ropes. They assumed the young man had allied with his grandfather's Rasputin. Henry II, who was careful not to publicly criticize Bennett, gave every appearance that he *was* allied with Bennett. And there was plenty for him to be cautious about. The 53-year-old Bennett was more than a hard-nosed head of an industrial police force; he was also an underworld kingpin. In the rough-and-tumble Detroit crime world, no one was more powerful than Harry Bennett.

Several of the men Bennett enlisted as part of his Ford Service maintained active careers in organized crime. "Even the most powerful gangsters defer to him," according to *The American Mercury* in 1940. Bennett never denied his connections to the syndicates, but he could rationalize them. Bennett was responsible for the safekeeping of one of America's wealthiest and most visible families. In the aftermath of the Lindbergh kidnapping, preserving the family was essential. Bennett believed he could take whatever measures were necessary, including befriending underworld figures who could offer protection. He claimed he had neutralized America's crime bosses by recruiting them, thus ensuring protection for Edsel Ford and his family.

Reporters who covered Ford at the *Detroit Free Press* and *Detroit News* during the 1930s and early 1940s wrote most of the big crime stories for their newspapers because Harry Bennett had all the inside dope. Having populated the Ford Service with dozens of ex-convicts and never hiding the fact, Bennett indeed promoted a sympathetic reputation for himself as a man willing to give criminals "a second chance."

Since joining the company, Henry Ford II was getting a close-up look at how the ex-pugilist operated. Bennett knew almost nothing about automobiles or engineering or mass production, but when an important policy matter came up, Bennett would get into his car and disappear for a few hours. Then he'd come back and say, "I've been to see Mr. Ford, and he wants us to do it this way." Young Henry caught on quickly. On one occasion when Bennett pulled this stunt, Henry II checked with his grandmother, Clara Ford, and discovered that Bennett hadn't seen his grandfather at all.

Ford Motor's sorry state of affairs was an open secret in the auto industry. "When young Henry came in here, the company was not only dying, it was already dead, and rigor mortis was setting in," says Jack Davis in the official Ford history, *Ford: Decline and Rebirth*. But Henry II couldn't begin a turnaround until he had driven out the crooks. In the process, he began to demonstrate a gift for winning at corporate infighting. On April 10, 1944, he got the board of directors to name him executive vice president. Using this authority, young Henry slowly began promoting his own people and neutralizing or dismissing Bennett's cronies.

A year later, the 83-year-old patriarch's health took a sharp turn for the worse, leaving him nearly incapacitated. Young Henry moved swiftly to fill the power vacuum. He continued to hide his deep animosity toward Bennett, though he did not respond to Bennett's repeated efforts to win him over. For a while, Henry the younger even appeared supportive of Bennett, at one point praising his "excellent background and knowledge." All the while, he was plotting a decisive strike.

With old Henry debilitated in the summer of 1945, Bennett's hold on the company began to loosen and finally unravel. Eleanor Ford, Henry's mother, struck first. In a shocking emotional outburst at a board of directors meeting that summer, she accused Bennett of destroying her husband. Bennett sat deadpan as she vowed not to let him do the same to her son.

A few weeks later, Eleanor got the old man's attention when she threatened to sell her voting shares on the open market unless he installed Henry II as president. That his mother had to stand up for Henry Ford II was an apparent blow to his stature, a further humiliation for "Edsel's boy," as he was known inside the company. But Eleanor Ford's threat was a critical step in the passage of power from Henry I to Henry II.

Most historians now believe that Henry II orchestrated the gambit himself. Bennett still believed he could bring young Henry into his own camp, and he began to flex his organization's muscle and even started to subtly intimidate the young Ford. He once took Henry II for a ride in his airplane in an apparent gesture of friendship that also carried a symbolic message—Bennett could crash and burn them both. Years later, Henry Ford II would concede that he was afraid of Bennett. But he betrayed none of it; his fear was overridden by contempt.

Late in the summer of 1945, young Henry and Ford executive John Bugas drew up lists of Bennett followers they needed to expunge. Those lists led to still more lists as the two men planned to eradicate not only Bennett and his ringleaders, but as many of their lower-level cronies as possible.

31

"Davis, Bugas, Bricker, and I hatched the whole deal to take over the company," Ford recalled in 1982. "We hatched it over at the Detroit Club in one of the private dining rooms. They kept bugging me and saying that the whole place was going down the drain."

On September 20, 1945, the patriarch—under pressure from his daughter-in-law and his wife, and in the face of his own frailty—called Henry II to his home and declared that he would step down as president and would turn over the job to his grandson.

Young Henry was wary. He knew that 26 years earlier the old man had given the job to his father, but withheld real authority. Henry II told his grandfather he'd only take the position if he had a free hand to do as he pleased. Henry I argued and the debate went on for some time, but the young man never wavered and the offer of the presidency was never withdrawn.

Young Henry moved swiftly. After leaving Fair Lane, he called for a board meeting the next day to ratify his grandfather's decision. At the meeting, Bennett grasped the fact that he had lost and left to go to his basement office in the administration building. Not long after, Henry followed him there.

John Bugas had urged Henry Ford II not to personally fire Harry Bennett. It was too risky. Bennett kept a pistol in the top drawer of his desk.

"Let me do it," Bugas said.

But the young man sensed that history would record and recount the moment. He stepped into Bennett's office and informed the little man that he was out.

Bennett snarled, "You're taking over a billion dollar organization here that you haven't contributed a thing to."

Thirty-three years later, Lee Iacocca would accuse Henry Ford of lacking the courage to fire him to his face. But no one who had been around Ford Motor Company for any length of time believed it. The courage of "Edsel's boy" was never in doubt.

Henry dismissed Harry Bennett, but it was up to Bugas to evict him. The former head of agents in Detroit's FBI office, Bugas had been hired by Bennett a few years earlier after he had uncovered a theft ring at the Rouge plant involving some of Bennett's cohorts. Bennett doubled Bugas' FBI salary, but the two clashed, and Bennett soon froze him out. Isolated and discouraged, Bugas allied with Henry Ford II when the young man joined the company.

According to later accounts by a newspaper friend of Bugas', the former FBI man slipped a .38 into his belt and walked into Bennett's office. When Bennett saw him, he shouted, "You son of a bitch!" and pulled a .45 automatic out of his desk drawer. Bugas pulled his own gun out and said, "Don't make the mistake of pulling the trigger because I'll kill you, Harry."

Bennett cooled off. "Let's talk about it," he said.

But Bugas turned and walked out of the office, not certain he wouldn't get a bullet in the back of the head. Later in the day, smoke began drifting out of Bennett's office. Some thought Bennett had set the place on fire in an act of sabotage. In fact, he was burning his papers.

Later in life, Henry Ford II told his Ford colleagues about the Harry Bennett years. "I didn't know anything, and I was scared to death," he said.

One former underling said that Ford would occasionally talk about those days after a few drinks. "He didn't know how many people in the company were loyal to Henry Ford I and how many loyal to Harry Bennett personally until after he had fired Bennett. He felt a great sense of relief when, after Bennett had been let go, there were no riots in the Rouge. He had half expected that."

With Bennett out, Henry and Bugas began combing the ranks of the company to expunge his allies. It was a deep purge that reached from the highest executive ranks down to the level of foreman at the Rouge plant. He took out sales staffers in far-off zone offices and managers of parts plants owned by Ford.

Henry had assembled long lists of men who were loyal to Bennett and scratched the names off one by one as he fired or demoted them, avenging his father's death in the process.

Bennett repaired to his home in Ann Arbor, setting himself up as a manufacturer's agent, living quietly until his death in 1979.

Henry Ford II brought immediate change to the company. Under Bennett's rule, employees couldn't smoke on Ford property. Afterward, the engineering department foreman put an ashtray on each engineer's drafting table. Suddenly, the atmosphere was more relaxed. Workers were encouraged to eat lunch and take breaks together. It was a new Ford Motor Company and in many ways the beginning of the modern auto industry. Henry II went on one of the most aggressive and creative hiring sprees in business history, even hiring executives from other companies—something his grandfather had never done.

Ernest Kanzler, Edsel's brother-in-law, advised young Henry to hire executives from rival General Motors, and he did so. Thus, the second Henry Ford would bring the influence of Alfred P. Sloan Jr. to Dearborn, taking on men who trained under GM's longtime president and corporate America's seminal organizational thinker.

It was Sloan's business strategies that enabled General Motors to overcome the seemingly invincible Ford in the 1920s and 1930s and come to dominate the American automobile industry. But in the post–Henry Ford II era, Ford would claim the mantle of "best-managed," in part because Sloan's theories were being freshly applied. Meanwhile, GM itself in the 1950s and 1960s had become doctrinaire and inflexible.

Henry hired a Sloan disciple named Ernie Breech from Bendix Corporation, a GM subsidiary. Breech had worked closely with Sloan and had gleaned lessons on precision thinking from the great man. He brought in a GM finance man named Lewis Crusoe.

He also hired several senior managers from Chrysler Corporation, automotive suppliers, and other established American corporations.

His new purchasing director, Albert Browning, had been a merchandising star at Montgomery Ward before the war and ran the purchasing operations of the U.S. Army during World War II.

Together they helped free Ford from the moorings of the evil Bennett and the obsolete dictums and ways of Henry Ford I. Young Henry was rebuilding the company with the same kind of energy his grandfather had put into building the company in the first decade of the twentieth century. In the process, Henry II invented a management concept that would become known as "the best and the brightest," a notion that would play a key role in American organizational theory and practice in the second half of the twentieth century.

Ford's new charges were faced with a massive undertaking. The Ford Motor Company in 1945 was in a disastrous state that reflected the hazy mind of the aged founder. It was the most poorly managed company in the auto industry, and possibly the most poorly run of any giant American enterprise of the day.

But Ford's product engineering was still grinding away, and the engineering staff was relatively robust compared to the rest of the company. This was one area in which Bennett had comparatively little influence. And there was the strength of an enormous Ford dealer network. It was everything else at the company that needed fixing.

Ford's emphasis was not on hiring car men. Ford had enough auto enthusiasts—from his grandfather on down. What was needed were businessmen, educated professional managers who could draw an organizational chart, read a financial statement, and undertake a cost analysis.

By conventional standards, no American auto company chief executive was less prepared for the job than Henry Ford II. But far from a hapless super-rich kid, young Henry brought with him a new world of influences—Yale, the modernized American armed forces, and his high-minded father.

He was the first head of a major American auto manufacturer born in the twentieth century, and he supplemented his grandfather's nineteenth century principles with the most up-to-date organizational thinking on the planet—a side effect of the war effort.

And Ford Motor Company survived. In a 1980 interview, Henry II said, "There was never, never, never a thought in my mind that it wouldn't be turned around. I didn't know how long it would take, nor did I know how to do it myself. But I never questioned that it could be done. And luck was on our side, and God was on our side, and the economy was on our side, and everything else."

What Henry Ford II accomplished changed the automobile business. Ford remained the second biggest automaker, after General Motors, but it would play a key role in the U.S. auto industry over the next 40 years—establishing a competitive force that prevented GM from becoming even more hidebound than it became later in the century. Without this rivalry, the entire U.S. auto industry would have been weaker and more vulnerable.

Without a strong Ford Motor Company, the car business would have missed out on several products that changed the transportation habits of Americans. Even the lugubrious failure of the Edsel in 1957 was a guidepost to the future. It spawned the idea of spinning off an upmarket sales channel, something Toyota—which couldn't take its corporate eye off of Ford in the 1950s and 1960s—would do successfully three decades later.

Henry II also redefined how carmakers were organized in Europe. He envisioned a pan-European Ford in 1969. And he was the first to believe that a company active in dozens of nations around the world should attempt to unify them in one worldwide organization.

Henry II was a Solomon-like figure who understood the big picture. During the next decades, he made prescient judgments while steering the company and made course corrections when necessary.

If one man laid the foundation of the modern auto industry it was the Deuce. Every industry requires a figure not driven by personal ambition, but a higher purpose. In the auto industry this figure was Henry Ford II.

In the two years leading up to his showdown with Bennett, Henry II had reached a painful conclusion about his company. Its ranks were swollen with intellectually inferior managers. After his years at the Hotchkiss School in Connecticut and at Yale, young Henry was struck by the scarcity of executives that he believed possessed superior intellects. Some of them were downright dullards, he felt.

Whereas Ford's nemesis, General Motors, seemed to bulge with the cerebral young men who had thrived in Alfred P. Sloan's thinking man's organization, Ford was filled with either Harry Bennett's hooligans or seat-of-the-pants engineers and managers. His grandfather had left school at age 15 and believed college was highly overrated. Several of Henry I's most talented engineers had come up from the factory floor and had done so well that he was convinced that higher education was a waste of time. This anti-education culture had taken deep root at Ford, and the best and the brightest young men from America's universities were giving Ford a pass.

Henry II knew he needed more smart people. One of his first decisions as president was to hire 50 college graduates each year. One of the members of the class of 1945 was a young engineer named Lee Iacocca.

After Henry had hired the college men, he made sure that each one took an intelligence test. Once inside Ford, the results of that entry IQ exam could follow an executive around forever. A low test score might even be used by a rival to thwart a manager's climb to the top.

A group of brainy junior officers who had helped keep the Allied war machine humming by applying statistical process controls and modern logistical theory to the battlefield joined the company in November 1945. They became known as the Whiz Kids, 10 young officers from an army air force statistical control group, who at war's end decided to offer themselves as a team to a single needy employer.

Their leader was Colonel Charles "Tex" Thornton, and their patron was Robert A. Lovett, assistant secretary of war. They were all friends who had worked closely together and gained each other's trust and respect. Most of the 10 were in their 20s, but they had self-confidence befitting men 20 years their senior. This confidence came from the massive responsibility they had undertaken during the war. They had achieved a giddy, youthful success that left them with a perfect sense of certainty about their abilities.

Henry Ford II had received a telegram from Thornton that read: "I would like to see you regarding a subject which I believe would be of immediate interest. This concerns a system which has been developed and applied successfully in the management of the Army Air Force for the past three years. Reference if desired is Robert A. Lovett, Assistant Secretary of War for Air."

Henry II and John Bugas met the Whiz Kids for the first time in December 1945. Eight of the ten filed into a room in the Rotunda Building in the Ford administration complex in Dearborn. Two of them stayed back in California awaiting the results of the meeting.

Tex Thornton did the talking for the officers. He explained briefly, but fluently, the sophisticated methods used to gain management control of the Allies' global bombing campaign. They collected data on the number of planes, bombs, airfields, fuel depots, pilots, crew members, and targets—generating an endless amount of facts.

The stat control team had compiled so much information that the data and numbers began to speak to them. They became incisive management tools. Thornton explained to Henry Ford II that the team would like to perform a similar miracle for the Ford Motor Company.

What Thornton and his friends didn't know was how open young Henry Ford would be to their brazen idea. They didn't know the degree to which the chaotic army air force in the early days of the war sounded like the Ford Motor Company the young president was trying to bring under control. They couldn't have found a more receptive audience anywhere in American business.

The Deuce decided on the spot to hire all 10 of them, and he told them so. When later in the meeting Bugas said something that made the decision sound tentative, Henry corrected him. He made sure Thornton and his men knew they were in.

Hiring the bright, young army air force officers was a brilliant stroke, but to Henry II it was something more. It was liberating. It would have gone against every bone in Henry Ford I's body and thus was a clear sign that Henry II was operating on his own—showing the direction he wished the company to go. Even if Bugas, his ally in battle with Bennett, counseled caution, Henry Ford II was casting a vote on the side of youth, brains, and a new day at Ford.

There were only 10 original Whiz Kids, but they would influence hundreds of Ford executives within a year or two and hundreds of thousands of businessmen across corporate America in another few years.

Not all of the Whiz Kids stayed at Ford. Thornton later became chairman of Litton Industries, a leader in the American corporate conglomeration movement of the 1950s and 1960s. Two of them, Robert McNamara and Arjay Miller, would serve as presidents of Ford Motor Company. J. Edward Lundy would become Ford's longtime financial czar and in many ways the most influential of all the Whiz Kids. James Wright would rise to group vice president of the car and truck divisions before leaving Ford to become president of the giant supplier Federal-Mogul. Ben Mills became general manager of the Lincoln-Mercury Division from 1958 until 1964.

In 1946, the Whiz Kids charged into the wilds of the Ford Motor Company. They were asked to formulate organizational charts, create job descriptions, devise methods of evaluating capital spending, identify profit centers, organize Ford into divisions, and set new product plans.

Each was a workaholic before the term was invented, striving everyday with maximum intensity. A few days into his job, Wright holed up at the Dearborn Inn near Ford's headquarters for a week and wrote a 57-page reorganization plan for the company. Miller completed the company's first 12-month financial forecast for 1946 in less than two weeks.

Henry Ford II had cleaned out a place for the Whiz Kids. He wanted them to have an opportunity to succeed, and he gave them the run of the company. Some of them would clash with the older General Motors veterans that Henry II hired at roughly the same time. But he let them fight their own battles—winning some and losing others—but he mostly protected them, allowing the best of the Whiz Kids to secure a place for themselves.

Had he taken over his grandfather's company at age 37 or 47, Henry II may have been less inclined to turn over so much authority to so many young men. But he was just 27 and was their contemporary. Only one of the Whiz Kids, Charles Moore, was younger than Henry.

Henry II was proud that a group of inquisitive young men were finding out what made his company tick. He would later push *Time Magazine* to do a cover story on the Whiz Kids because their influence clearly demonstrated the great improvements taking place at Ford.

The Whiz Kids brought order and process where there had been chaos and imprecision. They pioneered cost analysis, bringing to the company ideas freshly hatched in the nation's great business schools. Lundy came from Princeton, Miller from UCLA, and McNamara from Harvard, where he taught in the business school before joining the army.

Henry Ford I despised the very idea of business administration. He believed in organizing the plant, but saw no need to arrange the affairs of his administrative offices. He even banned organizational charts. So one of Henry II's biggest challenges was to find out who was in charge of what.

As a family-owned company—indeed, the largest family-controlled firm in the world—Henry I had run it as he pleased. His bottom line was simple: if the company's bank balance was bigger at the end of the month than it was at the beginning, then it was on the right track.

Old Henry's diametrical opposite was Alfred Sloan, who had set the standard for business organization in the automobile industry prior to World War II. Sloan rationalized GM's scattered brands and operations and created a perfect balance between central authority and decentralized divisions.

Sloan was the spiritual grandfather of the Whiz Kids, but the new generation took Sloan's ideas a step further. The Kids craved and devoured information—it was their sustenance. Just as they had in the army air corps, the Kids scoured the company for facts, data, figures—anything that would give insight into the mysterious inner workings of Ford.

Army air force stat control had begun as a gathering place of numbers and information; only later were the data and statistics analyzed and acted upon. The evolution would be the same at Ford. But first they needed the raw information—an accounting of everything in the vast industrial organism—its people, its machines, the cars it built, the number of workers needed to build them, and the cost of components. And almost none of this information was easily available. The Whiz Kids had to invent systems to collect the data before they could even begin to analyze it or implement changes based on it.

In the first decade of the twentieth century, Henry Ford I's young mechanics broke down the plant operations into ever-smaller units. Every minute mechanical operation in the factory was studied in search of ways to speed the moving assembly line. After years of effort, they had evolved something that could be called mass production.

Henry Ford II's young men did the same thing in Ford's business offices. In their early days, the Whiz Kids were called the Quiz Kids. They posed endless questions in an effort to understand what kind of beast they were dealing with.

Even the older men Henry Ford II hired—former General Motors executives installed in higher positions than the Whiz Kids—had never seen such curiosity. The young men believed that facts and figures would eliminate the need for guesswork in a company that had lived on guesswork for decades. None believed it more than Robert

McNamara. In a letter to a friend in 1946, McNamara wrote: "Ford must be rebuilt from the ground up. The extent of the decay which existed throughout the organization defies description. Channels of communication are poor, controls are lacking, organization is non-existent, planning is unheard of and the personnel problem is serious beyond belief."

In 1960, McNamara was named president of the company by Henry Ford II—the ultimate endorsement of the 1946 decision to hire the young team. McNamara's legacy was Ford's all-powerful finance department and its layer upon layer of systems for calculating costs; hiring, training, grading, and promoting managers; and measuring the value of advertising.

For men like McNamara and Lundy, academics at heart, Ford in 1946 was an extraordinary opportunity. It was a $1 billion test case—a blank slate from which to build the modern corporation. It was the Manhattan Project of financial controls—every bit as exciting as the manic push for perfection that Henry Ford I and his production wizards had carried out. The country's military sophistication and discipline—shaped by the demands of war—was fundamentally adapted for private business. Whereas other American companies were quick to adapt the technology developed for the war effort, the Whiz Kids adapted its organizational systems. The former supply officers transformed a company still rooted in the nineteenth century into one that influenced almost every large organization in America, including the U.S. government.

President John F. Kennedy's "Best and Brightest" administration in 1961 was patterned after the Ford Whiz Kids, right down to the selection of McNamara as his secretary of defense.

In time, the Whiz Kid culture would come under tremendous criticism. It would be held responsible for everything from the fact that Ford wasn't first with a minivan to the American travails in Vietnam in the 1960s. When Alex Trotman replaced Red Poling as chairman and

CEO of Ford in 1994 and the disciples of the original Whiz Kids were beginning to thin out at Ford, the company's leaders tried to reduce the influence of the finance department.

But one former Ford executive said, "If the finance department had too much influence it was because Ed Lundy hired guys with such high IQs. They couldn't help but be influential."

"Alex Trotman tried to lessen the influence of the finance guys, but do you do that by putting less able people on the finance side or raising the quality of the other side?"

The implication was clear. Ford's finance department was influential inside the corporation for the same reason it was influential outside of Ford. Those guys were good. McNamara, Lundy, and the original Whiz Kids had seen to it. In changing Ford, the Whiz Kids would change dozens of other companies as well. He would never admit it, but Iacocca saved the Chrysler Corporation in the early 1980s in part by applying the methods of the Whiz Kids.

While at Ford, Iacocca pitied himself as a kind of whipping boy for McNamara and Lundy's finance department. He scorned bean counters—even popularizing the term—for their lack of operating experience and product savvy, as well as their lack of line responsibility. Only Iacocca never realized how much he had come to rely on their methods. Arriving at Chrysler in 1979, he was appalled by the lack of fiscal reporting systems at a company that was supposed to have been dominated by accountants.

Bob Lutz started his career at General Motors' Adam Opel division in Germany, but Harold "Red" Poling, the tough finance executive he served under at Ford of Europe in the 1970s, turned him into a latter-day Whiz Kid. Poling, who would one day become chairman of Ford Motor Company, learned at the feet of the original Whiz Kids, Ed Lundy in particular. In Europe, he helped turn Lutz, the ultimate car guy, into a stickler on costs. Poling told him one day: "You know the difference between you and me? If we had a product program that was on track and it was going to produce a fine car that would be competitive, and would meet all its financial targets, and the devil came to you and said, 'Go $5 over the cost targets, and I will make sure that this is the best and most successful car of all time,' you'd say yes, and I wouldn't."

"You're right," Lutz replied. "I would say yes for $5; hell, I'd say yes for $50."

Poling told him: "You're willing to compromise financial discipline, but I won't. To me, financial discipline comes above everything else. It comes above creativity, above product. If you lose financial discipline, you've lost everything." Poling was repeating one of the Whiz Kid mantras. In his 1998 Chrysler retirement interview with *Automotive News*, Lutz said: "Poling was such a powerful influence on me that I began to think about it, and I thought: why can't you have both?"

Given what Henry was handed to start with, the systems and controls that he devised and encouraged were not just desirable; they were life-saving for Ford. Young Henry's attachment to financial disciplines would typecast his company for decades to come, and there would always be tension between creativity and analysis—with each getting the upper hand at one time or another.

CHAPTER THREE

Hell-Raiser Honda
Breaks the Mold

Japan's catastrophic world of 1945 was a breeding ground for Soichiro Honda's particular brand of genius. His appreciation for simplicity and opportunity grew out of the misery of post–World War II Tokyo.

Along with food and medicine, fuel was a precious resource in the bombed-out, burned-out city. Gasoline was strictly rationed, and a black market thrived. There was no fuel to run automobiles, so the remnants of Tokyo's rail system was forced to transport far more passengers than it had the capacity to handle. Lack of fuel often brought the trains to a halt. Honda hated to be packed in with the masses. He owned a car, but couldn't drive it because of the restrictions on the sale of gasoline. To get around, he fitted a bicycle with a leftover 50-cc gasoline engine that had been used by the Japanese military to power generators. He started a small business attaching surplus engines to bicycles and soon had a long line of customers. When the supply of motors ran out, Honda designed and built one of his own, but he was criticized by people who thought it outrageous to produce a machine that burned gasoline at a time of shortages. Honda responded by explaining that the efficiency of his motorcycles justified building and selling them.

Using profits from the piston ring business he sold toward the end of the war, Honda bought some forest land and squeezed the resin from the roots of pine trees. He mixed the resin with whatever gasoline he could scrounge, stretching the fuel, which was in short supply. Getting more out of less was how Soichiro Honda survived after the war, and the experience deeply influenced his career and his company. Twenty-five years later, fuel-efficient engines would establish the Honda Motor Company in the first rank of the world's carmakers and would change the automotive industry forever. The defining moment for the man and his company occurred the year Soichiro Honda retired, in 1973. It was the completion and application of the CVCC. The engine had been in development for two decades, and once it was perfected and on the market under the hood of the new Honda Civic compact, it opened the door for all Japanese carmakers in America. The Honda Motor Company had emerged as a threat to the world's established auto manufacturers. No longer was it just a jumped-up frivolous motorcycle maker with outsized ambitions. Honda was now the standard bearer of the Japanese invasion of the U.S. car market.

In a way, Henry Ford II and Soichiro Honda both descended from Henry Ford I. One was the grandson and the other the spiritual son. Honda, who was born near Hamamatsu, Japan, in 1906, would grow up to be the closest thing to the original Henry Ford that the second half of the twentieth century would see. Henry Ford was Honda's hero, and he was like him in many ways. Soichiro's father was a village blacksmith; Henry Ford I's father was a carpenter. Neither Henry Ford nor Soichiro Honda had much use for formal education. They both achieved substantial success at an early age without the benefit of advanced schooling, and the companies that would bear their names would not get off the ground until they were over 40. Like Henry Ford I, Honda hated reading and writing, yet was fascinated by scientific subjects. Both were born engineers—eager, intuitive, and self-taught. But along with their mechanical genius, each discovered a talent for leadership. Both Ford and Honda had more of a gift for the inspiration of others than any studied management style. Soichiro Honda went to Tokyo at age 16 to become an apprentice mechanic at the Arto Shokai repair shop. During his years in Tokyo, which included the calamity of the Great Kanto Earthquake of 1923, Honda discovered his passion for automobile mechanics and racing. He helped Arto Shokai build racing cars and eventually drove them in competition. He did so well at the repair shop that within a few years the boss helped him set up a branch office in Hamamatsu, starting with one employee.

A certain rowdiness also took hold of him during this time. Honda drank to excess, chased women, and drove recklessly. He was notorious in Hamamatsu. One drunken night, he threw a young geisha girl out a third floor window and nearly killed her, and once while driving a car full of girls he barreled off a bridge.

At first, Honda's age and lack of educational credentials kept him from attracting much business. The experience embittered him, and it was to be the beginnings of his hypercritical view of Japanese society. In his own company, Honda would value the energy of youth, and he would encourage and promote able young engineers no matter what their educational background.

Business gradually picked up at the repair shop, and Honda would eventually employ 50 men. But he grew restless repairing goods manufactured by others and decided that the real money was made in manufacturing. So Honda relied on his natural inventiveness to get started and patented a new way to cast metal wheel spokes to replace the wooden ones that were prevalent in Japan. Before long, he was piling up the royalties. Honda also dreamed of making automobiles. Once, he spotted one of Henry Ford's machines, a Model T, flying down a street in Hamamatsu. He chased after the car and then fell to the road and sniffed a drop of oil that had been left behind, inhaling heavily as if performing a religious rite. The young man loved speed, and by the early 1930s he was an avid race-car driver who built his own cars for competition and developed an understanding of engines and vehicle design. Honda's thirst for four-wheeled competition would re-emerge 30 years later when his company entered Formula One competition.

Honda's own racing career ended in 1936 after a horrific crash just before the finish line in the All Japan Speed Rally between Tokyo and Yokohama. While laid up with his injuries, Honda decided to devote himself entirely to his business, which was not going well. In 1934, at age 28, Honda had decided to manufacture die-cast piston rings in the city of Yamashita. It seemed like a good idea at the time. Every internal-combustion engine in the world needed piston rings, which required little in the way of raw materials, so upfront investment could be low. Honda rented a factory, bought machinery, and hired 50 workers, but struggled to get his manufacturing company off the ground and had trouble devising a way to successfully cast the rings. He had patented a method for casting spokes, but the piston ring problem seemed insurmountable.

With a factory and employees unable to turn out an acceptable product, Honda began to despair. He would spend nights on the factory floor trying to solve the problem, like the young Henry Ford I, who had to wrestle with the details of a moving assembly line. The rings Honda was able to make proved worthless because they soon fell apart in use. He finally took his problem to a professor at the Hamamatsu Technical School, who quickly alerted Honda to the problem—a necessary ingredient, silicon, was missing from the metal's composition.

Stunned by his lack of basic knowledge, Honda decided in 1935, at age 29, to enroll in the mechanical engineering department at the Hamamatsu Technical School. Soichiro Honda had only attended formal school for 10 years in a country where degrees are highly prized and a degree from a good university was considered essential for a successful career. An irony of Honda's life was his devotion to the pursuit of knowledge. He set up a quasi-academic research-and-development company within Honda Motor Company to protect engineers from the daily pressures and influence of commerce. All the while, he professed a distaste for university degrees and the apparatus of formal education. He bragged that he found better and more creative engineers by hiring young men who had not come from Japan's prestigious universities. Yet no company was more committed to pure research than Honda. No company gave its technicians more freedom to make mistakes. Honda hired engineers whose lack of a "quality" educational background prevented them from being considered for employment at Toyota or Nissan.

Honda would lower the boom on any college graduate who made a mistake. Once, when a piston designed by newly minted engineer Shoichiro Irimajiri broke down during the August 1965 British Grand Prix, Honda told Irimajiri: "I hate college graduates. A company does not need people like you who use only their heads."

But 30 years earlier, Honda had had to go to school to solve the problem of casting piston rings. He attended lectures and tried to apply everything he heard to the problem of the piston rings. The school refused to grant him a degree after he refused to take the final examinations, which only reinforced his loathing of the ways and strictures of higher education. "A ticket to a movie theatre will get you into a theatre, but you cannot even see a movie with a diploma," Honda said. Still, he learned something about casting piston rings, and by 1937 his factory was turning out serviceable, though not perfect, parts. Honda received an order for 50,000 piston rings from Toyota Motor Company, but when a sample of 50 rings contained only three that met Toyota's exacting standards, he had to look for other customers. Honda was able to sell piston rings at a reduced price to producers of lower-quality engines, though not to Toyota or Nissan.

The piston rings' quality improved over the next few years, and in 1942 Toyota acquired a 40 percent stake in Honda's company, called Tokai Seikai Heavy Industry. This much-needed financing would give Honda the resources he needed to get into the motorcycle business after the war. And 20 years later, Honda would be in the car business, competing with Toyota, whose 1942 investment would pay off handsomely in the modern era. The older, larger well-established company had a long tradition of quality and efficiency. When they were combined with the competitive prod of the maverick, aggressive young Honda company in the 1970s and 1980s, it would make Toyota the most competitive car manufacturer in the world.

Honda's company thrived during the late 1930s and early 1940s, and Soichiro Honda was as boisterous as ever. He once lowered himself into a septic tank to retrieve one of his supplier's false teeth and proceeded to put the teeth in his own mouth. He showed up drunk at a presentation to bankers and was promptly turned down for the loan he was seeking. Still, Honda profited during Japan's war years. His piston ring company built parts and production machinery for the Japanese navy. Serving the country's military gave Honda the opportunity he needed to demonstrate his originality. He came up with a simple machine for making piston rings and developed an automatic propeller-cutting machine. Both devices could be operated efficiently by the women who had moved into Japan's workforce during the war.

Honda believed the conquering Americans would nationalize Toyota after the war ended, depriving him of his principal backer. So he sold his remaining 60 percent share of Tokai Seikai to Toyota and began thinking about what to do next. At age 40 and with no company to run, Honda reverted to his raucous pre-war lifestyle. He turned his mechanical skills to making synthetic sake from medical alcohol, and he and his friends would spend hours drinking the homemade swill. His wife began to wonder if his youthful hunger for success had been destroyed forever. But Honda was biding his time, looking for the right opportunity. In the meantime, he rigged up a desalination device and traded the fresh water he made from sea water to farmers for rice. In 1946, Honda considered manufacturing textiles, but then another idea presented itself. He began rounding up two-stroke engines left over from the military and adapting them to bicycles. With the severe gasoline shortages keeping automobiles of the streets, Honda's garage-built motorcycles were a thrifty alternative to four-wheel transportation. In 1948, he formed the Honda Motor Company for the production of motorcycles. He started with 20 employees. Within 12 years, it was the world's leading motorcycle and motor-scooter maker.

In 1949, Honda introduced its 98-cc two-cycle Dream motorcycle, and much of what was learned in wartime production was applied to manufacturing the motorcycles. By 1950, Honda was building 1,000 motorcycles per month.

Soichiro Honda's rise began at approximately the same time as that of Henry Ford II, his hero's grandson. Henry II, who was 11 years younger than Honda, was born into fabulous wealth and great privilege. But like Honda, young Henry II failed to get a university degree. He was thrown out of Yale after turning in a term paper on the English author Thomas Hardy that he had received from a term paper–writing service. Long after Henry II restored his family's company to greatness, he was a commencement speaker at Yale. Like Honda, he was unrepentant, telling the audience, "I didn't write this one either." Honda was a mechanically adept, street-smart entrepreneur, and Henry II was the spoiled scion of one of the world's great industrial families. But they faced similar challenges after World War II. The war had helped Honda's little components company survive—much as contracts to build the bombers that attacked Tokyo had kept the Ford Motor Company afloat in the final years of Henry Ford I's failing stewardship. To succeed, both Honda and Henry II had to find the right people to help run and staff their companies in the chaotic days after the war.

Honda found a man named Takeo Fujisawa, who would be his Ernie Breech and Whiz Kids all rolled into one. Fujisawa became Honda's lifelong business companion, as well as his sales, marketing, and finance wizard, doing for Honda the engineer what Whiz Kids Robert McNamara and Ed Lundy (and later Lee Iacocca) would do for

Henry II. Soichiro Honda never met Henry Ford I, and Henry Ford II didn't know his grandfather during his creative and intellectual prime, but both were profoundly influenced by the elder Ford. Cars were in their blood. Henry Ford II would not allow his company to veer away from the production of automobiles, despite the American trend in the 1950s and 1960s toward the formation of giant conglomerates. "My grandfather built cars, and I build cars," he said in the 1980s, when auto companies were starting another diversification phase. And Soichiro Honda was not completely fulfilled until he was building cars—a desire that began to grow inside him the day he saw the Ford Model T churning through Hamamatsu.

But Honda would face obstacles to becoming a manufacturer of four-wheeled vehicles, and the biggest obstacle wasn't Toyota or Nissan or Mitsubishi, but the Japanese government. By 1959, Honda had grown into the world's largest motorcycle manufacturer, and it was anxious to begin producing four-wheel vehicles. But Japan's powerful Ministry of International Trade and Industry (MITI) did not want Soichiro Honda building automobiles. Honda had never thought of his company as a motorcycle manufacturer; he believed it was an engine company, with motorcycles as their first application. But MITI had a master plan for the auto industry—and it didn't include Honda. In fact, the ministry was proposing legislation to the Japanese Diet, the national legislature, that would not only ban new carmakers, but would also require some existing companies to merge. MITI sought to create a Japanese auto industry that would have the strength to challenge the best vehicle manufacturers in the world, and this master plan had huge implications for Honda. Without official backing, Honda had trouble setting up export operations and dealing with the legal complexities involved in exporting automobiles. The big banks were part of Japan's clubby zaibatsu network of companies, and Honda's maverick ways meant it was chronically under-financed. And this was why an American investment banker named Sidney Weinberg came to the Ford Motor Company in the early 1960s and proposed that Ford buy a share of Honda, which was then primarily a motorcycle maker.

The rising young Ford executive Lee Iacocca favored the idea, and Soichiro Honda was excited about the extra financing and was honored by the thought of partnering with his idol's company. But Ford's powerful finance executives, the aging Whiz Kids and their descendents, all opposed the idea. Meanwhile, stubborn Honda refused to bow to powerful MITI. He thought it critical to grow his company overseas, and he wanted to do that by producing cars. Honda had skirmished with the powerful ministry many times before. When he started motorcycle production after World War II, MITI officials were uncooperative, claiming that his fast-growth strategy "bordered on insanity." But in the end, the ministry's attempt to consolidate the Japanese auto industry failed. Many years later, Honda would shake his head with disbelief when in the late 1980s his old friend Iacocca accused Honda and other Japanese carmakers of being in league with MITI. "Japanese industry is not playing by itself," Iacocca wrote in his autobiography. "It's backed to the hilt in its close relationship to the Japanese government in the form of MITI."

In fact, Honda probably disliked MITI more than Iacocca, because for Honda MITI represented Japan's Tokyo University elite and other things he couldn't stand about Japan's establishment. Honda spent his entire life competing against the privileged and the powerful in his own country. He had been bullied by MITI, and if the old bureaucrats had had their way, Honda's motorcycle company would have never produced its first car.

And Honda would often rail loudly against MITI. "Probably I would have been even more successful had we not had MITI," he said in his final years. "MITI was not capable of making automobiles. I was." Honda introduced its first automobile in Japan in 1962, the S500 sports car. In 1966, the N360 mini-compact car debuted, and the first Honda automobile arrived in the United States in 1970. It was the tiny

N600 four-seater driven by a 600-cc, 36-horsepower engine and was priced at $1,398. Sales in the first year were 4,195.

What truly made Honda an automobile manufacturer was its revolutionary CVCC engine. With this powerplant, Honda vaulted to the front ranks of the automobile industry.

The CVCC engine project typified the good luck that followed Honda throughout his career. The Civic arrived in the United States in 1973, just as the world was reeling from the first of two major oil crises. The sight of long lines of people waiting to buy gasoline shook Americans to the core, and Soichiro Honda had the answer. Honda's fuel-efficient Civic caught on immediately. The Civic was the first car in U.S. automotive history to draw owners out of their standard-sized American sedans and into small cars. Owners of full-size Buicks and Oldsmobiles and Chryslers and Fords were trading their cars in to buy the new Civic in a market phenomenon never before seen in the U.S. car business.

Americans bought 32,575 Civics that first year, at prices starting at $2,150. Three years later, sales of the Civic reached 132,286. Even if tens of thousands of Civic buyers quickly returned to full-size cars when gasoline prices eased, many were impressed by their first experience with Japanese cars. And when they did buy larger cars in the early 1980s, they bought Honda Accords. Indeed, by 1989, the Accord was America's best-selling passenger car.

Honda had actually positioned itself for that advantage some years earlier. As the company first ventured into the U.S. car market at the start of the 1960s, one-third of its sales had been in Southern California, and Honda's managers soon realized that they were caught up in mounting public concerns about air pollution in the greater Los Angeles area.

Soichiro Honda knew then that he had an opportunity. He believed that Honda Motor Company was first and foremost an engine company, so engine problems—including the pollution they created—represented an opportunity for his company. In the mid-1960s, Honda

R&D began studying ways to build a pollution-free automobile engine, and in 1968 Honda withdrew from Formula One competition for several years so its engineers could concentrate on what became known as the "Clean Automobile Engine" project. Soichiro decided the solution had to be found in the internal workings of the engine, not with catalytic converters or any other attachments. By 1969, a special task force had been set up to run the project, and the problem became the company's central focus. Honda and his engineers knew they could achieve something that U.S. auto companies couldn't—or at least they could reach their goal before the Americans. "We thought that by tackling this pollution-fighting problem we, as a latecomer in the automobile field, would have an opportunity, a big chance," said Kiyoshi Kawashima, Honda's president at the time. The company's engineers had studied gas turbine systems and electrical engines, but these didn't fit Soichiro Honda's guidelines. The engine would have to be inexpensive to produce, which ruled out gas turbines; it would have to fit within the existing infrastructure, which meant no electrical engines; and it would have to be inexpensive to operate and maintain.

At this same time, the U.S. Congress presented a specific target in the form of the 1970 Clean Air Act. The Environmental Protection Agency established exhaust emissions standards that would take effect in 1975. While other automakers scrambled, Honda had a flying start. His clean team intensified its efforts and, at one point, 70 percent of the Honda R&D staff was working on the CVCC project. Among the members of the CVCC team were three future presidents of the company: Tadashi Kume, Nobuhiko Kawamoto, and Takeo Fukui. Shoichiro Irimajiri, the talented executive who set up Honda's first assembly plant in the United States many years later, was also on the team—having survived Soichiro Honda's ire at the British Grand Prix. A rotating group of engineers worked on the project—most were under age 30. The CVCC solution was settled on by early 1971, and it was no technical miracle, but rather the application of existing technology perfected through endless trial and error. CVCC was based on the principle of the stratified charge engine that had been around for years. No expensive retooling of production lines was required. The engine employed a very lean overall mixture and regulated combustion to suppress the production of pollutants. The design came out of endless tinkering and continual improvement. And one of the most insistent tinkerers was Soichiro Honda himself. He preferred spending his days at Honda R&D rather than concentrating on marketing and financial problems at the company's Tokyo headquarters. During the late 1960s, he spent part of almost every day working on the clean engine.

In 1972, a prototype was built and submitted for testing to the EPA. Word filtered back from Tokyo that Honda had developed an engine that could meet the 1975 standards. Panic swept through General Motors, Ford, and Chrysler. The Big Three had been arguing strenuously that the EPA standards were unrealistic and could not be met. Now Honda was on the verge of conforming. And even more, the engineers in Tokyo had an answer when American engineers claimed the CVCC would work only in small cars. Honda tested the concept successfully in V-8–powered Chevrolet Impalas. In the fall of 1973, the CVCC-fitted Chevys were tested by the EPA. Not only did they meet the new emissions standards, the CVCC improved the fuel economy of the original Impalas.

The CVCC project drew a sharp contrast between the way that American auto companies and Japanese firms—Honda in particular—attacked problems. Shoichiro Irimajiri was sent to Ford for three months in the 1970s to help with the CVCC, which Ford had acquired rights to under license. "I was on an assignment to provide Ford with technical assistance about the CVCC engine. I worked side by side with their engineers, their R&D center, and then I went to the spot—their test lab—to personally observe the tests, which, incidentally, had many errors. I kept thinking what a difference there is in Ford's management philosophy compared to Honda's."

The roots of the CVCC engine could be found in many places. Twenty years earlier, amid a financial crisis in 1954, Soichiro Honda announced that the young company would enter motorcycles in the Isle of Man Tourist Trophy Race in Great Britain. And he promised that the Honda bikes would win.

Honda's seemingly impossible boast energized the stricken company and created a goal-oriented culture. The clean engine problem would be attacked with the same fervor that motorcycle engineers had as they tried to squeeze more horsepower out of their engines. In fact, the development process was roughly the same in both cases—optimize the combustion process and complete the work under deadline. Both goals were met. Honda won the TT race in 1961. Some of the engineers who joined the company in the 1950s and 1960s—largely due to Honda's promise to win the TT—found themselves part of the CVCC team. One of them was Nobuhiko Kawamoto, a future president of Honda who would lead the company's Formula One team—another hotbed of CVCC engineers. Shortly after the company started building automobiles in the early 1960s, Honda did the same thing again. He announced that the company would build a racing car that would win at Le Mans. Just as his bold prediction in 1954 that Honda would someday win the Isle of Man TT caused people to think him foolish, his Le Mans boast caused many in the industry to shake their heads with astonishment. But Honda knew what he was doing.

By setting out an objective of building the world's fastest racing cars, he knew Honda would attract a better grade of engineer. Irimajiri, a motorcycle enthusiast, was one of them.

So it was that a version of the Civic was launched in the United States with the CVCC in 1975—in time to meet the EPA deadline. In fact, the CVCC's stratified-charge engine had met U.S. emissions standards nearly a decade before most other manufacturers could. Detroit's automakers filed for extensions of the emissions deadline. Testifying before a house committee in Washington, a Honda spokesman said:

"We do not intend to apply for an extension of time which certain automobile manufacturers have asked of the EPA administrators because we are capable of meeting those standards in 1975 and we consider it our obligation to do so." The publicity—against the background of the world's first oil crisis—gave the motorcycle manufacturer enormous credibility in America. The EPA ranked the 1975 Civic CVCC No. 1 in American gas mileage, averaging 27 miles per gallon in the city and 39 miles per gallon on the highway.

Soon Lee Iacocca would come calling with a proposal to buy 300,000 Honda engines to install in Ford Fiestas. But Henry Ford II killed Iacocca's proposal, and Ford missed this crucial opportunity to link with what would become, within a decade, the most aggressive and successful new car company in the world. What was the beginning of the end for Iacocca at Ford would become the true beginning of the Japanese automobile in the United States.

In 1982, Honda became the first Asian company to produce automobiles in the United States. The auto factory, built alongside a Honda motorcycle plant in Marysville, Ohio, began producing autos just a year after Japan agreed to accept voluntary quotas on its auto exports to the U.S. Honda's Japanese competitors soon followed with their own plants.

Soichiro Honda had always nurtured resourcefulness. He never wanted his engineers to remain in one narrowly focused job. He moved them around, challenging them and keeping them motivated, setting the template for the cross-functional platform teams of the 1990s. This approach was an extension of the way his racing teams were structured. Honda demanded in the late 1960s that his young engineers meet U.S. tailpipe emissions standards. But he had also ordered at that time that the Civic engine should be an air-cooled design, even though Honda's air-cooled 1968 1300-cc subcompact had sold poorly. Ironically, it was the CVCC project—the ultimate expression of Honda's dreams and vision—that brought him to realize that he was near the end of the line as an automotive engineer. He had long championed air-cooled engines, but the young men at Honda R&D—operating in the culture of youth and frankness that Honda had encouraged—rose up against him. In a dramatic encounter, a young Tadashi Kume argued that the air-cooled engine was a waste of time. The CVCC would have to be water cooled. Honda gave in. "Air cooling," he said, "is the limit of my technology."

Takeo Fujisawa advised Honda to either bow to the engineers' wishes and remain head of the company—or retire. He chose to remain—until the CVCC Civic had been introduced. Many years later, Kume became president of Honda. Soichiro Honda retired in 1973 at age 67. The Civic and its phenomenal engine were the crowning achievements of his life, vindicating a philosophy of work and method. The greatest technical advance in Japan's auto industry was achieved by young men who didn't necessarily have the highest educational credentials, but who reflected Soichiro Honda's belief in "ability first." Their success was the reason that, 10 years later, Ferdinand Piëch, the Porsche heir, engineer, and student of Japanese culture, considered quitting his job as head of development at Audi and moving to Japan to work at the master's company. Honda was an inspiration for Bob Lutz's Chrysler in the late 1980s as it organized for it's phenomenal product success in the pre-DaimlerChrysler years. And it was the reason Eberhard von Kuenheim, the longtime head of BMW, decided that Honda was the one carmaker in the world BMW would look to for guidance.

As he grew older, Honda pulled back from the company. There were no Harry Bennetts in his life, only a staff of gifted young engineers who had risen on merit. The automotive world had been fundamentally altered—not just by the advent of Honda's technology, but also by the opening of the rest of the world to the Japanese. Nothing would ever be the same again. Had there been no Honda, the auto industry would have been robbed of its single most inventive and influential post-war company, and the only successful automaker founded after World War II. In the 1980s, *Time Magazine* splashed "The Honda Way" on its cover. Each of the American companies benchmarked Honda. But Honda not only re-charted the course of the Big Three, it changed Toyota, the giant automaker that most reflects Japan's industrial establishment. Toyota was credited for its advances in lean production and quality control in the latter part of the twentieth century, but those attributes of Japanese business culture existed well before World War II. It was Soichiro Honda—the free spirit—who brought the spark to Japan.

Honda's unorthodoxy caused Toyota, which excelled in efficiency and quality, to also respond to technology and to adopt the skills of speed and flexibility. Maybe Eiji Toyoda, whose family started assembling GM cars in Japan in 1936 and selling them as Toyotas, should rate as one of our influential sextet. Or maybe we should accept that it was Honda's prodding that drove the ever-efficient Toyota to become the world's most consistently profitable automobile company.

CHAPTER FOUR

Eberhard von Kuenheim: Maker of BMW

Johanna Quandt looked like something out of *The Sound of Music.* Her white hair was tied in a tight bun as she greeted Henry Ford II at her grand home in Bad Homburg, Germany, in the summer of 1987. Ford would die of complications from pneumonia in Baden Baden, Germany, a few weeks later, but he wanted to see Mrs. Quandt one last time to try to convince her to sell BMW to the Ford Motor Company. Ford had been a supporter of Johanna's late husband, Herbert Quandt, in the days when many thought Quandt was crazy to try to salvage the Bavarian carmaker. And Henry had tremendous respect for Quandt's widow, who had been Herbert's secretary and his second wife. Ford was scheduled to meet her in the morning at her home just north of Frankfurt. But rather than zip into the Frankfurt airport on a Ford jet on the same day, Ford said he wanted to fly in the night before. Fog had been forecast for the Frankfurt area, and Henry Ford, always punctual and ever courteous—especially to fellow aristocrats—did not want to risk being fog-bound and late for the appointment. It would be rude.

Ford flew in the night before and arrived in time to meet Mrs. Quandt at her home the following morning. Ford and one of his finance executives, Bruce Blythe, sat on the veranda with Mrs. Quandt and BMW's chairman, Hans Graf von der Goltz, who was also the family's representative on the supervisory board. Graf von der Goltz joined BMW's board as Herbert Quandt's surrogate after Quandt died in 1982. After an hour or so of talking, Mrs. Quandt looked at her visitor and delivered her traditional rebuke: "Now, Henry, I know why you are here." Ford had wanted the acquisition of BMW to be part of his legacy. But as usual, Quandt wasn't selling. "Henry," she said in perfect English, "what would I do with the money?" It was a question Ford never had an answer for. But Quandt told her suitor that if she ever did decide to sell BMW she would sell it to him—because he had been so supportive of her husband when he bought the company—when so many thought it was crazy. Why was BMW Henry Ford II's last dream?

Bayerische Motoren Werke was badly in need of help in 1959. The company was sliding into bankruptcy and on the verge of being handed over to Daimler-Benz, where BMW would have lived out its days making axles for Mercedes cars. The crisis was averted when industrialist Herbert Quandt bought a controlling interest in the company and began the formation of the modern BMW. Quandt was the scion of a powerful Dutch industrial family whose wealth and influence stretched back more than 100 years—long before BMW began life as a manufacturer of aircraft engines in Munich in 1918. Motorcycles were added to BMW's product line in 1923, and the first BMW car appeared in 1928.

The company had taken over the Dixi Werks firm in Eisenach, Germany, which initially built British-designed Austin Sevens under license. By the mid-1930s, BMW was making a name for itself in the auto business. The precise handling 328 roadster won the 1940 prestigious Mille Miglia race in Italy. But unlike Volkswagen and Daimler-Benz, BMW failed to return to prominence after World War II and limped through the 1950s. Its main product during that decade of mediocrity was the bulbous 501, which had more in common with ungainly American cars of the era than racy pre-war BMWs. The 501 and the V-8–powered 502 sold poorly, and when BMW's fortunes began to sink in the mid-1950s, it was forced to license production of a three-wheeled bubble car from the Italian carmaker Iso. The Isetta, one of the lingering automotive curiosities of the 1950s, was the face of BMW until Herbert Quandt came along.

The company was in such grave financial condition that in December 1959 the supervisory board recommended selling out to its Stuttgart rival. But BMW's proud unions and shareholders raised a furor at the prospect of seeing the Bavarian company delivered to Daimler-Benz. Teaming with his brother Harald, Herbert Quandt quietly bought a 30 percent stake in BMW and kept it out of the hands of Daimler.

Quandt's main holding at the time was the Varta battery company, but he had been enthusiastic about cars his entire life. Quandt quickly began putting the company's house in order, making a series of executive appointments and then ordering his engineers to design and develop a car that would stand as a worthy competitor to Mercedes-Benz. He soon discovered that chief engineer Alex von Falkenhausen and his dedicated team had already made a start. They had drawn up plans for what would become the 1500, the precursor of modern BMWs. The 1500 was a small, lightweight sedan with a powerful engine that was more attractive and more technically advanced than other family sedans on the German market. Von Falkenhausen had conceived a light, responsive sedan body and stuffed it with a powerful 1500-cc engine. Designer Wilhelm Hofmeister carved out an elegant, symmetrical three-box shape that seemed to borrow from General Motors' 1959 Corvair.

BMW showed the 1500 at the September 1961 Frankfurt auto show. Unlike the 501, the new car had the soul of the BMWs of the 1930s. The company wanted to be a niche player, but its niche was in the middle of the market. The 1500 was an unpretentious family car—yet with agile road manners and surprising performance. The 1500 marked the beginning of the modern BMW, and von Falkenhausen and Hofmeister played decisive roles in the automaker's transition.

Another key figure was sales-and-marketing boss Paul Hahnemann, a loud and charismatic man who effectively ran BMW's day-to-day operations during the 1960s. Hahnemann, a former SS officer and Bob Lutz's predecessor in the job, saw BMW's brand potential as a maker of cars that suited younger drivers seeking an alternative to Mercedes-Benz. For Hahnemann, the company's image needed to be distinctly reflected in its products, and research showed that when Germans thought about BMW they still had the zippy cars of the 1930s in mind. The 1.5-liter 315 in 1934 and the 328 two-seater sports car in 1936 competed with the small Mercedes-Benz models of the era. Though the original 3-series was only made for seven years, its heritage became symbolized in BMW's instantly recognizable double-kidney radiator grille. Quandt's BMW followed the 1500 with the 1.8-liter 1800 in 1963 and the 2002 in 1968. BMW by then was not only gaining momentum in Europe, but beginning to attract attention in the United States. Auto journalist David E. Davis' famous 1968 review of the 2002 in *Car and Driver* was like a christening. Davis judged the BMW to be a car for discerning American drivers amid the growing sameness coming out of Detroit.

Quandt and Hahnemann had put BMW back on track. But the aging Quandt was having trouble maintaining control of his burgeoning car company, which was still only one part of his empire. Because Quandt was losing his eyesight (having suffered vision problems since he was a child), he evaluated new car designs by having designers make scale models so that he could rub his hands over the contours. Quandt had his second wife, Johanna, read all important business correspondence. He managed the company by listening intently to the voices of his executives. By 1969, just as the 2002 was making its mark, Quandt decided to put BMW into the hands of a new leader, someone not unlike himself. His choice was a surprise to the industry, but came naturally to Quandt. Eberhard von Kuenheim had spent 11 years as a production and sales engineer and later technical manager of the Max Mueller machine-tool company in Hanover, Germany. In 1965, Quandt hired the 36-year technocrat and put him in charge of coordinating technical matters in the group. Three years later, he gave von Kuenheim a particularly difficult assignment—head of Industrie-Werke Karlsruhe Augsburg, a machine tool company owned by the Quandts. Von Kuenheim had turned IWK around after only two years, and in January 1970 Quandt installed the 41-year-old Prussian aristocrat as head of BMW. At the September 1969 Frankfurt Auto Show, Quandt announced his decision that von Kuenheim would replace Gerhard Wilcke as chairman of the management board. Much could be heard in von Kuenheim's solemn baritone. The son of a proud Prussian family, von Kuenheim's slow, measured way of speaking filled the sightless Herbert Quandt with vision and confidence. BMW's senior executives, though, were shocked. The young machine-tool executive seemed unprepared for the job. BMW had reconstructed itself over the previous decade and had developed its own set of heroes. And von Kuenheim had no experience in the auto industry. The new chairman immediately clashed with Hahnemann, who called von Kuenheim's appointment the most expensive apprenticeship program in the car industry.

Within two years, Hahnemann was forced out. Some saw his departure as a huge mistake that would rob BMW of its momentum. With Quandt's money and commitment, Hahnemann had largely masterminded BMW's revival. Indeed, much of what he set forth in the 1960s, including the famous four-cylinder headquarters building, is still part of the BMW ethos. "Hahnemann feared nobody. He knew exactly what he was doing, and he knew everybody," said a former BMW executive. "But he was too much of a one-man show. You can rise and fall with such a man, and this is not what Quandt had in mind."

There were problems to be overcome. BMW needed a growth strategy. The build quality of BMW cars was still uneven, at least a generation behind Mercedes-Benz. And David E. Davis aside, the company still lusted for wider acceptance in America. So the most important executive hiring decision von Kuenheim would have to make was Hahnemann's replacement as head of sales and marketing. And Bob Lutz would make the world forget about Paul Hahnemann.

Together, von Kuenheim and Lutz would show the world that BMW had never been anything but the most admired automobile brand in the world. Von Kuenheim's 23 years in command was the longest span of power by any post–World War II auto CEO who did not own the company. Under von Kuenheim, BMW's sales revenues grew from 1.5 billion deutsche marks in 1970 to over 30 billion marks in 1993, the year he retired.

"I came in 1970 when BMW was selling 140,000 cars a year," said von Kuenheim. "The year before had turnover of one billion deutsch marks. That was a fixed point. Quandt wondered what to do with BMW, because it was very small. The experts said you could only succeed if you produce 500,000. We didn't have enough money, capacity, research or development people. When you are small you have only one chance—to produce more expensive cars. Higher turnover or higher volume. We went for the premium sector.

"How do you come out of that mousetrap to become bigger or go in a special sector niche? You go someplace where there is more or less no competition. We had a luxury sporty car. Good engine, good handling, and we got as high a price as possible. The VW Beetle sold for 4,500 to 5,000 marks in those days. I remember the BMW management board said, 'let's take 1,000 more, 20 percent more.' We had a fight on the board and decided 1,000 was not enough. We decided in 1970 to take 3,000 more," von Kuenheim said.

"It didn't work so well. It was a very bumpy road. The idea was right to go in that direction. But it was a company guided and controlled by engineers. We had excellent technical content. We had the best chassis, best engine, best handling. But we had no sales organization. And we were very provincial. Not a European company, not even a German company. It was a Bavarian company."

BMW began to make its first strides toward the top rank of world automotive brands when von Kuenheim and Bob Lutz decided in 1972 to take control of the company's national importers around the world. This was an unprecedented move that was tremendously taxing in time and energy. But the two men decided that it had to be done. The small Bavarian company had been flogging its motorcycles in overseas markets, but the car business was mainly focused on Germany. Hahnemann had put together a network of private distributors that was costing BMW a lot of money. The distributors were getting rich, while BMW was barely breaking even on the cars it sold outside of Germany.

"It was a very important decision to take control of the importers," said von Kuenheim. "They all were millionaires and we said we could use that money. I had very good help from a man named Bob Lutz. That was one of the secrets." When it was all over, BMW was able to control its brand and keep more of the profits from its cars. It was this strategic move that set BMW on a 30-year run as the world's most profitable—for its size—auto company.

Bob Lutz always felt that his single greatest contribution at BMW was getting the distribution under control. "BMW only sold through its own dealers in the United States," he said. "Everywhere else it had importers, and the importers were taking these horrendous margins."

Even in Europe, BMW had independent importers. "We already had the EC, and we had a separate importer for France, one for Belgium, one for Holland, and Italy," Lutz said. "In the U.S. we had a man named Maxie Hoffman. These guys all had multi-year contracts. They owned a lot of their own retail distribution, plus they had a 15 percent distributors' override, plus the 22 percent retail, so if they ran their own retail stores they're operating with a margin of well over 30 percent. We were essentially shipping them the vehicles at cost. We only made money on the vehicles in Germany. So I said to von Kuenheim, 'Hey, this isn't working.' He said this was the system that Hahnemann put in, and he seemed to be very friendly with these guys. Well, no wonder."

So young Lutz set off around Europe buying the import rights back from the entrepreneurs who held them. He moved around Europe with a young BMW lawyer named Hagen Luderitz. "It involved a lot of negotiating, a lot of threats, and a lot of knowledge of new EC law. Finally we got rid of Maxie Hoffman, and that was the last one; that was such a quantum change in the profitability of BMW. They were siphoning off the profit, and they were living like kings," said Lutz.

The extravagance of the private importers was unbelievable. The French importer had a 19-year-old son who wore white suede Elvis outfits and had a chauffeur in white livery who drove him around Paris in a white Rolls-Royce Phantom with white leather upholstery. Some of the BMW management board members had become used to the perks handed out by the distributors when they traveled around Europe. After Lutz had got rid of the French distributor, one member of the management board complained.

"I was just in Paris with my wife. We went to the Paris show, and I must say I am very, very disappointed with Mr. Lutz's performance here with our national sales company," said the man. Lutz asked why the man was unhappy.

"Well, back in the old days with our former distributor, my wife and I would go to Paris, and we'd be picked up at the airport in a Rolls-Royce, and we'd be driven to the Plaza Athénée and there on the cocktail table would be a nice gold watch for me and a diamond bracelet for my wife. And now I get to the hotel room and its just, 'Welcome to Paris. Your show tickets are enclosed in this envelope, please let us know if we can do anything for you.' This is an outrage. It was much better on the old days."

Lutz asked his colleague, "Did it ever occur to you, sir, who was paying for that gold watch and that diamond bracelet? It was coming out of the obscene profits made distributing our cars."

Lutz said there were a lot of personal linkages between distributors and senior people at BMW from the pre–von Kuenheim days. "These distributors weren't dumb," he said; they would entice the senior people at BMW with lavish bribes, such as cruises to the Greek islands.

According to Lutz, a distributor might say to a BMW man, "Just tell me when you'd like to go. I will make my yacht available to you, and I have a full crew. Tell me what kind of wines you like. Here, I'll give you this map. Show me what ports you'd like to see."

"Wow, is it OK?" the BMW executive would ask.

"Don't worry about it, nobody need know."

When Lutz tried to remove a distributor in Italy, the man asked him, "Mr. Lutz, do you like women?"

"Well, I'm sorry to say it is one of my weaknesses," Lutz said.

"Good, good, I just wanted to know," the distributor replied. "I have in the Mediterranean this beautiful yacht, just beautiful. And instead of talking about how you want to take away the distributorship from me, why don't we go on the yacht for 10 days. I have this beautiful countess, she is a little bit older, maybe 45, but she is for me. But her daughter is 19. I tell you the countess for me; the daughter for you. Nobody talks about it."

"Well, I could just see pictures of me fornicating this 19-year-old, the hidden video cameras are rolling. So I didn't fall for that one," said Lutz.

Hahnemann was in the center of the morass. "Hahnemann had to go because there were ethical violations of titanic proportions," said Lutz. "I mean absolutely titanic proportions. The mind boggles at the amount of money that came in through fictitious billings to the advertising agency and the fact that all BMW printed materials were printed by a publishing house that belonged to Hahnemann's mistress and it was never put out for bids. I think I would feel safe talking about it now because I think the statute of limitations has run on it. He was encouraged to resign under threat of prosecution. I was brought in because he had been canned." This was the mess von Kuenheim—and Lutz—inherited in the early 1970s.

Owning its own national sales companies allowed BMW to better control its brand image around the world and had the further effect of accelerating BMW's sales growth. The company needed volume to justify its company-owned worldwide distribution network. Von Kuenheim decided that BMW needed to capture 1 percent of the world market, or 370,000 units at the time. Many industry watchers believed BMW could not survive independently.

In the early 1970s, Lutz said he constantly heard the question, "How can BMW make it when they only produce 200,000 units?" Richard Gaul, a longtime public-relations boss who was a newspaper reporter covering BMW at the time, said, "In 1970, when Kuenheim took over he changed BMW from a small company owned by a rich investor into a real company." First von Kuenheim moved the company out of Munich by investing in a new plant in nearby Dingolfing. That was a big step in the evolution of the company. "This was a real brave decision, taken as it was during the first oil crisis," said Gaul. "Kuenheim's second big decision was moving the company out of Germany, which he did with Lutz by buying all our sales subsidiaries in all the countries. In 1983, we were the first to have our own distributor in Japan."

Von Kuenheim modernized BMW, but he still allowed the engineers to dominate the company. For many years, von Kuenheim didn't even give the top sales-and-marketing executive a seat on the management board. "He gives the engineers the feeling they are doing the most important job," said one BMW executive. And like Herbert Quandt, von Kuenheim seemed to have a sixth sense about everything going on at BMW. "The thing about von Kuenheim is that you could not lie to him," said one longtime BMW executive. "He knew everything." Said another, "Von Kuenheim was always the aristocrat. He could also be very scathing. With a movement of the hand, he could show that someone was not wanted. He could show that he was upset by simply mispronouncing your name." The press originally saw von Kuenheim as a kind of glorified clerk working for the owner of the company. But inside BMW, von Kuenheim projected an aura of grandeur. "When he came into a room, the room became quiet, because von Kuenheim himself was quiet. An alleyway would open up for him."

Von Kuenheim used the German language of his father and mother, employing old-style analogies that his managers had not heard since they were children. "He was the most demanding guy I ever met in every respect," said one of his former lieutenants. "In my first year I doubted I would be successful. He really brings you to your limits. He worked you every day, 24 hours a day. He always asked for intelligent solutions. If I complained that, 'Daimler has a lot of money to do things,' he would say, 'if you come up with an intelligent solution, you will have a lot of money as well.' He spoke in a very quiet way. He was very polite, but on the other hand very strict."

Von Kuenheim's vision was to be No. 1 in the luxury-car business. "In the mid-1980s, I remember he said he wanted to be attractive to old money. Young people were already buying BMWs, old money bought Mercedes," said a former BMW executive. Indeed, von Kuenheim brought a laser-like focus to Mercedes-Benz. "With this, he put BMW on track for its current success," said Jürgen Hubbert, the longtime head of Mercedes' passenger-car operations. A former BMW underling said: "He had the nemesis in Stuttgart. Mercedes was so old, had so much tradition. If von Kuenheim had a vision, it was that he wanted to be as good as Mercedes. And he did it with fewer resources."

But von Kuenheim's concept of chasing Mercedes was to be the leader. And it was often Mercedes trailing BMW's lead on some new technical development or business strategy. BMW made the decision to adopt electronic controls in its cars in 1978, at least eight years before Mercedes. The success of the BMW 3 series led Mercedes to bring out the 190 "Baby Benz" in 1984.

The 1986 7 series—the work of a BMW engineering team led by a young von Kuenheim protégé named Wolfgang Reitzle—was for years routinely called "the best sedan in the world." The 750iL version led to an industry-wide comeback of the 12-cylinder engine. Mercedes followed with a new S-class two years later that was a deep disappointment compared with the lithe 7 series. In the late 1980s, the 7 series outsold the S-class for the first time, which created a revolution in Stuttgart and caused heads to roll. Mercedes sought to redefine itself as a maker of lighter, more nimble cars.

In 1982, BMW held a gathering of its executives in Garmisch, south of Munich. Von Kuenheim gave a speech that included one paragraph that got a lot of attention. He said BMW's long-term goal, within 10 to 15 years, was to be No. 1. The goal was extremely ambitious. BMW still had a limited product lineup, and it would still be four years before the great 7 series of 1986 debuted. But the target was also very unspecific. BMW's sales people thought von Kuenheim wanted to become No. 1 in sales volume over Mercedes. Engineers interpreted von Kuenheim as wanting to be No. 1 in engines. "You could transfer it to any part of the business," said Gaul.

Von Kuenheim had learned from Soichiro Honda how important it was to give people goals to shoot for—especially, big overarching corporate goals. In Honda's case, it was racing—to win the motorcycle Tourist Trophy and Le Mans. Now von Kuenheim had laid out the big corporate goal. In his speech, today the stuff of legend at BMW, von Kuenheim didn't even mention Mercedes-Benz. But for many years afterward, people in the company would preface statements with the reverential "As von Kuenheim said in Garmisch." It was the spirit of Garmisch that led to the decision to offer 12-cylinder engines before V-8s on the E-32, the 1986 rendition of the 7 series. When the E-32 was nearly finished in 1983, Wielfried Ball, the engineer responsible for the body, had the impression that the car was too narrow. He built a prototype that was 2.5 centimeters wider and a little shorter than the car that was planned. Then Ball went to Reitzle, who went to von Kuenheim, who said BMW should make the change even if it meant spending several million more deutsche marks in development.

The 7 series' noble stance was a key to its success, say BMW engineers today. When the E-32 was launched, Jaguar's XJ12 was the only other V-12 sedan in the world. Von Kuenheim decided that the new 7 series needed one—and sooner rather than later.

The 12-banger version came out two years after the inline six and one year before the V-8. It was not a rational decision—certainly something Ford's bean counters would not have stood for. But von Kuenheim insisted. The V-12 would be another salvo against Mercedes-Benz.

In the late 1980s, BMW engineer Max Reissboeck was working on the E-36 generation of the 3 series that would debut in 1992. Reissboeck, who was a car enthusiast, had built for himself a small station-wagon version based on the then-current E-30 by making the roof a little longer and taking out the trunk. He was driving the makeshift wagon to work, and people took notice. The car even came to the attention of von Kuenheim, who asked Reissboeck for a look at the car.

Von Kuenheim liked it so much that he decided there and then that he wanted to produce the vehicle, and he asked Reissboeck to turn it over to the engineering department as a prototype. It became the first BMW Touring model, giving BMW drivers a place to stow skis and other gear without having to strap it to the roof of the car.

While the 7 series was making its debut, BMW opened its sprawling "FIZ" (Forschungs-und Innovationszentrum) engineering center. The glass-and-steel R&D center in Munich was the first facility in which a car company had brought together research, development, logistics, and quality control under one roof. The FIZ cost 1.2 billion deutsche marks, employed 6,000 engineers, and inspired almost every automotive technical center in the world. Chrysler's engineering center, which opened in the early 1990s and which Iacocca would regard as one of his greatest accomplishments, was a knockoff of von Kuenheim's FIZ.

In 1992, BMW decided to build an assembly plant in the United States—von Kuenheim again leading and Mercedes following. BMW set up shop in Spartanburg, South Carolina, for production of the Z-3 roadster and later other models. Not long afterwards, Mercedes set up its own U.S. plant in Vance, Alabama, after long insisting it would never produce a Mercedes car in America. "We have to maintain, secure, and build up the position we have achieved in the American market," von Kuenheim said at the time. "This is becoming increasingly difficult to do from Germany." The interaction between BMW and Mercedes was not unlike that of Honda and Toyota in Japan. Mercedes and Toyota were the older, bigger brothers. Without the competitive spark of Honda and BMW—which time after time proved faster, nimbler, and more creative than the older companies—Mercedes and Toyota would have been far more complacent and far less competitive.

Von Kuenheim also brought a manufacturing culture to BMW, and manufacturing was the crucial third leg of the stool with engineering and marketing. The machine-tool executive was a great believer in quality and in-plant flexibility—a philosophy inside BMW that became as strong as the "ultimate-driving-machine" sensibility.

While the famed Toyota Production System focused on eliminating the waste of time and resources, BMW became the most avidly adaptable carmaker in the world, able to produce countless variations of its cars on demand.

One of the keys to BMW's success was its customer-oriented sales and production process, which placed so much responsibility on functions such as logistics. No two BMWs on the assembly line are precisely alike. The mass customization concept allowed BMW buyers to design their own cars almost piece by piece. By 2000, BMW was far ahead of the world leaders in build-to-order delivery times. It could accept precisely specified customer orders much later than other manufacturers—a capability that descended directly from von Kuenheim's creed of flexibility.

Von Kuenheim had a vision for BMW, and he knew BMW had to have "the right behavior." He said, "We needed to treat people correctly—our customers, our suppliers. Letters had to be answered in the same week. We had to treat suppliers as gentlemen, something not seen in the previous few years. Some assemblers are now killing suppliers. We had to bring out the right style." It was the reason BMW led the way with electronics. "When I was a machine-tool businessman [I remember calling on Mercedes-Benz]. A Mercedes executive told me, 'I will never use electronics.'" Von Kuenheim filed that away for later use, and when he took over BMW a few years later he resolved to implement electronic controls in his cars as soon as possible.

"One of the early things I did when we got together was to go around one of the BMW plants," remembered Ralph Robins, the longtime chairman of Rolls-Royce plc, the aerospace engine manufacturer that formed a joint venture with BMW. "Electronics in aero engines were even more complex than in automobile engines. But I was impressed with what I saw at BMW, and I asked if they would do an engine management system for an aircraft engine. They did a beautiful piece of equipment, a one-off. I told von Kuenheim he should be in that business—engine management systems. But it was never built for serial production because everyone's got a bit of not-invented-here syndrome in this business. Today they are putting even more effort into electronics, while DaimlerChrysler is backing off; BMW has had difficulties—as Mercedes has, with electronics. But BMW isn't backing off."

Robins was astounded by the capability he found at the German carmaker. "It was a very high-class engineering outfit. I was amazed.

I'm used to having a company with a lot of high-class engineers. We had 5,000 of them. But BMW had that many, too. I was amazed at the degree of intellectual capability. [Von Kuenheim and I] went to dinner on a number of occasions. I remember once walking into a restaurant with him in Munich and the whole restaurant fell silent. He was treated as a very important citizen of Munich."

BMW had to speed up, so von Kuenheim relied on Bosch and other German suppliers to fulfill many of BMW's production needs. In the early- to mid-1980s, BMW had the industry's lowest level of in-house production. Von Kuenheim changed the way automakers dealt with suppliers, uncovering a whole new way to mine technology from companies—a method that borrowed a little from the Japanese keiretsu. His strategy was to ask his vendors to innovate. In return, he would treat their parts as more than commodities and would protect the technology. He would not take what Bosch or Siemens or the transmission maker Zahnradfabrik Friedrichshafen (ZF) had to offer, and then bid the technology to others who could build it cheaper. The strategy, as much as anything, had to do with BMW's advances, and it deeply influenced the way all automakers and suppliers interacted. BMW started it all, and in large part it was because von Kuenheim had himself been a supplier. Loyalty was something von Kuenheim believed in deeply, because it was ingrained in him from his youth. He would be loyal to the Quandt family and to his young executives and to his suppliers, and he demanded loyalty in return.

As he approached his own retirement in the early 1990s, von Kuenheim was looked upon as the great sage of the industry. In 1992, his last year as chairman of the management board, BMW had surpassed Mercedes-Benz in sales for the first time and had defined the market for sporty luxury sedans. It had a lean, flexible management team, great products, excellent margins, and a crystal-clear brand identity.

When Ferdinand Piëch began looking for a new head of his family's Porsche sports car company in 1991, he decided the right man was von Kuenheim's favorite son at BMW—Wolfgang Reitzle. The goal was not just to acquire Reitzle's obvious product know-how, but also to somehow gain access to the magic of von Kuenheim himself. But it was von Kuenheim who refused to allow this to happen—by apparently refusing to let Reitzle out of his contract. Thus Piëch decided to look for a "von Kuenheim" of his own. He found him in the Porsche organization, just as Quandt had found von Kuenheim 25 years earlier within his own group. Like the BMW maestro, Wendelin Wiedeking was 39 and virtually unknown when he took over a deeply troubled Porsche in late 1991. Like von Kuenheim, he was a surprise choice—a production specialist taking over a company known for its engineering prowess and marketing strength. Like von Kuenheim, he brought his company to new heights through flexible manufacturing principles.

Von Kuenheim's influence was incalculable. "Everything we did at Audi in 1993 to 1997 was in a way following what von Kuenheim had done," said a senior Audi executive. "BMW had a coherent relationship between engineering and brand. It was a company, not just a bunch of engineers. Von Kuenheim did that better than anyone." Von Kuenheim assembled more good young executives for a company its size than any automaker in the world; so many, in fact, that it was able to withstand the loss of several of them in the bloodletting that occurred during BMW's tragic attempt to fix Rover Group. "The great failure of Piëch was his inability to create a team. He left VW weaker than he found it," said a former Volkswagen executive. Piëch failed on the human side. "He was not able to create coherence."

But von Kuenheim built a powerful cadre of senior executives that included many qualified successors. "There may have been too many successors," said the VW executive, "but it is better to have too many than too few." Von Kuenheim's style of management was to always have two executives competing for every job and to let them fight it out. The competition between Bernd Pischetsrieder and Wolfgang Reitzle in 1993 was the most striking example.

It is likely that von Kuenheim learned the technique from his employer. It was the Quandt family that hired Bob Lutz before confirming von Kuenheim in his position of complete authority—and left the two to sweat it out.

After Lutz had settled for the secondary role, he became annoyed by the "kitchen cabinet," another distinctive von Kuenheim management tool—and voiced the complaint to him. "Von Kuenheim worried about my public personae because we were about the same age," said Lutz. "So there was this tension. The thing I didn't like about his management style, and I've told him this, is that he tended to manage not through colleagues, his co-members of the vorstand who under German law are kind of his equal—except he had a stronger vote. If he wanted a sales problem solved or wanted questions [answered] about sales or marketing, he rarely came to me, he had this special group of assistants. They were young Cologne business-school MBAs and PhDs who were carefully selected by him.

"It was a cluster of assistants. He had an assistant for production, an assistant for engineering, an assistant for product planning or for sales and marketing. It was like a kitchen cabinet, a parallel cabinet," Lutz said. "So he rarely went to his direct reports, the guys he should be talking to, and he put everything through his assistants, who would burrow down into the organization and get the information for him bring it back up to him. Then at a board meeting he would say, 'Mr. Lutz how many of the 3-liter coupes do we have in stock, are we moving those?' And he would already know the answer."

A former BMW executive said von Kuenheim assembled the talented young staff as a way to get to the heart of his company. "Yes, von Kuenheim had a kitchen cabinet. That was what the Monday morning meetings were all about." Von Kuenheim went home at 6 p.m. on Fridays and arrived at 9:00 a.m. on Monday morning, but he never took home files and folders and work; he went home for the weekend and read a book, usually about history.

One former assistant recalls: "He would start talking about the book he had read over the weekend. He would say 'did you know about this?' and I would say, 'No, can you please tell me.' It would be a book about the Prussian army or something." Indeed, von Kuenheim consulted on Monday mornings not with members of the management board—the board met the following day—but with his special aides for sales and marketing and production and engineering and personnel and legal affairs and other disciplines. They were young, and they were loyal above all to von Kuenheim. He sat with them for two or three hours, probing them, absorbing their facts and seeking out their opinions. Von Kuenheim was a good listener. To one of his former assistants, he was strict, but he listened. "That was the preparation for the Tuesday morning board meetings. That's where he got his knowledge. The staff got its material on Friday and it had to prepare for Monday morning. Out of those meetings he [von Kuenheim] came to a conclusion. He may have known what he wanted to do before, but he was open to listening to new ideas for solutions. He tried to balance and weigh."

"I got along very well with him straightaway," recalls Ralph Robins. "We were both technocrats. He thought it unusual that I was an engineer running a British company. That wasn't unusual in Germany, but at the time it was unusual in the U.K. We hit it off very quickly. BMW had come from nothing, and it pursued a very consistent policy. He took it to a very strong position. When we met, he decided he wanted to take the company back to its roots." BMW had started building engines for World War I–vintage German fighter planes. Von Kuenheim had had so much success developing cars he could sell at a premium that he had begun to look around for other businesses where he could do the same. "BMW had become successful selling premium cars," said Robins. "Where else could you get a premium price for a product? The aerospace industry was seen to be one. What came out of it was a world-class aero engine plant in Berlin and a world-class car

[Rolls-Royce] factory in Goodwood. It all went very well." Robins and von Kuenheim were a good fit from the beginning, which made the difference when Volkswagen would buy Rolls-Royce the carmaker a decade later but fail to gain the rights to the name—which belonged to Robins' Rolls-Royce plc.

Robins was an engineer and car fanatic who had been a young engineer at Rolls before the auto and aero sides of the business were unceremoniously split up in the early 1970s. What impressed him was BMW's technical prowess. But he was even more impressed by von Kuenheim himself. "We had a fit right from the beginning," he said. "He was very straightforward to deal with. He had the respect of everyone there. He was a very clear-cut decision maker. We had a unique relationship." The two men met in the mid-1980s. "I remember walking into a room and Wolfgang Reitzle was there. Then von Kuenheim came into the room. It was clear who was going to make the decision. I accepted that he had a very, very good knowledge of the auto industry, and he accepted that I had a good knowledge of the aerospace industry."

That Bob Lutz would even consider leaving the cocoon of General Motors so early in his career was a measure of his self-confidence. He was a German-speaking Swiss-American, who had joined GM at the company's New York Overseas Planning Office. He came out of Stanford's famed business school after a long career in the United States Marines. Lutz's European roots and language ability made him a natural for GM's Adam Opel subsidiary in Rüsselsheim, Germany. Working under future GM vice chairman Alexander Cunningham, Lutz was a man in a hurry. He was already 32 when he reached Opel and had no time to lose. He quickly moved up the ranks, displaying a rare product insight and uncommon self-confidence. Within 10 years of joining GM, he would be running Ford of Europe. It was possibly the fastest track any post-war auto executive was ever on. The Lutz legend was taking root.

He had seemed destined to scale the heights of the world's largest company. But in 1971 Lutz stunned Cunningham by accepting BMW's offer to become Hahnemann's replacement. Partly it was for money—eight times as much, Lutz said. But what really drove Bob Lutz was driving itself. Driving cars. Once back in Europe, the fighter pilot rediscovered the joys of the autobahn and of tearing through Germany's perfectly paved back roads. The country was one giant race course. He believed he could sell cars that handled and performed well—and Opel models came up short. He had a hard time making the GM bosses back in Detroit understand that Europeans wanted a driving experience different from American customers. What Lutz absorbed during his three years at BMW would ignite him and would in turn influence Ford, Chrysler, and ultimately General Motors. He carried BMW's driving sensibilities to those companies—and tried his best to pass them on. It was as though he was on a mission to make the rest of the world's cars like BMW's. Lutz hit the ground running in Munich. Von Kuenheim called him "schnelle Bob" or "fast Bob." Lutz saw it as his job to exploit and enhance BMW's status as a driver's car—an alternative to Europe's tedious mainstream offerings and the loose-handling floaters from Detroit. Some said he understood the brand better than von Kuenheim himself. Lutz was paying close attention from Rüsselsheim. He was racing against BMWs on the autobahn and peering into the cars to see who drove them. Lutz saw a great brand under construction.

One of the first things Bob Lutz did in Munich was to reverse von Kuenheim's decision to modify the BMW logo by getting rid of the letters "BMW" and the black border, leaving only the blue and white propeller. Lutz also immediately began to put his stamp on BMW's products. He sketched a coupe on a napkin that would become one of the company's most legendary cars, the 6 series coupe—later realized in full form by Paul Bracq. In 1971, von Kuenheim decided BMW should commit itself to racing—canceling a decision made by Hahnemann. Lutz's first step was to form a separate competition group, BMW Motorsport GmbH, which began turning out hot versions of BMW production cars.

Lutz's most important job at BMW was to cement the company's place in the American market. One problem was that BMW was a mystery to most Americans. A generation in the United States grew up thinking BMW stood for "British Motor Works." Lutz had to carve out name recognition that went beyond readers of enthusiast magazines.

In 1974, Lutz put BMW's U.S. advertising account up for review and ultimately chose the upstart firm of Ammirati and Puris to create a new campaign. The agency was selected over older and more established shops. Ralph Ammirati and Martin Puris had been copywriters at a trendy agency called Carl Ally that had done some clever ads for Fiat in the U.S. that Lutz admired. Now that the two men were on their own, Lutz wanted them to create something extraordinary for BMW. And they did. Ammirati and Puris began hammering away at themes that in time would help send BMW into the front ranks of the world's consumer brands. The ads emphasized "new luxury" founded on speed and driving sensation, handling and power. Puris came up with the tagline: "The Ultimate Driving Machine." The ads contrasted BMW with the mushy dynamics of most cars on American roads in the early 1970s. They turned BMW's spartan interiors into a plus point.

The oldest of the American baby boomers were turning 29 when the first Ammirati & Puris ads broke in print and on television. It was the first wave of what would be the biggest demographic change in history. There were more 17- and 18-year-olds in America in 1975 than anytime before or since. And these were highly impressionable TV-era teenagers being exposed to the early BMW advertising. What Lutz and Ammirati and Puris did in the mid-1970s was to help fuel the American baby-boom lust not only for BMWs, but for quality goods of all kinds—even if the vast majority of those kids had to get through college and find a very good job before even thinking about becoming luxury consumers. Those kids never strayed far from their ideal automobile, even if tens of thousands eventually bought a Mercedes or an Audi or even a Saab. BMW advertising helped form their impressions. It wasn't only driving enthusiasts who bought BMWs in the 1980s, it was a new class of young professionals who a generation earlier would have bought Cadillacs.

The image created by Lutz's campaign told affluent young Americans about something they didn't know they needed—and barely knew existed. Lutz was gone by the time the ads began in earnest—having left for Ford of Europe in 1974. But he was the father of that perfectly timed, massively influential promotional barrage. For a while, von Kuenheim was expected to take over leadership of Quandt's entire empire, and Lutz was viewed as a possible successor. But there was a tension between the two men that caused Lutz to leave. They both understood BMW's values. But von Kuenheim would survive Lutz's departure just as he did Hahnemann's. And BMW's brand qualities never shifted even slightly during the 23 years he was in command, something that's never happened anywhere in the auto industry—before or since. Von Kuenheim planted the BMW ensign so deeply in the soil that it never once swayed.

By the 1980s, BMW was the consumer brand most identified with rich, free-spending yuppies. The compact Three Series, launched in 1982, was a yuppie's dream car. In fact, it was so closely linked with young urban professionals—with all their negative connotations—that the label became a kind of albatross by the end of the 1980s, becoming more of a marketing problem than an advantage. But the brand was by then much too strong, and BMW had become deeply embedded in American culture. No automotive nameplate in the world could boast more positive associations. It was the brand of dreams. After the mid-1980s, every car marque in the world aspired to BMW-like status, and BMW became everyone's benchmark—even Lutz's. At his first European auto show after moving to Chrysler—the March 1987 Geneva show—Lutz faced a roomful of European journalists. He knew the drill. "If you turn this Chrysler LeBaron upside down," Lutz said, "it has everything a BMW has."

It also had some things that BMW didn't have, like road noise, engine noise, scuttle shake in the convertible model, and a poor automatic transmission. Nevertheless, it was the best-selling open car in the United States within four years. Lutz was the consummate professional who—despite his flawless taste for good cars—could sell anything to anyone, and would continue to do so.

CHAPTER FIVE

Lee Iacocca Confronts the Ford Family

T he longer Henry Ford II ran the Ford Motor Company the more capricious he was when it came to hiring and firing his top lieutenants. The heavy politics at Ford during the 1960s and 1970s grew out of Henry II's impulsive behavior. He would discard executives for no obvious reason, sometimes literally because he didn't like the cut of their clothes. You never knew where you stood with him.

"Always keep your people anxious and off balance," Ford once told Lee Iacocca. Success at Ford depended not only on initiative and results, it meant giving the company's powerful finance division a wide berth; and, first and foremost, it required staying out of trouble with the Deuce. Across town at General Motors, the bureaucracy was set in stone. One had to follow rigid rules to move up the corporate ladder, but these rules were so easy to understand they could have been made into a book. You picked up your boss at the airport, prepared his reports to higher-ups, hit your financial targets, and tried not to stand out too much. At Ford, the rules were always changing—and so were the players. One day Bunkie Knudsen was in charge and the next day he wasn't. One day Henry was in a good mood and could share a joke and see your point and the next day it was off with your head.

Everyone's luck seemed to run out eventually. Until Phillip Caldwell replaced Henry II as chairman in the 1980s, every No. 2 man under Henry II had his career cut short in some dramatic way.

The conflict that came to a head in 1978 between Henry Ford II and Lee Iacocca was standard Ford boardroom soap-opera fare. But for the automotive industry, the conflict was a decisive event that brought radical change to the global auto business. Everything changed after Iacocca left Ford for Chrysler.

As Henry Ford II grew older, a generational divide opened up in the company. Some of the men in Iacocca's generation—born in the 1920s—had begun to question the finance-minded Whiz Kids, who were all born in the 1910s. The younger men tended to be more market oriented and less numbers driven, whether they were in sales or engineering or even finance. It was as if a two-party system had developed in the company.

By the late 1960s and early 1970s, the young guys were pushing the chairman to build a small front-wheel-drive car to confront rising foreign competition. By the late 1970s, after Honda's breakthrough with the CVCC engine, small front-wheel-drive Japanese imports had begun to eat into Ford's market share and earnings. A group of young executives was challenging Henry II's willingness to leave the small-car market to others. One of the critics was a product executive named Don Frey, a contemporary of Lee Iacocca's who had more to do with the actual development of the Mustang than anyone else. Frey had been an engineering professor at the University of Michigan before he joined Ford. He was a voracious reader and liked to talk about the books he had read. "Maybe he's a genius," Henry Ford II once said. "Maybe not. But he's certainly a pain in the ass."

As Henry II grew older, the main thing he seemed to want from his executives was that they *not* be a pain in the ass. In the 1960s and 1970s, almost anyone who fell out of grace with Henry Ford did so because, to one degree or another, they got on the Deuce's nerves. And this was the worst possible sin to Ford. Becoming a pain in the royal ass eventually cancelled out anything you may have achieved and might still have to offer.

The most notable of the royal pains was, of course, Iacocca.

No matter how talented an executive, or how brilliant and inventive and productive and successful you were, if you got on Henry's nerves you didn't stick around.

Henry II's first gulp of air at Ford Motor Company had not been the joy of creating a breakthrough car or solving a production problem but getting rid of Harry Bennett and his henchmen. Having been only 27 years old when he took control of the company, Ford was consumed with self-doubt, even if his actions never betrayed it. But by the late 1950s, as he passed 40, he began to act less like a self-doubting prince and more like a monarch. Plus he was growing less and less tolerant of anyone who disturbed his peace. He was confident enough to cut himself loose from his mentors, the last being Ernie Breech, the veteran GM executive Henry hired in 1946 to guide day-to-day operations while the young man watched and learned.

Breech installed a tidy management structure, and Henry II allowed the Whiz Kids to infiltrate the finance department and eventually take control of the purse strings. The finance department, the organizational expression of young Henry's fear of chaos and failure, allowed Ford to dig itself out from the mess old Henry had left. By the 1960s, Finance was led by J. Edward Lundy, a shy, single, and single-minded original Whiz Kid, who would become a cult figure inside Ford. He kept a low profile, but wielded legendary power.

With the elevation of Lundy and fellow Whiz Kid Robert McNamara in the late 1950s, Henry Ford II had begun to rely heavily on his finance generals. In an environment of supreme cost discipline—a kind of "Big Brother" setting, as one former Ford executive put it—Iacocca developed a knack for taking limited resources and creating something special—from building gimmicky sales programs in the 1950s to repackaging the mundane Ford Falcon into the fire-breathing Mustang in 1964. Iacocca was the lead campaigner among dozens of talented young engineers and executives who had grown up in Ford's meritocracy in the 1950s. Many of them would later save Chrysler from ruin under Iacocca's flag.

As Iacocca moved up the ranks at Ford, he brought with him a new kind of young executive—men like Frey, Norman Krandall, Bert Andren, Hans Matthias, and Hal Sperlich. They were mostly car enthusiasts who began to believe that the company was taking huge risks by failing to invest in important new vehicle concepts. Increasingly, they were throwing themselves up against Lundy's finance department barricades.

Henry II was 41 when he began a love affair with the Italian-born Cristina Vettore Austin. He met her in March 1960 at a dinner for Princess Grace of Monaco. In 1963, he divorced his wife, Anne, and in 1965 married Cristina. It was in those years that Ford executives back in Dearborn began to notice that Henry was becoming less tolerant of the younger product planners and engineers. He sat through fewer meetings with them than he did earlier in his career. He didn't see ideas take shape and thus fall into allegiance with them early on. He only saw fully developed ideas, and when they surprised him, his gut instinct was to shoot them down. It was a new Henry Ford. McNamara's departure in the autumn of 1960 may have had something to do with it. "When I was at Ford, Henry II was too busy to get into trouble," McNamara said. "He was learning the ropes and doing a first-rate job at it."

Ford's new Whiz Kids, who had followed in the wake of Iacocca's personal success, had begun to exasperate Henry Ford II.

Norman Krandall was the point man on what became known as the Mini/Max project in the late 1960s. It was a concept for a spacious, one-volume vehicle, a small family van with car-like driving characteristics that could fit in a garage. It was a concept that in time would become the minivan, one of the world's most ubiquitous vehicles. In the late 1960s, Krandall had assembled data to demonstrate that the market for such a model would approach 800,000 units. Ford's finance staff didn't believe it and didn't want to risk the billions of dollars that would be needed to create a new front-wheel-drive platform for the vehicle. Krandall left Ford in 1978 after his deepening frustration over the slow movement of the Mini/Max project led to a showdown with Lundy.

Meanwhile, Henry was himself growing a little dizzy with everything happening around him. And the more disoriented he became, the angrier he got. During the late 1960s and early 1970s, Ford sat through countless meetings in which young engineers and product planners, most of them acolytes of Lee Iacocca, wanted the company to build small front-wheel-drive passenger cars. There was always another meeting where Ford had to listen to proposals that went against his fundamental product beliefs—that small cars meant small profits. Ford wanted to continue building large rear-wheel-drive sedans that offered high profit margins. His finance staff beat back the challenges, but the younger firebrand executives such as Sperlich and Krandall were coming up with new studies and new data that suggested that the Ford Motor Company was straying off course by not building a small front-wheel-drive car.

And this drove Henry crazy. In a series of interviews with a Ford historian in 1982, he said: "A lot of people in the past, maybe even today, tend to say, well, this is what the survey says, and thereby relieve themselves of making a decision. I think that's bunk. If people don't think they know what the public is going to want they shouldn't be in the job." Iacocca, who had taken over as Ford's president in late 1970, was more politically astute than Sperlich and Krandall, but by the mid-1970s had become engaged in the great small-car debate. He joined Sperlich in pushing for a front-wheel-drive car. Henry turned them down—for the United States. But he approved such a car for Europe. It would become the Fiesta, which made its debut in July 1976 as the company's first small front-wheel-drive hatchback.

Iacocca later contended that Phillip Caldwell, then chairman of Ford of Europe and the man who inherited the power taken away from Iacocca, opposed the Fiesta project. But it was Iacocca who had been forced to carry the fight to Henry Ford, and this was the start of Iacocca's undoing despite the fact that the Fiesta became a major success.

The war between Iacocca and Henry Ford was full of intrigue and was a two-sided story if there ever was one. But it wasn't the usual corporate death match because so much rode on it—the very future of the automotive industry, in fact. If Iacocca had stayed at Ford, its product lineup would have been vastly different in the 1980s—for better or worse. The company would have almost certainly worked closely with Honda. If Ford had produced the first minivan in 1980, as Krandall and Sperlich had proposed—four years sooner than Iacocca was able to at Chrysler—the dominoes would have fallen his way. General Motors would have brought out a similar concept that it was preparing in the 1970s. But the front-wheel-drive garageable van had become a losing proposition for Iacocca at Ford. After years of pushing for small cars and small vans, Sperlich had raised so much ire in Henry Ford that the chairman in 1976 ordered Iacocca to get rid of him. Sperlich's strongly held beliefs were largely bred while he ran Ford's European operations, a position Iacocca gave him in 1971 to keep him out of Henry's direct line of fire. After Ford, Sperlich went off to Chrysler as head of product planning—waiting, as it turned out, for Iacocca to arrive in 1978 and green-light the minivan project that had been stalled at Ford.

"Henry Ford had a gruff demeanor, but he was polite," says a Ford executive of that era. "What Henry didn't like about Hal Sperlich was that Sperlich would get so excited that he would forget about being polite. You could be blunt with Henry Ford, but you just had to be polite and Sperlich wasn't." The same man said that if it hadn't been for

Sperlich's abrasive ways, if it had been anyone other than Sperlich who was pushing the minivan concept, Ford would have gone for it. He just couldn't abide Sperlich.

Firing Hal Sperlich was relatively easy for Ford. But it would take him three years to get rid of Iacocca—a sign of Iacocca's enormous power base in the company. Iacocca in 1975 felt he could no longer ignore the Japanese threat, so he devised a plan to get Ford into the small-car business quickly and inexpensively. In late 1975, he boarded a plane for Tokyo to meet, and attempt to strike a deal with, Soichiro Honda. Though Iacocca would emerge as America's most vigorous Japan basher, he found that he liked Soichiro Honda and was deeply influenced by his style and thinking.

After all, it was Soichiro Honda who once said, "It is not in my nature to spend money sparingly when I am having a good time." Here was a man whose name was on the building, who was strong minded and temperamental, yet had none of the arrogance of Henry Ford II. It wasn't Honda's lack of self-importance that impressed Iacocca so much. Iacocca could be as pompous as any captain of industry. It was the reality of what Honda had managed to construct for himself—a large company that he could call his own.

"Honda is a genius," Iacocca recalled years later. "He is like old Henry Ford. He went to the lab every day, put on a white coat, and worked on engines." For now, Honda had the front-wheel-drive technology that Ford needed, and Soichiro Honda welcomed Iacocca to Tokyo as though he were a long-lost son. Here was an American car executive unlike any other he had come across, a cigar-chomping plain-talking man—the sort of man Soichiro Honda could trust. Honda liked Iacocca's relaxed body language. Honda was deeply honored to be called upon by the president of the Ford Motor Company, the institution founded by his hero, Henry Ford, the man whose spirit resided inside Soichiro Honda. Honda had tried to model himself after old Henry Ford, and Iacocca's visit was a symbol of all he had achieved.

Honda was enthusiastic about doing business with Ford, just as he had been very open to an investment banker's proposal for Ford to buy a stake in Honda a decade earlier. Honda invited Iacocca to his home in the fashionable Ikkebukuro section of Tokyo. Iacocca lived in Bloomfield Hills, Michigan, the stunningly upscale enclave of America's automotive aristocracy—an area far more grand than Soichiro Honda's neighborhood. Still, Honda laid out a lavish feast for his guest and received permission from the local authorities to close down traffic in his Tokyo neighborhood and put on a huge fireworks display. Iacocca was thrilled as the two men drank sake and cracked jokes, keeping their translators busy. Iacocca gave the great man a Mustang as a gift. Honda presented Iacocca with a beautiful cloisonné vase. And the two men bonded in Tokyo.

The visit turned out to be a turning point in Iacocca's life and career. Honda was like no automotive executive he had ever seen. He could only think how great it would be to control his own company and his personal destiny, answering to no one.

The atmosphere for doing a business deal was perfect. The next day, Iacocca laid out the details of his proposal to Honda. He wanted to buy 300,000 CVCC engines and transmissions and install them in a special wide-body version of the European Ford Fiesta that would be sold in the United States. Ford would pay $711 per engine, getting a state-of-the-art small-car engine that exceeded U.S. emission standards and would immediately make Ford a major force in the small-car competition against General Motors.

By the time Iacocca jumped into his limousine at the Imperial Hotel and headed off to Haneda Airport, the agreement was sealed. Within 18 months, Ford Fiestas would be rolling off the line at the company's Wayne, Michigan, assembly plant with Honda engines. Lee Iacocca had reacted quickly and decisively to the challenge of rising gas prices and found a way to use changing world conditions to strike a blow against GM.

It was pure Iacocca—a stroke of brilliance like the Mustang. Iacocca believed he had done the deal of a lifetime and had provided Ford with a forceful response to Japanese small-car competition—and a leg up on General Motors. Beating GM to the punch was uppermost on Iacocca's mind, and with Soichiro Honda's engine he knew he could do it.

The problem was that Iacocca had failed to consult Henry about setting up a joint venture with Honda, and the chairman demolished the idea in the famous "Jap engine" outburst. Iacocca was distraught. "What the hell can you do?" he asked his friend Hal Sperlich.

"We were stupid to turn him down," Sperlich said years later.

But it was also a shred of evidence Iacocca felt he might be able to use someday in a showdown with the Deuce. Look how Henry had abused his position and harmed the shareholders in the process. It was inexcusable, Iacocca thought. Now he had to tell his new friend Soichiro Honda that there would be no engine deal.

Henry Ford had hated the secretive way Iacocca had gone about arranging the Honda agreement, and Iacocca had truly become a real pain in the ass. It had been hard enough for Iacocca to get the job of president of the Ford Motor Company. It would be even harder for him to hold on to it. Somewhere along the line, Iacocca began to think the unthinkable, to consider leveraging his personal power base inside Ford in a way that might just allow him to withstand the inevitable face-off with Henry. The visit to Soichiro Honda in 1975 might have got him into hot water, but it also helped fuel his worldview and personal ambition. The sheer, intoxicating pleasure of unquestioned authority! How easily Soichiro Honda wore it. What must it be like? Iacocca really wanted to know.

Several times in his career Iacocca would try to acquire such authority, and he did achieve something like ultimate power at Chrysler in the 1980s. But what he really wanted was to cross the great divide that separated the professional manager from the owner— Henry II's territory. Iacocca's last attempt would come after retiring from Chrysler and joining with billionaire Kirk Kerkorian in an ill-fated bid to take over Chrysler.

But Iacocca came close to toppling Henry Ford in 1978, which was by itself an extraordinary and overlooked personal achievement. It was something he seemed to have been planning for years.

Iacocca might have guessed his days were numbered in December 1970, when at 46 he received what he would call the greatest Christmas present of his life—being named president of Ford by Henry Ford II. He knew the line about the Indian rope trick that was often repeated inside Ford—when you reach the top, you disappear. Under Henry Ford II it had happened to Ernie Breech, John Dykstra, Arjay Miller, and Bunkie Knudsen. It might have happened to Robert McNamara if President John F. Kennedy hadn't asked him to become U.S. Secretary of Defense only a month after being named president of Ford.

Iacocca had clawed his way up the ladder at Ford. He must have known deep down that he couldn't last out his 15 years until retirement—unless he built a power base that could bear up against the man who led the family that controlled 45 percent of the voting rights. Whether by design or instinct, Iacocca set up a vast network of loyalists inside Ford that was meant to accomplish what Knudsen and Miller could never hope for—their own base of allegiance. Iacocca's was already strong enough by 1969 to have helped knock Knudsen out of the box.

"Inside Ford there were very clearly an Iacocca camp and a Henry Ford II camp," said a senior executive from that era.

What Iacocca didn't fathom was how Henry Ford II would view the first attempt by an employee of the Ford Motor Company since Harry Bennett to create his own private organization. Iacocca, like Bennett, viewed Ford employees in black or white terms. Either they were with him or they were against him. In the mid-1970s, Iacocca began to organize his partisans, and he started asking them to stand up and be counted. In the end, not all of them would.

Dealers were on his side, though. It seemed all 6,600 of them were for Iacocca. He also had a better relationship with most suppliers than Henry Ford. And several members of the board of directors seemed to be Iacocca men. But in setting up his battalions, in focusing so much on separating those loyal to him from those who were not, he put Henry Ford's guard up.

Henry took the threat seriously, but such was his respect, his fear, that he decided not to strike until he was able to strike hard, much as he did against Bennett 30 years before.

It would help if he could prove that Iacocca, like Bennett, was a crook. In 1975, the Deuce spent $1.5 million to investigate allegations that Iacocca was illegally feeding all of Ford's travel business to a New York friend named Bill Fugazy. The detailed inquiry turned up nothing.

Meanwhile, Ford's financial performance had held up well in difficult economic conditions. So Henry hatched another plan. He would have to take Iacocca out in stages. He hired the world's most prestigious management consultants, McKinsey and Co., to review Ford's top management structure. The consultants came back with what they knew they were hired to do—find a way to cut into Iacocca's power. Taking McKinsey's recommendation, Henry on April 14, 1977, announced formation of an office of the chief executive that would include Henry Ford, Lee Iacocca, and Phil Caldwell, as vice chairman. Then a few months later came another move. The corporation announced that Iacocca would henceforth report to Caldwell, not Ford.

Iacocca was being cut off at the knees. His use of the beloved company plane even had to be approved by Caldwell.

Caldwell was in many ways the opposite of the carousing Ford. Once, at a company gathering, the fastidious teetotaler turned down the Deuce's offer of a drink.

"I don't drink," Caldwell said. Ford offered him a cigar.

"No, thank you," Caldwell said, "I don't smoke."

"What the hell *do* you do?" Henry asked.

Henry Ford II really *did* like Iacocca—at least for a long while and despite saying otherwise in emotional moments. He just couldn't trust him. In the 1960s and early 1970s, Iacocca and Ford traveled through Europe together, enjoying each other's company. They smoked cigars, drank Italian wine, and shared a similar sense of humor. "They were too much alike," said one Ford executive from that era.

Iacocca said many years after his wars with Ford: "I tried to remember the years beginning in 1960, when we were buddies. We hunted together, we went to parties together, and we caroused in Europe together. So I try to remember the 16 good years, and not the two bad ones in 1977 and 1978."

Iacocca had allies on the board of directors in 1978—Franklin Murphy, chairman of the Times-Mirror Corp.; a Boston financier named George Bennett; Joseph Cullman, the CEO of Philip Morris; and Henry's younger brother, William Clay Ford Jr. As Henry Ford began to push for Iacocca's dismissal in 1978, Iacocca began to take matters into his own hands. In June, he took the corporate jet to Boston to confer with George Bennett and Cullman.

In his autobiography, Iacocca dismissed the trips as innocent. He claimed he had been requested to meet with board members in an attempt to solve the crisis brewing about his future. Others saw it as a bold attempt to arrange backing on the board for a showdown. Either way, the board of directors had been engaged. It would have to choose between Iacocca and the grandson of the founder—the man whose courage saved the company from hoodlums in 1945. As negotiations carried on between the two sides, substantial support arose for Iacocca—throwing Henry into a rage. Most of the directors liked Iacocca, and many considered him a terrific car man and a strong leader. And he'd been making money for the company. They couldn't understand why Ford was so intent on humiliating Iacocca.

Indeed, there were nagging doubts about Ford's capability after 33 years in charge. Was "Crazy Henry" disease creeping into his behavior? Would he repeat the late-life excesses of his grandfather? But Iacocca asked too much of the board. There was no compelling cause to unseat Henry Ford II, and the board had no stomach for the fight. Lee Iacocca was terrific, but Henry stood for the family. There was no crisis afoot that justified tearing the fabric of one of the great family businesses in history. "It's either him or me," the chairman finally told them.

On July 13, Iacocca walked into the Deuce's office and pressed Ford for an explanation. Why was he being fired? The Deuce could only say, "I just don't like you."

Iacocca had nowhere to turn. His best chance was the man sitting there in the room—Bill Ford. But though Bill had a pained look on his face, he wasn't going to stop his brother. Iacocca just didn't have the votes to stay at Ford. William Clay Ford, the deferential younger brother, had the power to preserve Iacocca if he had really wanted to— in the form of stock ownership.

William Ford was the third man in the room the day Iacocca heard his fate. At the end of the meeting, Bill Ford was in tears. Bill and Lee walked out of Henry's office together. "There was nothing I could do," Bill said.

Iacocca later wrote, "I imagined that his brother Bill, who owned twice as much stock as Henry, would say one day: 'Look, my brother's gone nuts. We've got to replace him.' I know that the idea had certainly crossed Bill's mind."

Henry Ford believed he was ridding the company of another Harry Bennett. While being interviewed for a corporate history in 1980, Ford was asked to reflect on his old nemesis from 1945. "Harry Bennett was the dirtiest, lousiest son of a bitch I ever met in my life, save one," Ford said. That "one" was Iacocca. "Iacocca really did feel he could take over the whole enchilada," recalled one senior Ford executive who was a young finance staffer at the time and watched the soap opera close at hand. "But he really didn't have a choice. It was an act of desperation. He was going to lose one way or another, so he might as well try to take over control of the company." It was a hopeless cause, said the executive. Even if the board of directors had picked a new chairman and deposed Henry Ford II, the family would have retained voting control. "It would have replaced the board of directors with another board, which would have reinstated Henry Ford II," said the executive.

Another senior Ford executive from that period said a key reason Henry Ford II got rid of Iacocca was because Lundy was getting close to retirement age and Lundy's counterweight was going to be missed. "He didn't want Iacocca to go off half-cocked. Ford needed someone like Caldwell who was more down to earth and finance oriented, what with Lundy as well as Henry Ford himself ready to retire."

While Iacocca claimed that Henry Ford was out of touch, the Deuce's supporters saw it differently. Ford was always punctual, always well prepared for every meeting—and he remained that way late in his career. He always read the material, and read everything from the previous meeting on the subject, even if that meeting had occurred two years earlier. He was never much for the details of finance, nor was he a math whiz. Lundy would make sure to prepare the financial reports for Ford in the exact same format every time—the same columns of numbers, so that Henry got accustomed to it and could quickly find the numbers he was looking for.

Amid two energy crises, they claimed Iacocca was himself delusional—trying to find another Mustang-like smash. According to Douglas Brinkley's family-authorized history, *Wheels of the World*, published to commemorate the company's 100th anniversary: "The more rash he [Iacocca] became in looking for the big hit, the more conservative Ford grew in refusing to put his faith, and the company's money into a miracle model far adrift of the rest of the pack. To his ears, front-wheel drive seemed a gamble and so did the launch of a whole new type of vehicle in the van wagon. While the company waited, he and Iacocca didn't find a middle ground. In fact, they split further and further apart."

Brinkley recorded that Robert Alexander, a longtime Ford executive, thought that Iacocca was reckless when it came to Henry Ford II. "Lee was really looking for battles," Alexander said. "It was as if Lee was swelled up. He made the victory of (Bunkie) Knudsen, where he had taken him out single-handedly. Maybe he was contemptuous of Mr. Ford; maybe it blinded him where he believed that he could take on anyone."

Henry's men argued that Ford Motor was adrift in 1975 because of a lack of leadership from Iacocca, whom they saw as old-fashioned, a huckster, a manager full of burning ambition and intrigue. Personal survival was his creed. And he did make mistakes. The Pinto was a big one—a disaster. He was a great consumer of perks—a basic error in a company headed by a member of the founding family. It wasn't just the money Iacocca was spending with his frequent Ford flying—his most conspicuous consumption—it was what it symbolized. It was a veiled challenge to the authority of the Fords. But Iacocca persisted. He also enjoyed showing off during meetings, using engineer-speak he didn't think Henry could follow. It was more than just showing off or intimidation, it was part of a strategy to prove that he was the more competent to lead the company.

Iacocca was also becoming one of the most famous businessmen in America—far better known than his counterparts at General Motors and Chrysler. The success of the Mustang had put him on a higher plane. He could simply not suppress himself as Dykstra, Miller, and Knudsen had done as president. He would act as if Ford were the Iacocca Motor Company.

Lee Iacocca saw himself as the chairman's equal—and his superior when it came to executive ability. Iacocca was challenging the class barriers not just in the auto industry, but in the American social aristocracy as well. And in a way Iacocca seemed to cherish the feud. By fighting back, by winning a sympathetic following inside the company, he had already won a kind of victory over the Deuce.

Henry Ford II had little to say about Iacocca in public. But in an interview with David Lewis after his early-1980s retirement—the contents of which were sealed until 10 years after his death—Ford discussed his nemesis.

"Iacocca, until the oil embargo and government regulations got very difficult, was a good executive. But Iacocca . . . let me put it another way . . . Iacocca was an extremely intelligent product man, a super salesman. It didn't make any difference what he was selling. He was very imaginative, very bright, very quick. But when it finally came down to 1974, '75, he got lost all of a sudden. Completely. He got himself into a blue funk over products. I never developed product lines. That wasn't what I thought my job was. I approved products, but I didn't develop them. I could say no, or I could say yes, or I could suggest ideas. But I didn't do the development work. But then our development work became terrible, and it changed all the time. We never had a good program for any duration. . . . He thought he was paying proper attention. But he got thoroughly confused in his later years as to what the hell to do, and he had a new program every two to three months. The organization was totally discombobulated."

Once gone from Ford, Iacocca ached to trump his former boss by building something as big as Ford and declaring himself the proprietor. In the weeks after his dismissal, he contemplated a consortium made up of Chrysler, American Motors, and possibly Volkswagen. "The entrepreneur in me was getting restless," Iacocca wrote.

After joining Chrysler that fall, Iacocca was in a position to make the consortium a reality, but Chrysler was in such bad financial shape that American Motors and Volkswagen weren't interested.

Then, in 1981, Iacocca came up with a plan to merge Chrysler with Ford. Many viewed it as nothing but a power grab. Iacocca said he would step aside after 12 months to avoid a conflict with Henry. But no one at Ford believed he would really walk away. They said Iacocca believed he had enough loyalty still embedded at Ford to be named CEO by acclamation. In the end, Ford's board of directors barely gave the idea a hearing.

Iacocca was sympathetically portrayed in the aftermath of the firing, easily winning the public relations war with Henry Ford. He was cast as the dynamic professional manager who had pulled himself up by his bootstraps, while Henry Ford II had degenerated into a boozy, ill-tempered, ineffectual heir who Iacocca said "never had to work for anything." It was a grand caricature. Henry Ford II was in many ways the greater innovator, the big picture guy, if not the operational genius. He brought new thinking not only to the American car business after World War II, but to all of American business. He created the prototypical post-war corporate management technique that focused on financial controls and systems.

If Iacocca had stayed at Ford, it may have meant the beginning of the end of Ford family dominance of the company. With Iacocca gone, Henry Ford II could retire with the company safely in the hands of the obedient Caldwell. Ultimate power stayed with the family, including Henry Ford II's son Edsel and his nephew William Clay Ford Jr.

By surviving the challenge of Iacocca, the family had survived for good. Donald Petersen, who succeeded Caldwell in 1985, two years before Henry died, tried to keep the two young cousins under control. They had forced their way onto the board, but Petersen refused to give them any committee assignments, and they were the only two members of the board that Petersen would not allow to use company planes.

In 1987, Petersen sent Bill Ford to one of the company's farthest out-posts, Ford of Switzerland, a tiny backwater within the company. Still in his 20s, Bill Ford shook visibly when a reporter came to see him. The young man seemed to lack the will to manage and did indeed retire from active management a couple of years later and took a seat on the finance committee.

After holding over a dozen Ford operating or staff jobs in nine years, Bill Ford was dizzied by the details of one post after another and worried that he was losing sight of the big picture. Some industry watchers thought Bill was giving up. All the Ford family seemed to pull away from the day-to-day affairs of the company, leaving it to the pro-fessional managers. But when Bill "retired" to spend more time run-ning his father's National Football League team, the Detroit Lions, he was actually setting himself up for greater control at Ford, not less. On the finance committee, he was learning more of what he needed to know rather than visiting dealers in the Australian outback, as his older cousin Edsel was doing.

Henry Ford II had one final person to fire before he died. He wanted to fire Don Petersen because Petersen was cutting him out of the flow of information. Petersen was ultimately fired because the board of directors worried that he was having a nervous breakdown. During a board meeting, Petersen once threw his Rolex watch down the length of a table when he didn't get his way on something, then stormed out of the room. The board members worried that running Ford was too much for him. Petersen had to go. And Henry Ford II had foreseen it.

Iacocca believed the auto industry would consolidate, that a few major groups would someday control almost every car brand. He believed so much in the idea that it became a kind of industry axiom. He was interested in big mergers. He had spent hours with Sperlich developing the global car company concept that would align big automakers from the United States, Europe, and Japan. But Chrysler couldn't pull it off; the company was retrenching when Iacocca arrived. Had he remained at Ford, Iacocca would have had a platform for realizing that dream.

The immediate consequence of Iacocca leaving Ford for Chrysler was that he took his crew with him. Not long after joining Chrysler, Iacocca sent T-shirts to 14 Ford executives with the words *Bored with Ford?* printed on the front. Iacocca not only brought his product cohorts over from Ford—men like Hans Matthias, his former chief engineer at Ford Division—he recruited ex-Ford sales guys like Gar Laux; purchasing executives like Paul Bergmoser; operations men like Gerry Greenwald; and finance specialists like Steve Miller. Iacocca took so many able executives away from Ford that it surely damaged Henry II's company. Those left in power were mainly men who had sidestepped the ire of the aging chairman; they tended to be the Lundy designates and compliant favorites such as Caldwell and Poling.

Had they not been left leaderless, many other Ford managers would have resisted the call of the Japanese import companies, the ranks of which were swollen by talented Ford sales-and-marketing executives who joined the Japanese companies' California import offices. If Chrysler had collapsed outright without Iacocca, Ford would have benefited far more than General Motors from its failure.

The negative impact on Ford of the departure of Lee Iacocca and his acolytes was blunted by the revival of the American economy during the mid-1980s. Ford and General Motors both bounced back, and Ford had a heyday under Donald Petersen with success fueled by strong sales of the 1985 Taurus and Sable and a new aerodynamic look that had been bequeathed to Ford in North America by Bob Lutz's European organization.

Lutz would have stayed, too, and may have become Ford's chief executive in time, but he was sidetracked by Poling, his old boss, with whom he clashed in Europe. Lutz finally joined Iacocca at Chrysler in 1986—much later than those who left Ford in the first wave. He had his troubles with Iacocca at Chrysler, which might have happened at Ford had both remained. But with Lutz in a high position at Ford, it seemed unlikely that the second generation of the Sierra-inspired Taurus/Sable would have fallen flat in the marketplace. A more successful Taurus/Sable would have strengthened Ford during the 1990s.

The big loser under those circumstances would have been Toyota's Camry, the Taurus competitor that in the 1990s became America's best-selling passenger car. The Camry was an astounding climb for the Japanese company, but its place in the pecking order had been helped by Ford's mistakes; the company was never able to reach full speed. Ford in 1946 was a makeover, almost as sapped of energy as Toyota was at the end of World War II. But a phenomenally successful hiring spree and can-do spirit ignited by the young chief executive created a new Ford that influenced hundreds of large corporations around the world. Yet Henry Ford would not let Ford continue on the course he had started in 1946 with the Whiz Kids and later, the product-savvy Iacocca-Sperlich generation of executives. Henry Ford had created the perfect corporate structure—a strong cost-control bureaucracy combined with a dynamic car development organization. These two sides would clash, but it was a good system of checks and balances. Unfortunately, the Ford Motor Company was never given the freedom and support it needed to achieve its full potential.

Ford had the size, the talent, the financial discipline, the geographic breadth, and the shareholder commitment—in the form of family ownership—to become something more than it was at the end of the twentieth century. It might have developed into the kind of company in the 1980s and 1990s that another family-controlled company did in fact become. That company was Toyota.

A landmark change in auto industry rankings occurred in 2004: GM had eclipsed Ford in U.S. sales in 1921, and never looked back; but now the Ford Motor Company was being overtaken again. Toyota leapfrogged over Ford to become the world's No. 2 automaker by volume. Had Henry Ford II been able to liberate within the company the energy and leadership of Lee Iacocca—or his equivalent—that might never have been possible.

CHAPTER SIX

Ferdinand Piëch

Ferdinand Piëch was not the usual 26-year-old engineering graduate when he began working at his family's sports-car company in April 1963. He was the grandson of Ferdinand Porsche and a member of a family worth billions. He was also a world-class eccentric.

The Porsches and the Piëchs were automotive nobility of the highest order. Besides the Stuttgart car manufacturer, they also owned Porsche Holdings, one of Europe's largest car distributors. Without the family connections it seems unlikely Piëch could have risen to the top of Europe's biggest auto manufacturer—Volkswagen. No CEO in the history of the auto industry (except possibly the first Henry Ford—"Crazy Henry") ever possessed a personality more bizarre than Piëch. He could be utterly strange—even a little creepy. Many of his CEO peers felt that they couldn't hold a normal conversation with him. There was no one like him anywhere in the upper ranks of the global auto industry. He was an abuser of power, a despot surrounded by yes men when he ran VW in the 1990s.

Although Piëch was usually distant and mysterious, he could turn cuddly if an attractive young woman were around. Before a gala dinner speech in Brussels in 1996, an animated Piëch talked non-stop for two hours to a young Mercedes-Benz executive at the head table. The woman was there to receive an industry award. Piëch spoke hardly a word to the many notables at the table that night, which included two other European automotive chief executives.

Women were drawn to him from his days as head of the Porsche racing team in the go-go 1960s. His wealth and power were enticing, and Piëch played it to the hilt. He wound up marrying four times and had thirteen children by at least three women. In one relationship, the wife of a Porsche cousin walked out on her husband, moved in with Piëch, and bore him two children. He eventually left her for the children's nanny, whom he married.

Piëch's inscrutability generated fear, which he used to powerful effect throughout his career. When he looked at subordinates their eyes would widen, as if they were antelopes just noticing that they had fallen under the gaze of a lion. But Piëch's rough style and idiosyncrasies tended to mask the giant contributions he made to the global auto industry in the second half of the twentieth century.

As a young boy, Piëch idolized his grandfather, Professor Ferdinand Porsche. Porsche, who in turn doted on Piëch, was treated like the Pope, and Piëch was wowed by the admiration shown his grandfather. Piëch spent endless hours with the professor, listening to tales of his grandfather's life, how he solved this technical problem or won that race. The relationship infused the young Ferdinand with a colossal appetite for success. He wanted to emulate this famous man, and Piëch absorbed his grandfather's ideas and love of tinkering and experimenting.

As a teenager, Piëch spent summer vacations helping his uncle Ferry Porsche build the first Porsche 356 sports cars. Ferry's son Ferdinand Alexander "Butzi" Porsche was there, too. But while Butzi was playful and friendly, the family began to notice that Piëch, the son of Ferry's sister Louise and her lawyer husband Anton Piëch, was astonishingly intense and single-minded. He also seemed blindingly talented. Young Piëch absorbed the fine points of a motor so fast that the older engineers at the company's shops in Gmund, Austria, and Stuttgart-Zuffenhausen were in awe. Many of them had worked with Ferdinand Porsche before the war and would shake their heads in wonder as Piëch peppered them with questions and challenged everything they said and did.

Louise Piëch headed the car distribution side of the family business. Many sales directors from Europe's carmakers got to know her well because she was their distributor in Austria.

"She was an incredible person," said one of them. "She was the first in the office and last to leave every night."

At a private party celebrating her 85th birthday, the usually stoic Piëch was nearly in tears as he spoke of her, surprising the group by using his boyhood name for her.

"He molded himself after her," said someone who knew both of them well. "She was a big influence. She was such a strong character, but she was friendly, the opposite of Ferdinand."

Piëch's father became the managing director of Volkswagen in 1941, at the height of World War II.

"Anton Piëch never got the recognition for the rebuilding of the company after the war," said a former VW executive. "I think Ferdinand felt he had to complete his work."

The youthful Piëch's self-confidence was boundless. Yet life was not perfect. As the son of Louise rather than Ferry Porsche, he had the wrong parent if he wanted to inherit real power in the Porsche sports-car company. Louise had agreed to let Ferry run Porsche, but she insisted that her own children be given as much chance as Ferry's sons to take the helm when the time came for him to step down.

Piëch's rival would always be Butzi, a happy-go-lucky young man who loved cars as much as his grim cousin, but seemed to have far less of the burning personal ambition and almost no taste for the business politics that went with it. It was 28-year-old Butzi who, in 1961, put pen to paper and wound up with the design for the successor to the Porsche 956, the 901 road car. It would eventually be called the 911 and be forever known as Butzi's handiwork.

Piëch didn't begin full-time work in Zuffenhausen until after the car was nearly ready for production, but when he came out of the Zurich Technical University he was like a race car exploding out of a slipstream. He showed up at Porsche in the spring of 1963 and threw himself into his work with a ferocity that stunned the older men at Porsche.

Piëch quickly made his mark on the design of the 911 race engine. Rather than spending his first year deferring to his elders, he demanded changes even if it meant delaying the completion of the project. Six months before the car went on sale, Piëch insisted on switching from a wet-sump to the dry-sump lubrication used in one of Porsche's race cars. Against all odds, he re-engineered the part and got it replaced.

Butzi's design became a defining moment in Piëch's life. It was the achievement he was obligated to match and exceed. Some believe he spent the rest of his career attempting to do so. The family rivalry toughened Piëch for later battles. Throughout his career, he would win one after another—even in situations where fame and money and power could not possibly help him. Despite his great personal wealth, Piëch was, improbably, a self-made man.

Nothing like his easygoing cousin, Piëch was fanatical about cars, and he had an obsessive-compulsive drive that both inspired and frightened the tough, veteran engineers he worked alongside. A young man searching for ways to excel, Piëch soon took complete charge of Porsche's sports-car competition programs.

The track was the best possible outlet for his competitive drive. To win races, he needed to constantly come up with new ideas about design, fuel efficiency, and safety. He also had to squeeze more power from smaller engines and coax money out of sponsors and his uncle's factory.

Butzi had not only designed the 911, but also the 904 racing car. Yet compared to his younger cousin he seemed almost docile. Butzi's father tolerated Piëch's eccentricities and abrasiveness. Not only had his sister insisted upon a role for her son, but there was no denying that his nephew was exceptionally gifted. By 1965, Piëch's uncle gave him complete charge of Porsche's test and development department, though he had already laid claim to the position.

The first thing Piëch did when he took control of the development and test department was to call the staff together and demand that the group achieve something extraordinary. He wanted a new generation of sports cars that would knock Ford and Ferrari off their perch.

Piëch and a more senior engineer, Helmut Bott, would sometimes confer all day in one of their offices, hashing over concepts they would later take to their race-car designers. Piëch had found a mentor in Bott. The older man was warmhearted and easygoing, and the two got along well. Bott's technical brilliance dazzled Piëch.

The 26-year-old instantly built a power base inside the company. He assembled a small team of young and dedicated engineers. It was a tight-knit, highly efficient unit with no regard for rigid departmental boundaries. It included men like development engineer Hans Metzger and test driver Peter Falk. Some in Porsche's engineering department realized they couldn't work with the iron-willed young man and soon left; Piëch pushed some others out. They would either rise to his level of intensity or would have to leave.

Piëch was an exasperating genius who worked all day and all night and demanded that his staff work right alongside him. He believed engineering was an act of physical endurance and would test the staying power of his top lieutenants throughout his entire career. Piëch himself never needed much sleep; he would often show up on a factory workshop floor unannounced in the middle of the night, gazing over an engineer's shoulder to make suggestions.

An excellent driver, Piëch years later ordered Volkswagen's top executives to accompany him on grueling test drives of new vehicles. He held at least four of them a year—on and off road, on proving rounds in the desert, on ice, in mountains, and on speed circuits. During the tests, proximity to Piëch signaled the current hierarchy. Whoever had Piëch's favor was ordered to join his car or follow closely.

The entourage was accompanied by VW factory physicians, who had to follow the high-speed group in a fully packed car that could be used as an emergency room. The doctors' biggest worry was not an accident; it was that VW's top executives would suffer heart attacks, physical collapses, or dehydration. Piëch pressed on with little regard for rest or even bathroom stops. He would often go all day without so much as a lunch break. His energy was unflagging.

If Piëch had never set foot in Audi, if he had simply retired to life on a yacht after his uncle banned family members from managing the sports-car company in 1971, his legend would be secure.

Piëch was a modern version of Enzo Ferrari's wild-eyed fanaticism in the 1920s. He and his team worked at a furious pace, designing, developing, and racing five different designs between early 1966 and the spring of 1968. They developed the 904, Carrera 6, 910, 907, and 908. Engine sizes grew from four to six to eight cylinders.

The 904 dominated the 2.0-liter production sports car class for Porsche in the mid-1960s, setting the standard at Daytona, Sebring, and Le Mans in 1964 and 1965. But in 1965, the 904 was defeated in hillclimb competition by Ferrari's Type 166 Dino Spyder.

Piëch went into overdrive. In an attempt to compete with Ferrari, he first tried converting the car from a coupe to an open-topped car. When that failed, Piëch tried a design that would take Porsche to the top of the sport. The tube-frame spyder car called the "Ollon-Villars" after its first event was the basis for the next generation of Porsche race cars. The 906, or Carrera 6, reflected Piëch's belief in low weight, low drag, and more power—three concepts that he would carry to Audi and Volkswagen production cars many years later.

The Carrera 6 weighed 1,235 pounds, 250 pounds less than the 904. Piëch had the new body refined in the wind tunnel, a first for Porsche. The spherical windshield previewed closed racing cars of the future. The doors were gullwing and had a sloping louvered Plexiglas rear cover over the engine. Elements of this design continued in Porsche's racing cars long after Piëch had left the company.

But Piëch believed Porsche needed something more to compete with Ferrari and Ford at Le Mans. He decided to fit a 12-cylinder engine to a simple lightweight chassis and create an all-new racing machine. The company's board of directors resisted. Porsche was a small manufacturer and couldn't afford such a huge investment. Ferry Porsche saw the engineering benefits and promotional value of the 12-cylinder project, but the high cost worried the practical patriarch.

Piëch wouldn't be denied. For years, rumors floated about the inducements Piëch made to win approval for the 12-cylinder, and this was the first great demonstration of his willpower. He convinced Porsche's board to spend the money to develop the 5-liter 917; approval was granted in July 1968.

Rumors of the 12-cylinder began to circulate in early 1969. At Ferrari, they thought Piëch was insane. But he was going ahead, and in the process he transformed the 24 Hours of Le Mans into a battle of the budgets between Ferrari and Porsche.

The first 917 was shown at the Geneva auto show on March 12, 1969. The International Racing Federation required 25 cars to be produced for homologation. Normally, approval would be granted when officials were shown a few ready-made cars and some components. But after convincing his uncle, Piëch ordered all 25 cars to be built. When officials came to Stuttgart in April, the 25 917s stood in a perfect line.

The motor-racing world was stunned.

For several months, the team grew to about seven designers as they toiled under tremendous pressure from Piëch. During his Porsche racing days, he developed the habit of fostering internal competition among the engineers in his department—an effort to drive them to greater performance.

Piëch succeeded in beating the Ferraris and Ford GT40s. The 917 won the 1970 24 Hours of Le Mans, while at the same time dominating the Can-Am series. It became Porsche's most famous purpose-built race car, as well as the most powerful ever, at 1,100 horsepower. In a 1997 *Motor Sport* magazine poll, the Porsche 917 was voted the greatest racing car of all time.

Piëch introduced unconventional methods to guarantee the reliability of his race cars. He brought cars to Volkswagen's high-speed test track in Wolfsburg for endurance runs and set up test programs with accurate reproduction of severe racing conditions on each circuit.

By the late 1960s, Piëch was not only running the racing department, he also managed a department of 200 production-car engineers. He was on top of the world when Ferry Porsche ruled that family members could no longer run the company.

The problem of nepotism had been festering ever since Piëch joined the company in 1963. As Piëch grew more powerful, the rivalry among the third generation of Porsches grew more intense. Piëch had debated engineering strategies with Butzi Porsche and his younger brother, Peter Porsche. Not only were there business feuds, there were extramarital affairs.

By 1971, Ferry had had enough. He expelled all members of the third generation from the company's management and decided that Porsche would thereafter be run by non-family managers. Piëch partisans felt Ferry took action mainly to prevent his nephew from gaining control. By then it was obvious that Butzi had no chance of competing with his more illustrious cousin.

The success of the 911 had fuelled the rivalry between the pair, as each sought more credit for the car. The arguments spilled over to the other siblings and their parents. But Louise Piëch also supported the decision. The poisonous atmosphere meant the cousins could never share power.

"After I ascertained that the necessary harmony and cooperation could not be created," Ferry wrote in his autobiography, "I drew the inevitable conclusion and said, 'Then nobody's going to be boss!'"

Piëch had expected to spend his entire life working for the Porsche sports-car company and was said to be stunned and embittered by his uncle's decision. But this would be the only real career defeat Piëch would ever suffer. In the end, some observers believed that things worked out as Piëch had planned them.

Piëch knew he could never succeed Ferry Porsche as head of the sports-car company; he would always be No. 2 to his older cousin or to Butzi's younger brother, Peter Porsche.

"It had to be a Porsche," Piëch said.

By engaging Butzi and Peter in battle, Piëch forced the older generation to banish them both—to a life of relative obscurity running Porsche Design, the Austrian company that made watches and other goods that sported the Porsche logo, including high-tech spectacle frames, watches, pens, and TV sets. But Ferdinand Piëch went out to make his mark in the world and prove to his family that he was a great engineer and leader worthy of his grandfather's reputation and respect.

The two sides of the family continued to battle. "It was difficult to keep the Porsches and Piëchs marching in step to reach the necessary accommodations to manage," said Peter Schutz, a former Porsche chairman.

Ferry and Butzi Porsche's ideas were usually opposed by Louise and Ferdinand Piëch. When Porsche introduced its 928 model in 1978, Ferdinand publicly proclaimed the sports car overpriced.

Piëch now had to settle on a personal strategy. BMW seemed a possibility. Herbert Quandt had installed the young machine-tool executive Eberhard von Kuenheim in the top job in 1970. Von Kuenheim had no experience in the auto industry, and some didn't think he would last. By 1971, however, it was clear that von Kuenheim was a powerful presence and that BMW would not be big enough for both he and Piëch.

So Piëch headed off to Stuttgart to do consulting work for Mercedes-Benz, taking on a six-month engineering contract. Afterwards, Mercedes-Benz chairman Joachim Zahn offered to put him in line to succeed Hans Scherenberg as Mercedes' development chief, but Piëch turned him down. He thought the development budget was too low.

"I want the technology to come forward," he told Zahn.

But the plan was probably for Piëch to go to the Volkswagen group all along. Gerhard Richard Gumpert, VW's distributor in Italy, organized a temporary job for Piëch at Italdesign, the fledgling independent Turin design studio headed by Giorgetto Giugiaro. The young designer had just completed work on the first-generation Golf and Scirocco coupe.

From there, Piëch moved to Audi-NSU in August 1972, managing the special projects department. Three years later, he was named head of research and development. A few years later, Giugiaro would design the landmark 1983 Audi 100 for Piëch that would mark a major turning point in automotive design.

A few months before Ferdinand Piëch joined Audi, Bob Lutz had moved to BMW. The two Bavarian brands were well on their way, and within a decade BMW and Audi would be putting enormous competitive pressure on Mercedes-Benz.

Piëch and Lutz were like two young heavyweight contenders. Their careers took different paths, but they took the measure of each other's progress and might have ended up at the same place at the same time exactly 20 years later.

Lutz was five years older than Piëch, but they each began their careers in 1963. Lutz had spent several years in the U.S. Marine Corps before starting his auto career at General Motors in the United States.

Both Piëch and Lutz jolted their companies from day one. Lutz started at GM's New York planning office and was soon assigned to Adam Opel in Germany. Piëch began in engine design at Porsche. Within two years, Piëch was master of all technical development at the company and head of the racing team. He was turning Porsche into a competition powerhouse in the 1960s. Lutz, meanwhile, was lighting a fire under Opel sales in France and Germany.

They were the two hardest charging young men in the European auto industry in the 1960s. Both were in a tremendous hurry. Lutz was getting promoted so fast at Opel that GM couldn't raise his salary fast enough. They both all but took over jobs in their companies before they were actually promoted into them. Piëch was a member of the family that owned the company. Lutz sometimes acted as if he owned General Motors.

And both were spurred by developments at BMW. Mercedes was the top dog, but the revolution in Munich is what really interested Piëch and Lutz. A tremendous brand was being built before their eyes. When zooming along the autobahn in Bavaria, Piëch tried to pass all BMW drivers, hoping to convince them to buy an Audi instead. Lutz quickly agreed to join BMW when Eberhard von Kuenheim offered him a job and a big salary increase. Besides his sales and marketing responsibilities, Lutz re-launched BMW's racing programs. Piëch quickly picked up racing responsibility at Audi after his years of success at Porsche.

Both were aristocrats who loved cars. Piëch would drive Audi to new heights with a string of technical achievements, while Lutz played a central role in making BMWs known as the "ultimate driving machine," both in Europe and the United States.

The joint success of Audi and BMW shocked sleepy Mercedes-Benz into action. Throughout the 1970s and 1980s, Mercedes frequently found itself following Audi and BMW in technical leaps forward. Audi's Quattro all-wheel drive led to Mercedes' 4Matic. BMW was first with a V-12 engine, and its success with small sport sedans coaxed Mercedes to bring out the 190 "Baby Benz."

Mercedes had to push hard to stay at the leading edge in technology, which spurred innovative suppliers such as Robert Bosch. This in turn helped to establish the entire German automotive industry as a world leader in luxury performance.

Piëch and Lutz were constantly aware of one another. When Lutz went to Ford of Europe in 1974, Piëch feared that he would introduce better powertrains at a company known more for styling than engine performance and technology. Piëch was quick to dismiss anything that came out of the Ford of Europe stable. When Ford came out with its CVH engine in the late 1970s, Piëch—by then Audi's head of research and development—strode onto the Ford stand at a motor show with his entourage, studied the engine for a while, and sniffed, "This doesn't scare us."

Lutz did beat Piëch to the punch in design, though just barely. Ford brought out the aerodynamic Sierra in 1982. Piëch's low-drag Audi 100 was introduced a year later. Together they would alter global auto design for the next 20 years.

Piëch was always on guard for personal competitors and feared that some day Lutz would emerge as a candidate to head Volkswagen. The Swiss-American Lutz seemed perfect for VW, with its big presence in the U.S. market.

But Lee Iacocca hired Lutz at Chrysler in 1985, otherwise Lutz would have been a candidate for the Audi job in 1988. When Carl Hahn stepped down as Volkswagen's chairman in 1992, Piëch outmaneuvered his closest challenger for Hahn's job, another ex-Ford man named Daniel Goeudevert, who had been hired by Lutz.

Lutz appeared uninterested in vying for the VW job because he was the natural successor to Lee Iacocca at Chrysler. By the time Iacocca had reached over Lutz to bring in General Motors Europe head Robert Eaton as his successor, Piëch had already sewn up the Volkswagen CEO position.

Either way, it would have been hard to stop him. Piëch had been campaigning for the job since the day in 1972 when he joined Audi.

WHILE TESTING THE NEW Quattro all-wheel-drive system in a disguised standard Audi 80 in 1979, Walter Treser and Ferdinand Piëch drove up the Stelvio Pass between Austria and Italy for winter testing. Piëch spotted two men struggling to attach snow chains to a truck. He stopped and asked the men if he could help. Treser recalled: "When they waved us by, he took off at full speed with a big smile—without snow chains or special winter tires. He left those guys in disbelief that such a humble Audi could drive in such poor snow conditions. He really enjoyed the fun of proving something that way."

In the late 1970s, Audi's research-and-development center in Ingolstadt, Germany, was a hotbed of technical advances. In the vast building known by Audi employees as "Palazzo Piëch," the industry's technology agenda was being written.

As much as the ideas themselves, Piëch seemed to love the process of engineering—the rigor and the discipline of taking raw ideas and applying them to production vehicles. He saw technology as the only way to build the Audi brand. The pre-war "NSU-Audi" name had vanished until the mid-1960s, when Volkswagen took a majority share in the company. It was a brand with aspirations of grandeur, but it seemed to creep along, never building any real momentum until Piëch came along. The company's slogan "Vorsprung durch Technik" was the personification of Piëch—the belief that technology was the answer to all problems in the auto business. Audi was the test-bed to prove his theory and the springboard for his ambition.

The ideas he sponsored and pushed into production at Audi usually came from others. Piëch was a wonderful grower of ideas. He never sought to collect patents; his aim was much higher. It was victory—on the race track or in the showrooms. It was something he learned under the duress and deadlines of race team management at Porsche. Engineering was a team sport that needed a coach—a stern taskmaster—and Piëch fit the role perfectly.

"He was a great man for solving problems with other people's ideas," said a former VW executive. "He knew immediately when he saw a good idea, like Picasso seeing an African mask and making it into art. When he came up with the platform-sharing strategy at VW in the 1990s, that was really just Toyota's strategy. Only Toyota didn't have a name for it."

Piëch's grandfather Ferdinand Porsche had built cars and racers for Auto Union, the predecessor of Audi. But there was another reason Piëch picked Audi over Mercedes-Benz and BMW. Audi was a brand trying to find its way, and thus it was open to free-thinking young engineers. Piëch felt he would be able to build the kind of team he had had at Porsche. He could create Audi's product engineering in his own image more easily than he could at its south German rivals. Mercedes was considered far too "establishment," and BMW was already on its way with von Kuenheim in command. Audi was the best chance he had to realize his ambitions. Indeed, Piëch's Audi had a greater impact on the technology of the auto industry than any other auto company in the final two decades of the twentieth century.

"Piëch brought top-level engineering to volume manufacturers," said a rival executive. "He turned Audi into something that could compete with BMW and Mercedes and in the 1990s kept Volkswagen, from a product point of view, very much the target for other Europeans."

Piëch decided that Audi must be a premium brand and was frustrated by the brand's lack of independence from Volkswagen. He decided 15 years before he become Audi's CEO that the VW subsidiary needed its own marketing, customer service, distribution, and dealer network. It had to be totally separate.

"Piëch is a very systematic fellow, very influenced by Asian philosophy," said a former colleague. "He took a long-term view. He knew where he wanted to go, and he took the steps. From the day he arrived at Audi, he had a strategy. When he took over R&D in Audi in 1975 he knew want he wanted to do."

The design of the 1983 Audi 100 was a revolution in aerodynamics, with its 0.30 drag coefficient—an all-time low for a production car. The car turned more heads than any in the history of the German autobahn when it arrived. Two generations of car designers would opt for aerodynamic purity as a result. It was a complete reformation of post-war design—as revolutionary as the Chrysler Airflow of 1934, which had little influence on the industry.

But as evocative as the 1983 Audi 100 was, it was the 1980 100 that established Audi as one of the industry's technology leaders. A version of the 100 that year carried the name Quattro because it had all-wheel drive. It was the first mass-produced high-performance car with permanent four-wheel drive, and it elevated Audi in the eyes of world's automotive press and the general public.

The full impact of what Audi had achieved was not fully understood for years. The off-road revolution of the 1990s stemmed indirectly from it. The sport utility vehicles that overtook passenger sedans in popularity grew not only from Lee Iacocca's revitalized Jeep brand and Bob Lutz's first Ford Explorer, SUVs came from the public acceptance of all-wheel drive that began with Piëch at Audi. What started as an add-on for luxury and performance cars became a feature that drivers in all segments discovered and soon demanded.

If Piëch was the driving force behind the first Audi Quattro, the father of the concept was an engineer named Jörg Bensinger, head of Audi's road-test department in the late 1970s. Bensinger had the idea while in Finland in February 1977.

He was driving one of Audi's all-wheel-drive off-road Iltis vehicles after having just come out of one of the conventional Audi sedans being tested in rough conditions. Bensinger wondered if it would be possible to distribute the power of a sports car onto four wheels as a way to improve rally-car performance. The British company Jensen had been building its four-wheel-drive Interceptor FF (Ferguson Formula) since 1966 in very low numbers, but four-wheel drive was nowhere to be found on the passenger-car landscape.

Bensinger took his idea to Piëch, asking to adapt the Iltis four-wheel-drive system to an Audi sedan. Piëch was skeptical at first, but after thinking it over decided it was right for Audi. The all-wheel-drive system offered an opportunity for Audi to strike a blow at Mercedes-Benz and BMW.

"We must convince the public of the advantages of four-wheel drive and that we can do it at Audi," Piëch told Bensinger. "The customers see something technical coming from Mercedes and they say OK, it must be better."

Piëch sanctioned an unofficial prototype, installing the Iltis system in an Audi 80. It was only a test. No code name was assigned to the project. But soon Piëch was taking on the Quattro challenge, just as he had the development of the V-12–powered Porsche 917 race car a decade earlier.

Piëch formed a small group of engineers who toiled away in secrecy. Suspecting that they were on to something big, he wanted to preserve the concept for Audi, and not allow bigger-name German companies, or even Volkswagen, to steal their thunder. It was the way Piëch had always worked—with great intensity and mystery.

The group included Treser, who at the time was one of Audi's senior project managers; in the early 1980s he became better known for running Audi Sport's operation. Treser eventually started his own sports-car manufacturer and designed a revolutionary interior-seating configuration for the Opel Zafira small van many years later.

Treser clashed with Piëch, as did most engineers who worked closely with him. But the two men respected each other. Treser recalled the first time he met Piëch. In 1976, Piëch invited him to talk about joining Audi. The two met at the Munich airport, and Piëch arrived with a briefcase under one arm and a couple of engine components under the other. Together they got into an Audi 200 prototype and drove off.

"That was typical Piëch," said Treser, "doing two or three things at once."

Six years earlier, Piëch had turned down the top Mercedes' research-and-development job because the research budget was too small. He had told them that he wanted the technology to go forward. The Quattro would be Piëch's chance to show Mercedes what he had meant.

The Quattro team was working at breakneck speed. Treser built the first prototype, using the Audi 80 and Iltis running gear, in March 1977. It was crude—using permanent four-wheel drive with no center differential. It was not ideal for a passenger car.

Several prototypes were made. Piëch and his men raided the Volkswagen parts bin and took components from several Audi models. The prototype used a new turbocharged five-cylinder engine; the suspension and transmission from the Audi 100; the floorpan and some running gear from the Audi 80; and the body of the soon-to-be-released 80-based Audi Coupé. The gearbox was a completely new design. Instead of bulky transfer cases, a hollow shaft was used to transmit power to the front and back.

Testing carried on through the remainder of 1977. In January 1978, a prototype was shown to Werner Schmidt, VW's sales director. Piëch's team went to Turracher Höhe in Austria—Europe's steepest mountain pass, with 23 percent grades. Piëch slapped summer tires on the car and no snow chains, and the Quattro flew up the mountain pass without a hitch.

In April, the prototype was tested at the Hockenheim Ring. The car put out only 160 horsepower but turned lap times only a fraction slower than vehicles capable of 240 horsepower.

In May, Volkswagen's group development chief, Ernst Fiala, approved the project. But VW Chairman Toni Schmucker—a sales specialist, not a technician—wasn't sure that the high development costs would be worthwhile.

Piëch arranged for a final test—a drive up a steep grassy slope that Audi engineers had doused with water—for the ex–Ford man that summer. Schmucker was given three vehicles to try: a front-wheel-drive Audi 80, a rear-wheel-drive car of another make, and one of the Quattro prototypes.

After Schmucker's Audi 80 failed to make it up the lawn, Piëch put the VW boss in the Quattro prototype. The four-wheel-drive car negotiated the slope easily. Schmucker came away wildly impressed, and the project was soon approved.

A year later, Piëch took the newest prototypes to the Sahara desert, and in September 1979, rally driver Hannu Mikkola test drove the latest prototype. The following March, the car was on the Audi stand in Geneva. Audi designer Hartmut Warkuss put wider plastic wings and spoilers on an existing monocoque coupe body.

Treser, who came up with the Quattro name, went racing with the car. Mikkola led by six minutes at the 1981 Monte Carlo Rally before slamming his car against the wall of a bridge. In 1982, the Quattro won its first Rally Championship.

The Audi Quattro and the short-wheelbase Quattro Sport won nearly ever major competition, which led to applying the successful technology to passenger cars both at Audi and at Volkswagen. The original plan was to build only 400 units for homologation, but within a few years there were Quattro versions of Audi's entire model lineup.

Piëch was always jotting ideas on scraps of paper. Wherever his imagination led, his pen followed, like a modern-day Leonardo. He was able to sketch a complete engine in freehand; while on a bullet train in Japan, Piëch drew VW's "W" engine configuration for some of the engineers accompanying him. He once drew a diagram of the Quattro four-wheel-drive system on the back of an envelope.

Piëch invented a test to check the smoothness of eight-cylinder engines. He placed a coin on its rim on a level surface in the car. If it stood on end while the engine ran, the motor passed Piëch's test. It was the kind of test Henry Royce would have tried in 1906.

Indeed, Piëch's personal style seemed to route through a wormhole in the decades directly after the automotive industry was founded— and he was a reflection of those unconventional men. As the ultimate throwback, Piëch was precisely what the auto industry needed in the latter part of the twentieth century—a time when the industry had begun to turn to commodification and trivialization of cars.

Consumer brand management had taken root at archrival General Motors just as Piëch was beginning his tenure as VW's chief executive in 1993. He believed GM's brand management was just another way of saying that cars could be sold like beer or potato chips or toothpaste. Were it not for Piëch, the industry might have settled for less, for easier and less expensive technical solutions. Why put four-wheel drive on a passenger car? Why bother making a Skoda as good as a Volkswagen and a Volkswagen as good as an Audi and an Audi as good as a Mercedes?

Piëch, more than any single individual, promoted and maintained Europe's technical advantage over the rest of the automotive world in the second half of the twentieth century. With Japan gaining an upper hand in manufacturing efficiency and America's laser-like focus on the bottom line, what else was there for the Europeans but technology? Ride dynamics, low-end torque, all-wheel drive, anti-lock brakes— these were the things that allowed the Europeans to compete with Japanese carmakers at home and in America.

After 115 years, the cars of Europe and the United States remained fundamentally different. Part of the reason for this was infrastructure.

Europe's roads were carved out centuries before the long, straight, and flat American highways. And fuel costs were two or three times higher in Europe than in America.

But the dissimilarities also reflected the different focus of each continent's carmakers. The first great automotive engineering breakthroughs occurred in Germany, France, England, and Italy. Europeans spurred America's automotive pioneers. As the great North American auto companies took hold—General Motors, Ford, and Chrysler—the size and scope of the Europeans diminished. Still, the U.S. companies could never dominate in Europe.

General Motors and Ford have had huge European subsidiaries for decades, but they did it with indigenous companies—Opel and Ford of Europe—that produced European cars in Europe. There would be no all-conquering American Coca-Colas or McDonald's in the car business.

The global auto business benefited from a strong and powerful European industry. American cars were never exported successfully to Europe, but the best of Europe could always count on sales in North America. Piëch's grandfather's Beetle was the only model in history to have achieved broad success on both sides of the Atlantic until the Mercedes and BMWs and Piëch's own Audis in the 1980s. The latter-day cars did it by remaining true to European motoring principles. Technology made it possible—handling, advanced powertrains, and designs that appealed to American car buyers.

Piëch was the most persistent proponent of advanced technology in the last two decades of the century. He did not ignore customers, but they were abstract to him. The cars and the technology were real. One of the low moments of his career grew from his disregard of the special sensibilities of American customers.

In 1986, Audi 5000 owners in the United States began slamming their cars through their garages or into oncoming traffic. It was a malady called unintended acceleration. In some cases, the results were tragic—and a complete mystery.

No engineering problem, no computer glitch, no accelerator malfunction could be found. But the accelerator and brakes pedals were positioned closer together than American owners of Cadillacs and Lincolns were accustomed to. American luxury-car drivers were inadvertently stomping on the accelerator when they were trying to bring the car to a halt. It was the ultimate difference between the two markets, with disastrous consequences.

Audi's sales plummeted. The brand was all but dead in the United States, losing 80 percent of its volume within a couple of years. And it took a decade to recover. Piëch, with his minimal feel for people or customers, had miscalculated. He believed only in the technology, just as the industry pioneers did 100 years before him.

Despite Audi's technical prowess, Piëch was frustrated that the brand had failed to match the marketing power of his great rival BMW. And this led to disagreements with Audi's CEO Wolfgang Habbel in the mid-1980s.

Piëch had a house in Tenerife and would stop in Madrid to do little deals with Juan José Diaz Ruiz, who at the time was head of the VW-Audi distributor in Spain. He would ask Diaz Ruiz to order cars with higher levels of content. Diaz Ruiz would tell him that the equipment cost too much, and Piëch, the head of product development, would offer the distributor special deals—something he had no authority to do. Habbel hated that. Piëch grew frustrated and began to openly conspire against the older man. Habbel fought back.

In 1986, Piëch was invited for tea at the Habbels. The CEO informed Piëch that he planned to get rid of him. The following year, Habbel announced that he would be staying an extra year as CEO, which so enraged Piëch that he called his lawyer and told him he wanted out of his Audi contract. Piëch told his wife that he wanted to go to anywhere, even to Japan. He was convinced that he could work as an engineer for a Japanese firm. Honda was his first choice. He was talked into staying at Audi for the extra year and began to position himself for replacing Habbel in 1988.

But Volkswagen Chairman Carl Hahn had a different idea. He wanted Helmut Werner, the head of German tire maker Continental to replace Habbel, not Piëch. But Piëch had prepared for the day well. He was extremely popular within Audi for having stood up to Wolfsburg for many years. The so-called "Audiana" in Ingolstadt hated being owned by VW, and Piëch fed their sentiment. Audi was behind him. Faced with the fiercely determined Piëch, Werner moved to Mercedes-Benz, leaving the Audi job to Piëch. Werner become chairman of Mercedes before being run off by another tough corporate politician, Jürgen Schrempp.

Once installed as head of Audi, Piëch set out to show the world that he was a better marketer than his predecessor, and he was determined to repair the damage of the unintended acceleration controversy in the United States.

Although Hahn had long seen Piëch as his potential successor—once telling a reporter that it was "unavoidable" that Piëch would succeed him—they had a distant relationship while Piëch ran Audi.

"He didn't seem to like the idea," Piëch wrote in his autobiography. "I assume that he would have preferred my career to slow down a bit." Hahn tried to get Piëch to accept the job of Volkswagen research-and-development chief, succeeding the legendary Fiala. But Piëch felt that as Audi's CEO it would be easier for him to head the entire group, and he was annoyed by Hahn's mixed messages. "Hahn knew that I was the right person—and he feared the idea," Piëch said.

Piëch had at least one rival: Daniel Goeudevert, the former Ford of Germany boss. He was a specialist in sales and marketing, Piëch's perceived weakness. Goeudevert was named vice chairman, deputy to Hahn, who tried to offer an alternative to Piëch, who in turn tried to make a deal with Goeudevert.

"One day we had the opportunity in the car to talk undisturbed," recalls Piëch. "I suggested to Goeudevert that, in case I was chosen to succeed Hahn, he would take responsibility for engineering and sales. I asked him if he could imagine such a mutual understanding and if he was prepared to strike a deal on that.

"German is not Goeudevert's native language, so he could have misunderstood. When I asked him again, and he changed the subject again, I knew what he thought of such an idea."

As the VW supervisory board prepared to make a choice, some members talked individually with the two men on the same day.

"Goeudevert was convinced he won the job and went home," writes Piëch. "After answering dozens of other questions, I went to bed. At nine, Franz Steinkühler, deputy to Klaus Liesen on the supervisory board, called me and said the outlook was not so good. I went to bed and slept very well. At two in the morning Steinkühler called and said: 'You are it.'"

Piëch was named head of VW in late 1992, but he had left some bitterness in his wake. To become head of VW Group, Piëch had had to show strong financial results at Audi. He had to demonstrate that he was not only a great engineer, but a great manager. He did so by building cars without firm orders in 1991 and 1992.

"He knew he had to present enormous results, he had to skim on costs and invoice, invoice, invoice," said a former Audi executive. "At the end of 1992, Audi had huge stocks because of the cars it built without orders."

Piëch's successor, Franz-Josef Kortüm, lasted barely a year as he tried to get rid of the excess stocks of Audis in a declining market, as the first Gulf War stifled demand and the European economy collapsed.

"He [Piëch] did me a lot of professional harm," said one executive. "But he was the only engineer with a global vision for product. We will all look at the great period of the 1990s and credit him for it. He was a guy who moved the industry."

IF PIËCH HAD ONE SHORTCOMING, it was that he worried less about marketing failure than any executive of his era. In the late 1990s, Piëch the engineer wanted to prove that highly economical and eco-logical cars were technically feasible. He ordered development of a version of the company's tiny Lupo that would consume just three liters of fuel per 100 kilometers. The car was placed on the market, where it sold poorly.

Piëch made his last business trip as VW chairman in a prototype with a fuel consumption of one liter per 100 kilometers. Piëch felt that pursuing highly economical and ecological versions of series cars would justify his commitment to develop luxury and sporty models with enormously powerful and thirsty engines—such as the 1,001 horsepower Bugatti Veyron that was unveiled in 2003.

Later in his tenure at Volkswagen, Piëch took criticism for overdo-ing luxury at the "people's car" company. He bought Lamborghini and Bentley and spent money to develop Bugatti. The luxurious Volkswagen-badged Phaeton sedan in 2002 showed how little he wor-ried about brands. It was technology and performance that concerned him. He put the VW emblem on a car that challenged the Mercedes-Benz S-class and BMW 7 series in every way except for image appeal.

The official business case for the move was that if Mercedes could attack Volkswagen's bread-and-butter cars with smaller models such as the A-class, VW had to fight back with cars that would chal-lenge Mercedes. Piëch was simply trying to prove once again that brand images were as malleable as clay and that only technology and performance truly mattered.

CHAPTER SEVEN

Iacocca the Savior
of Chrysler

L ee Iacocca almost went to work for Chrysler Corporation in
1962 rather than in 1978. A conflict-of-interest scandal involving Chrysler President William Newberg had blown up that
year. Newberg owned part of a Chrysler supplier, and when it came to
light he was forced out. Heidrick & Struggles, a headhunting firm in
Chicago, contacted 38-year-old Iacocca about joining Chrysler as executive vice president. Nobody had heard of Iacocca outside Detroit
because the Mustang wouldn't come out until 1964. But Iacocca had
been running the Ford Division of the Ford Motor Company for two
years and was building a solid reputation in the industry. To Iacocca,
the Chrysler job sounded pretty good, but he turned it down because
he liked his chances at Ford. He did, though, tell the headhunters to
keep him in mind if they knew of an opportunity for him to run his
own show.

Chrysler had given the job instead to an accountant named Lynn
Townsend, the man who was chief executive when the No. 3 U.S.
automaker took a deep plunge into desperate financial trouble in the 1970s.
Iacocca would wonder to himself, "Would things have been different at

Chrysler if I had taken that job? Maybe. But you can't ask yourself where you might have been if you had taken that turn instead of this turn. You might be dead."

In the days and weeks of inactivity after his dismissal from Ford in July 1978, Iacocca mostly sat back and reflected. He could be seen sometimes in the den of his 15-room split-level home in Bloomfield Hills, puffing on a cigar, while his teenage daughter, Lia, hosted friends down the hall. He would pad about the house, relaxing in "Lido's Lounge," a bar area in his home.

Iacocca was angry, but it was not a particularly traumatic time for him. So many job offers were pouring in that he knew he could bide his time. Auto suppliers called. Aerospace companies were interested. Business schools offered deanships. There were reports of more than 50 offers to become a CEO within a few weeks of his dismissal from Ford. Charles Tandy wanted him as his successor at Radio Shack.

Renault CEO Bernard Hanon talked to Iacocca about joining the French company, which was about to acquire American Motors and launch an assault on the U.S. market. Iacocca would have been head of AMC.

Iacocca knew two things about his future. He wanted to stay active, and he wanted it to remain in the auto industry. When Iacocca was in the car business he was also in the steel business, the glass business, and the tire business. He was running a consumer-products marketer and he was a defense contractor. He was in a hundred businesses at once. There was nothing in the business world like autos.

It didn't take Iacocca long to realize that an opportunity would open up across town at beleaguered Chrysler. He simply had to wait for the call. In a sense, this was ordained. When Lee Iacocca walked out of Henry Ford II's office on July 13, 1978, he may as well have stepped into his Continental Mark IV and driven straight to Highland Park 15 miles away. Chrysler was the only game in town if Iacocca was going to achieve the kind of absolute power he craved after his years as No. 2 at

Ford. And Chrysler needed the help; it was in terrible shape. Its cars weren't selling, it was losing record amounts of money each quarter, and it had piled up so much debt that any white knight had to think twice about coming to the company's rescue. When the Federal Loan Guarantee Act that saved Chrysler was passed at the end of 1979, the company was in hock to 400 banks and insurance companies to the tune of $4.75 billion. In January 1980, the company nearly ran out of money completely.

Iacocca's first overture from Chrysler came quickly, in August 1978—an SOS from Chrysler Chairman John Riccardo, a man so far in over his head that it was beginning to take a toll on his health.

The two men met for the first time at Detroit's Pontchartrain Hotel. They took elaborate measures to keep the meeting a secret, entering through side doors at different times. But deep down each must have understood the inevitability of this fateful meeting.

Lee Iacocca joined Chrysler on November 1, 1978, as president and chief operating officer. It was agreed that he would become chairman and CEO when Riccardo retired the following year. The day Iacocca's appointment was announced, Chrysler reported a quarterly loss of $159 million, the worst in its history.

Iacocca was greeted as a savior. When he walked into the first officers' council meeting a few days later, the other executives gave him a standing ovation. But once installed at Chrysler, Iacocca began to smell a rat. No American auto company had allowed itself to sink into such a poor condition since Ford in the early 1940s. Iacocca had expected to find an organization more or less comparable to the one he had just come from. What he discovered was a company utterly unlike anything he had ever seen. The country's 10th largest corporation looked as if it had been cobbled together by a host of amateurs. There was absolutely no organizational logic to Chrysler in 1978.

One overworked executive was in charge of *both* manufacturing and sales—a situation that helped to preserve Chrysler's famously foolish "sales bank"—its practice of building most cars not to order, but on spec—in the hope of finding a buyer.

Within days, Iacocca realized that Chrysler would need a complete overhaul, and there was no one to do it but him. "My greatest disappointment," Iacocca would say about his early years at Chrysler, "was starting from scratch." Iacocca was not yet CEO, but Riccardo had given him authority to do whatever he needed to do to fix Chrysler's operations. "I knew it was bad, but I didn't know it was that bad," he once recalled. "What I didn't know was how rotten the system was; how bad purchasing was; how many guys were on the take; how rotten it was to the core. That stunned me."

Iacocca found two huge problems. Chrysler lacked fundamental cost-analysis business systems, and it didn't know how to use its people. Chrysler had taken the concept of broadening the skills of its executives to ridiculous extremes. The company was moving people into jobs they were not equipped to handle. Iacocca remembered that not only was the controller unable to provide good financial data—because the company didn't have them—but that the controller didn't want to be controller in the first place.

Chrysler was terrible at positioning its personnel. It was full of square pegs in round holes. A successful manager in one part of the business would get a totally unrelated job until the company was filled with executives in positions for which they were unsuited.

Ford's Whiz Kids were the ultimate bean counters, a derogative term Iacocca helped popularize, if he didn't invent it altogether. But they were also believers in management training and the proper utilization of executive talent. They were numerate, but they were curious, too, and they knew that data could unlock secrets. For Townsend and the Chrysler accountants, the numbers were simply a shortcut. But the Chrysler numbers weren't reliable. It was like managing a major league baseball team by consulting no more than the box scores.

Executives at the highest levels were placed in jobs unrelated to anything they had ever done before. Townsend, who was Riccardo's predecessor, had had no true feel for the auto industry and how it really operated. He had managed the Chrysler Corporation by consulting a list of plant shipping schedules each morning, a daily sales sheet each noon, and a report on new orders just before he left the office every night at 6:30 p.m. With his cheat sheets, Townsend felt he could remain on top of things. He had no gut feel for what a purchasing manager did—or for what a body engineer or a zone manager did. Townsend was a numbers guy without intuition. Within three weeks of joining Chrysler, Iacocca ordered a top-to-bottom reorganization of the executive team. Within 27 months of taking over Chrysler—by early 1981—he had removed eight of the corporation's nine executive vice presidents. When Iacocca joined Chrysler, it had 35 vice presidents. Within three years, 33 of those had been fired. He recalled "feeling so bad for some of these guys because they'd plead and say, 'Hey boss, I didn't want this job, give me a chance. I don't want to be diversified.' I was friendly with most of them I fired. They were happy to get the hell out."

Iacocca had expected much of what he found at Chrysler. He knew, for instance, that labor relations were lousy, and it was certainly no secret how poorly Chrysler's cars were being built. In 1975, Chrysler introduced what some considered the worst cars ever produced by a U.S. auto manufacturer in the post-war era—a pair of compact twins called the Dodge Aspen and the Plymouth Volaré. The build quality of the cars was so poor that they quickly began to fall apart in owner's hands, leaving Chrysler with huge warranty bills. The cars were rushed out months too early. The first customers were, in effect, guinea pigs, used by Chrysler for what should have been the testing phase for the new models. More than three and half million cars were recalled for free repairs. A variety of problems plagued the cars—from engines that stalled to brakes that didn't function properly. In 1980, when Chrysler was trying to bail itself out, it had to pay over $100 million to honor anti-rust warranties alone. Iacocca knew from his suppliers that Chrysler's purchasing department was by far the least efficient in the U.S. industry. But he was surprised to find that Chrysler's vaunted engineering, long considered the strength of the company, had been starved by the previous management. The engineering operation was still a source of pride in Highland Park, but morale was plummeting. And meanwhile, Iacocca discovered that cars in the pipeline were behind schedule.

One of his first acts was to promote his old Ford colleague Hal Sperlich from vice president for product planning to group vice president in charge of all product development. For years, Chrysler's products—with one or two notable exceptions—had been pale imitations of what Ford and GM were building and selling. The stodgy design meant that the customers the company was attracting were older and less affluent than Ford and GM buyers. Chrysler buyers also put more on credit and replaced their cars less frequently. And Chrysler's owner loyalty rate was barely more than half that of Ford and a third of GM's. The company's dealers were less financed than other auto retailers and tended to be located on the poorer side of town.

None of this was a complete surprise to an auto man as savvy as Iacocca. What surprised him most was the lack of earnest financial controls. The kind of fiscal management Ford had turned into an art and science was nowhere to be found at Chrysler. The company's executives didn't have realistic financial projections on vehicle programs or new factories or the wherewithal to understand the true costs of doing business. Iacocca had spent much of his career at Ford finessing his way through finance director J. Edward Lundy's kingdom. Any time he and his team tried to get a new car into production—including the Mustang—they had to maneuver through a minefield of blue pinstriped suits, often Ivy League MBAs who found ingenious ways to pick holes in product proposals. They were expert at slow-walking projects, maintaining the net of financial discipline so tight that the company could be threatened with obliteration—as it was in the 1940s.

Iacocca knew how to play the Ford game. He had learned to operate effectively within that framework, though he was a product guy and a merchandiser and a natural antagonist of the finance lords. He had in fact moved the company away from the conservatism of Robert McNamara and Lundy's men, who never really quite forgave him. At Chrysler, Iacocca had expected to find something similar—a financial College of Cardinals that might have been tough and even destructive, but kept things under control. In fact, he had counted on it. Everyone knew that Lynn Townsend had come from Touche Ross, the great Detroit accounting firm. Riccardo, his successor, had also been a Touche executive before joining Chrysler. But where Ford was awash in systems, Chrysler was a Fortune 500 company with almost nothing of the kind. It was a top-down, shoot-from-the-hip enterprise. Townsend and Riccardo were "basically a couple of accountants," Iacocca wrote. As big-time accountants, they thought that they could control Chrysler by combing through summaries spat out daily by the plants and sales departments. There was accounting, but no accountability.

At meetings, Iacocca was stunned to see how little the other executives knew about what was happening in their company.

At the first board of directors meeting Iacocca sat through, there were no slide presentations or financial reviews and certainly no Ed Lundy look-alike. The lack of control had allowed the company to ship hundreds of thousands of cars that it knew could not be sold—cars that had no customer. Dealers hadn't ordered them and couldn't handle them, so the cars piled up in massive parking lots the company had had to scour the Detroit metropolitan area to find.

Chrysler epitomized the kind of American behemoth that had become so vulnerable to the Japanese onslaught. No corporation—at least in the automotive industry—was more tightly wedded to the sanctity of the quarterly earnings report, the mentality the Japanese slaughtered in the 1970s and 1980s. Townsend's mantra was "shipping schedules." Chrysler tried to meet the schedule and attain the volumes that kept the factories humming and quarterly profits streaming. But when sales plunged with the second oil crisis of the 1970s, cars were being shipped to empty fields.

The cars became weather damaged, and some even started to rust while they awaited a dealer who could be browbeaten into taking them. One executive said Townsend's philosophy was to "stack cars like cans of beans on a shelf." More than anything else, it was the "sales bank" that brought Chrysler to the edge of bankruptcy. Its bulging inventory became a joke in Detroit—a visible sign of a failing company—acres of cars with no buyers, spoiling the resale value of Chryslers on the road—cutting even deeper into brand loyalty. College kids were hired in giant phone banks to try to peddle the unwanted cars to dealers. Iacocca was stunned when at one of the first meetings he attended, a decision was made to take 10,000 cars out of the production schedule. A few days later, 50,000 cars were removed from the plan. Iacocca couldn't understand it. There had been no economic catastrophe. Why was Chrysler cutting production so drastically? It was because no more cars could be squeezed onto the giant parking lots. By the summer of 1980, the sales bank had soared to 80,000 cars.

The mess at Chrysler was the worst jolt of Iacocca's career because he hadn't seen it coming. He had a sickening, helpless feeling. He was in command of a huge enterprise that he could not begin to understand. It was as if he spoke a different language—as if he had been given control of a giant auto-making collective in the Soviet Union that just kept grinding out lousy cars to keep workers occupied. Things were so bad that Iacocca even stopped being mad at Henry Ford for a while and began to get steamed at his new boss—Chrysler's board of directors. "I was really mad before I got fired, the way Henry did things," he said years later. "But the actual firing, that was only a summer of being pissed. Once I got here I didn't have time to be mad at Henry or anybody. I was up to my ears in problems."

How, he asked, could Chrysler's management get such a slipshod approach past the distinguished group of businessmen who sat on the board of directors? It was so bad that Iacocca became deeply alarmed about the immediate future—about cash flow, something he'd never encountered at Ford. Within a few weeks, he came to the realization that Chrysler just might not survive.

"It hit me like a ton of bricks," Iacocca wrote in his autobiography. "We were running out of cash." Iacocca had heard the stories about the mess young Henry Ford II found at his grandfather's company in 1945, and he saw some of it first hand as a young trainee in Dearborn in 1946.

He'd also heard the stories during late night bull sessions with some original Whiz Kids, men like McNamara and Arjay Miller, who were there and who had helped to fix it. He thought about them as the enormity of the problems at Chrysler dawned on him.

But there was no evidence that Iacocca ever truly doubted that he was the right guy for the job.

Chrysler needed someone special to step in, and if one looked out over the American corporate-leader landscape in 1978, there weren't many choices that made more sense than Lee Iacocca. "I didn't plan it that way, but by getting canned in 1978, I got thrown into a situation where I became a leader," Iacocca said. "You need to have a war to make a general. Fortunately the war doesn't let you know what's coming tomorrow, or you'd go nuts. Some days at Chrysler, I wouldn't have got up in the morning if I had known what was coming." In the process, Iacocca rediscovered his old self. After eight years as president of Ford, getting fired was a shot of humility. His lost youthful hunger had come back to him, and he lost some of the imperial style that marked his triumphant years both at Ford and then much later at Chrysler. Henry Ford II had inadvertently put Lee Iacocca back at the top of his game.

Back in 1956—when Iacocca had been dealt a bad hand at Ford by McNamara trying to promote their cars with safety features—Iacocca had come up with a sales promotion that saved the model year. Now he had to do it again.

A few years later, Iacocca would become a national hero, best-selling author, and the subject of speculation that he might run for U.S. president. He would break out the foot-long cigars once again and sound and act like Henry Ford II. But from 1979 through 1981, he was all business—and at full-throttle concentration there was none better than Lee Iacocca.

Chrysler not only needed Iacocca, it needed the Ford Motor Company. Iacocca gave his new employer the kind of modernizing Ford had received in 1946. For the most part, Chrysler's rescuers were ex-Ford executives who had learned from the old heroes of Dearborn. Henry Ford II's turnaround of his family's company in the 1940s was the model of all great automotive industry turnarounds in the second half of the century—the 1979–1981 rescue of Chrysler, the 1992 revolution at General Motors, and the 1991–2001 revival of Nissan by Carlos Ghosn and Renault. Iacocca was a strand of Ford DNA that transformed the cellular structure of Chrysler.

At first, just about everyone opposed the idea of U.S. government–backed loans for Chrysler. Not only were liberal Democrats from non-auto manufacturing states against the loans, but business titans such as Walter Wriston, head of Citicorp, and Tom Murphy, the chairman of General Motors. Ford Chairman Phil Caldwell wouldn't say it for the record, but it was clear that he vehemently opposed the idea. So did the National Association of Manufacturers and the Business Roundtable—on ideological grounds.

Chrysler's crisis and plea for welfare was fair game for critics. And the bailout became the subject of ridicule by late-night comedians and editorial cartoonists. Iacocca could have turned himself into a national joke. Instead, he became the opposite. Iacocca said his best moment at

Chrysler was in August 1983 when the company paid off the government-guaranteed loans at a luncheon at the Washington Press Club. "Nothing is ever going to top it," Iacocca said. "I hated being in the government's pocket for that money, and when we got out, how sweet it was."

But getting into the government's pocket in the first place might have been the greatest achievement of Iacocca's career, greater than the Mustang, greater than the first minivan.

Lee Iacocca had been preparing his entire life for the challenge he faced when he arrived in Highland Park in the autumn of 1978. It was as if the Ford Motor Company, where he had catapulted up the corporate ladder, was just a rehearsal for the job of his life.

Iacocca was 54 when he joined Chrysler. He'd succeeded at Ford to a degree that no one, including his beloved father, Nicola, could have possibly imagined. He'd earned more money than six generations of Iacocca men. If he'd retired after Ford and spent the rest of his life playing golf, tending to his vineyards in Italy, or lying around his house in Boca Raton, he would have been one for the record books. No one would have forgotten Lee Iacocca.

But his career became an automotive industry version of the life of Winston Churchill, who was put out to pasture, then suddenly thrust back into the middle of a crisis. Iacocca would play Churchill to Townsend's—and Riccardo's—Neville Chamberlain. The worst days at Chrysler were like Churchill's in the war cabinet rooms during the Battle of Britain. Some reflect back that Iacocca could not have possibly screwed up because he had nothing to lose. Chrysler's mess hadn't been his doing. Yet had Chrysler swerved into bankruptcy or been acquired by Ford or General Motors at a fire sale, Iacocca's legacy would have been diminished. He had staked his reputation on turning Chrysler around.

The utter chaos he found at Chrysler may have shocked Iacocca, but it also empowered him. It gave him the ability to operate with more freedom than he ever knew at Ford. Now he could call upon a lifetime of lessons learned.

While a zone manager in western Pennsylvania in the 1950s, Iacocca absorbed one of the fundamental lessons of his business life: an auto sales executive was only as good as his dealers. He would repeat it over and over again to anyone he met in those days. When Iacocca became a superstar in the 1980s, the conversation would inevitably turn to him whenever auto people gathered. And those who had met him in the 1950s always recalled the same thing. "I'm the best because I've got the best dealers," Iacocca had told them in the 1950s.

As he ascended the ranks at Ford, he drifted away from the entrepreneurs who moved the metal and helped the company get through hard times. But at Chrysler, his first instinct was to get the tired masses of dealers on his side. He knew the company could not dig itself out until he had convinced the badly abused retailers that he meant what he said—Chrysler's cars and trucks would improve and that he would treat the dealers with respect.

Iacocca hired Gar Laux, who had become a dealer himself after retiring from Ford. Laux's job was to gain the confidence of dealers and to motivate them for what Iacocca knew would be a long haul—the wait for a new compact model in late 1980 that was known internally as the K-car. Iacocca and Laux had to get them excited about the K-car-based front-wheel-drive "garageable van" that would arrive in late 1983. And just as he did as a young man at Ford in the 1950s, Iacocca began to take things into his own hands.

Once, early in his career, Iacocca had himself driven a Pennsylvania dealer's stock of used cars around the man's sales area and tried to sell them one by one. He had checked county registration lists to see who had the oldest cars and thus might want to replace them. He helped get the dealer out of a jam. Now Iacocca poured himself into the sales and marketing of Chrysler's humdrum vehicles. He fell back on his knack for the great promotion. His most famous come-on was the "56 for 56" campaign in which he convinced tens of thousands of Ford-wary buyers that they could buy the 1956 models for a payment of $56 a month if they put 20 percent down. Iacocca came up with the gimmick himself after taking over an underperforming region in a disappointing sales year for Ford. The promotion worked brilliantly and was the big break of Iacocca's early career. The "Iacocca Plan" made him a household name in the far corners of the corporation. Twenty-five years later, he was telling Americans: "If you can find a better car, buy it"—one of the most famous taglines in American advertising history and another original Iacocca idea. He became the television pitchman, appearing in the commercials. It was another first for Chrysler, like the loan guarantees and the labor concessions he would get. And in the process, he influenced a generation of CEO pitchmen, none of whom would be as effective as Iacocca.

As quickly as he could, Iacocca installed the business practices of the Ford Whiz Kids and their offspring at Chrysler. He became the missionary for the financial beliefs that he had disparaged and often tried to circumvent. He began to live by the mantra of Whiz Kid and former Ford President Robert McNamara—what gets measured gets managed. Ford had been a tremendous business education for Lee Iacocca, just as it was for hundreds of other automotive managers in the United States and Europe. Dozens graduated from Ford to other companies, and not only car manufacturers. During the 1960s, 1970s, and 1980s, no corporation in the world was afraid to hire a manager trained at the Ford Motor Company. Ed Lundy once said, "We run a high-power business school, and from the jobs our alumni get, I believe a first-rate one."

At Chrysler, Iacocca arranged for an influx of Ford talent. Henry Ford II had performed his post-war miracle with extraordinarily intuitive hiring—bringing in the best and the brightest—from General Motors and from the American military. Iacocca had to do something similar. He brought in Laux, Gerry Greenwald, Steve Miller, Ben Bidwell, and Paul Bergmoser from Ford. And those senior Ford executives brought over their own Ford favorites, who in turn brought over some of theirs to Chrysler, until the effect was what Henry Ford II did in 1946—hiring his way out of a crisis by not only bringing in big shots at the top, but managers further down, too. In 1946, Henry II hired older men like Ernie Breech and Lewis Crusoe from GM, but he hired the Whiz Kids too. Financially troubled General Motors would do something similar in 1992—bringing in hordes of people from outside GM. But they didn't come from Ford or Chrysler, they came from consumer brand marketers—a miscalculation that was rectified in 2001 when Bob Lutz was lured out of retirement.

At Ford, Iacocca had learned to take existing vehicle platforms and raid the parts bin to create something new and exciting at relative bargain rates. He and his team had taken the underpinnings of the Falcon to get the 1964 Mustang into showrooms and would use the same strategy to get the K-car–based minivan into production at Chrysler.

With the Mustang, Iacocca had learned how to build a sense of anticipation. Fifteen years later, he created such a storm of interest in the basic front-wheel-drive K-car that it seemed the future of the nation depended on it. The "K-car" codename became part of the national parlance, so much so that it had to be used on the Plymouth Reliant and Dodge Aries nameplates, otherwise Chrysler would have wasted $100 million in free publicity.

Iacocca's years making elaborate, airtight business cases for Ford's finance department helped him take the case for saving Chrysler to the United States Congress. The House and Senate Banking Committees would never grill him as hard as Henry Ford II's numbers crunchers had.

What's more, Iacocca knew his way around the nation's capital. He had learned how power is wielded in Washington while calling on Richard Nixon with that great door-opener, the Deuce. He looked and felt comfortable in Washington and succeeded in uniting America's oldest, strongest, and most antagonistic interest groups—big business, big labor, and big government—in a common cause. He struck a chord with both fiscally conservative Republicans and UAW Democrats. Everyone got the message because Iacocca was delivering it. Of course, he had a good product to sell—the salvation of Chrysler—and he not only knew how to sell it in the seat of power, he knew how to take his case to the American people. Without a spokesman able to summarize both the bleakness and opportunity at Chrysler, the federal loan guarantees would have been dismissed as pork barrel for failed faceless industrialists—much as the Lockheed federal loan guarantees were viewed in 1971.

Iacocca was pulling together all his skills and rounding up all his experience. He was utilizing everything he had learned and everyone who had influenced him, whether he had liked them or not. It was the same thing Bob Lutz would do at Chrysler a decade later. John Riccardo was still chairman when Chrysler asked for the federal loan guarantees. He was a Detroit fat cat right out of central casting—a cranky U.S. auto executive who blamed all his problems on federal regulations. He was Chrysler's own worst enemy—and a lightning rod for the anti-loan guarantee forces.

Riccardo resigned on September 18, 1979, which meant Iacocca was now chief executive and the lead spokesman for the bailout. Not long afterward, he testified before a hearing of the House and Senate banking committees. Expecting another irritable CEO like Riccardo, Iacocca gave a spirited, passionate, and humor-laden defense of the loan guarantees. And unlike Riccardo, Iacocca found he was treated with respect. "If you do what you did for Ford with Chrysler," Congressman Stewart McKinney told him, "you are going to be a man that needs a big bronze statue put somewhere." Iacocca cracked, "I hope it's not a live statue." The room broke up with laughter.

Once when he brought up the fact at a congressional hearing that the Washington, D.C., subway system was getting a federal loan guarantee bigger than Chrysler's, he called it "a showpiece for the capital." "It's a transportation system," answered one congressman. Iacocca replied, "What the hell do you think Chrysler is?" Iacocca had surprised himself when it came to public speaking. As he rose at Ford, he never considered himself much of one. And he wasn't. When nervous or unprepared he'd lapse into corporate jargon or dealer lingo while addressing big groups. He'd forget who his audience was and start to ramble. A Dale Carnegie class in 1956 helped, and Iacocca forced himself to give speech after speech until he found that he enjoyed it and had become very good at it. Indeed, it turned out he was built for the limelight. As Ford's president, many of his public appearances meant playing second banana to Henry Ford. The Deuce made the wisecracks at the company's annual shareholders' meeting or financial press conferences, and Iacocca would puff on his cigar and play off him.

But Iacocca thrived as the public persona of Chrysler. Under the most intense media scrutiny any American business enterprise had ever experienced, he was having the time of his life. Iacocca had trained for stardom at Ford, and now he was a performing on a wider American stage. He gave the anonymous automotive industry a name, a face, and a purpose. The country got a look inside the auto industry as he related its complexity, its cost burdens, its social obligations, the low, grocery store–like profit margins, and the brutal new Japanese competition.

Iacocca was bringing the auto industry into living rooms. He was the Johnny Carson of Detroit. He made believers of millions. No auto company titan since the first Henry Ford had made such an impact on the public consciousness. Iacocca was magnetic, and he was able to convince entertainers like Frank Sinatra, Bill Cosby, and Bob Hope to help for nothing.

In the end, Lee Iacocca convinced Americans that Chrysler's rustbelt business was worth saving and could be fixed. He had to answer the fundamental question that divided Congress and the Jimmy Carter administration—not whether Chrysler could be saved, but whether it *should* be saved. Chrysler built out-of-date gas guzzlers, was an inefficient manufacturer, and, by its own admission, sometimes shipped junk. So why bother? Chrysler's financial chiefs—Greenwald and Miller and others—received and deserved tremendous credit for putting together the rescue plan. But it was Iacocca who assembled the arguments and fought the fight in the court of public opinion. Allowing the tenth largest corporation in America to file for Chapter 11 protection would have kept creditors at bay. But customers would have stopped buying Chrysler's cars, afraid they wouldn't be able to get them serviced. Suppliers would have stopped shipping parts. The company would have died instantly. Iacocca knew this, and he was aware that the U.S. government knew it, too.

Iacocca would get his opportunity, but he still had to make the case. He did it by calling upon the main lesson he learned in the early days at Ford, while trying to get Pennsylvania dealers to fill up their lots with Fords. Iacocca had the knack of making the other guy feel he had no choice but to do what Iacocca wanted. In 1956, he convinced dealers that it was in their best interest to order more cars because he had a plan for selling them. He told the U.S. government that it could allow a company with 200,000 employees to go bankrupt, or it could back loan guarantees. It could pay now or it could pay later.

In December 1979, Congress passed the Chrysler Corporation Loan Guarantee Act, providing $1.5 billon in loan guarantees. The bill was signed into law by President Jimmy Carter in January. Chrysler also got $655 million in concessions from its 400 lenders. But this was only the beginning of the struggle. Iacocca still had to convince the American public to buy Chrysler's cars and trucks, and he had to whip the organization into shape.

Iacocca would remember these times as the most exhilarating of his career. He would have done it for nothing. In fact, for a couple of years he did just that, because he worked for a dollar a year. Of course, there would be a huge payoff for him when Chrysler was healthy again. Iacocca achieved a public stature that surpassed Henry Ford II and for a while that seemed all he would ever want. He had earned it the same way the Deuce had—by preventing a great company from dying.

After that, nothing would ever enthuse Iacocca quite so much—not the renovation of the Statue of Liberty or the Ellis Island Commission; not Chrysler's later bouts with financial ruin, nor the idea of running for president. Winston Churchill, another cigar-chomping executive, returned to power in 1951, but it was never the same—just as it could never quite be the same for Iacocca later in his career. When he retired in 1992, a longtime associate acknowledged Iacocca's self-absorption. "There's only one way you run the engine of ego, and that's with heavy praise and adulation," the associate said. "He's got that ego, he needs that constant filling of his emotional gas tank. But he was a truly outstanding guy. In some ways, he'll prove to be the last of the charismatic leaders. Lee will be the last of the emotional guys. But it took a guy with that charismatic presence to turn Chrysler around."

Iacocca had, by example, taught future business leaders how to save companies. He had applied the lessons learned at Ford in 1946 to the modern world. If Iacocca had not joined Chrysler in 1978, everything would be different. Scores of talented managers would have remained at Ford; Chrysler could not have stayed independent; the American minivan would have arrived years later, if at all; someone else would have bought American Motors and Jeep; there would be no DaimlerChrysler. And Bob Lutz would have stayed where he was.

CHAPTER EIGHT

The Cars Make the Real Stars

The industry's great car guys are futurists, able to prophesize what the contours and capabilities of automobiles will be a half-decade before they appear. This is really more art than science. And none were better at it than Bob Lutz and Ferdinand Piëch, the half-century's most instinctive diviners of the coming look and feel of automobiles. Lutz and Piëch share credit for the great divide in auto design in the early 1980s, the shift from straight lines and sharp angles to curved edges and soft corners—a trend in exterior styling that held up for two decades. Lutz's car was the 1982 Ford Sierra. Piëch was the father of the 1983 Audi 100.

There weren't the high-powered in-house designers in those days. Patrick le Quément, who later was the head of design at Renault during its glory years, shaped the European Sierra, which begat the Ford Taurus in North America. Independent designer Giorgetto Giugiaro was called on by Piëch to do the Audi 100. The Sierra appeared first, and the Audi 100 arrived soon afterward with a wind-cheating drag coefficient of 0.30. It was even sleeker than the Ford. The Audi had a stunning, bullet-shaped motif compared with the quadrangular Mercedes and BMW models it sought to compete against. Many automotive journalists rank it as the most influential design since Piëch's grandfather's original Beetle. No car turned more heads on the German autobahn when it first appeared. Not everyone liked it at first, but the 100 quickly grew on the auto world. The car was sold in America as the Audi 5000 and, ironically, four years after introduction, the 5000 caused the uproar that brought Audi to its knees.

American buyers, unaccustomed to the Audi's close pedal configuration, were stomping on the accelerator while thinking it was the brake, causing what became known as "unintended acceleration." Without the significant amount of negative publicity that suppressed Audi's U.S. sales for years, the company might have pulled up alongside BMW and Mercedes in the 1990s. Instead it had to wait another decade. By the mid-1980s, coefficient of drag—a measurement usually reserved for aircraft—became as common in car talk as horsepower and luggage space. Every automaker bragged about low wind resistance—none more than Ford.

The American architect Louis Sullivan's famous dictum, form follows function, became Ford's slogan. In 1979, Ford's new head of North American operations, Donald E. Petersen, decided to take a fresh look at Ford's future product plans for the 1980s.

The company was preparing new squared-off versions of the Thunderbird and LTD sedan that had been designed under veteran North American styling chief Gene Bordinet, who had been designing cars for three decades and was nearing retirement. The new Fords had gone through several levels of approval, but Petersen—who started his career in the early 1950s as a product planner—thought they were ugly.

In 1979, he paid a visit to a senior designer named Jack Telnack in the Dearborn styling studio. Petersen looked over the works in progress and asked Telnack if he was happy with the cars.

"Would you want to have that car parked in your driveway?" asked Petersen looking over one of the clay models.

Telnack, famously, said he would not.

"Then show me what you can do," Petersen said.

As the story goes, Telnack got busy on designs that would perk up the Ford product lineup in the 1980s—the aerodynamic "jellybean" cars. Petersen had shaken things up and would eventually take enormous credit for it. The Telnack saga would become part of Ford corporate lore, often repeated when Petersen later became chairman and CEO. But the North American aero cars came to Ford from Europe—and from Bob Lutz.

When Bob Lutz retired from Chrysler in 1998, the car most closely associated with him was the Viper, Chrysler's low-volume challenger to the Corvette. It was an important car in that it showed that Chrysler, after all those years of K-car derivatives, was still capable of generating some excitement. The Viper was also a kind of audition for Lutz and his new team. And it was a huge morale builder inside the company. But it wasn't the car Lutz was most proud of as he looked back on his career. Neither were the hot-selling LH cars that debuted in 1992—the first result of the newly formed platform team inspired by Soichiro Honda. The car Lutz thought of as his greatest achievement was the Sierra, a mid-size family sedan that struggled in the marketplace after its debut.

The Sierra was a pure Lutz play—well ahead of its time in terms of design. Launched in October 1982, the rear-wheel-drive hatchback replaced the Cortina in England and the Taunus in Germany. Within a few years, its rounded shape would blend in naturally with other cars on the road. Indeed, a decade after its debut the Sierra was still in production and the design seemed wholly contemporary and was flattered by many imitators. But in 1983, Ford's European dealers didn't like it much—especially in Britain, where salesmen called it an inverted soap dish or jelly mould. Its aero look was out of step with the boxy times.

The radical design was not the only problem. Ford didn't introduce a notchback until 1987, and Ford's European salesmen and marketers had wanted a front-wheel-drive car. The rear suspension on the

Taunus had been widely criticized. Ford of Europe's sales executives wanted a successor with an independent rear suspension, and Lutz got it. But Ford executives at the time remembered Lutz fighting with the finance overlords during the Sierra's development. "The Sierra was a clear example of what happened with Lutz in Europe," said an executive who was with Ford of Europe at the time. "Accountants could not care less about the design—whether it was advanced or not—so long as it made its numbers. But the Sierra was hurt by the fact that it didn't have front-wheel drive. The battle was lost because it cost too much money. The bean counters won the war. The styling was innovative, but the hardware, the expensive stuff, he could not get." Twenty-two years after the car's debut, Lutz didn't regard the fact that the Sierra had rear-wheel drive as a defeat. Ford at the time simply didn't have the money to ditch the Cortina-Taunus platform. "I was perfectly comfortable because we knew we would get a dynamically better car than anybody else's and we did," Lutz said.

"GM could afford to make the switch to front-wheel drive and we couldn't. It wasn't so much the chassis as the expense of east-westing all the engines and east-westing the transmissions. So we had to stay with all the north-south stuff, and we were able to do a new independent rear suspension.

"There was all kinds of hand-wringing—Renault is front-wheel drive, Peugeot is front-wheel drive, Volkswagen is front-wheel drive, GM is now—we were the only guys who were rear-wheel drive, and my point was 'yes and we are in very good company, called BMW and Mercedes-Benz.' If we do a primitive rear-wheel drive we will not be successful, if we do a sophisticated rear-wheel-drive chassis we will be successful. One concern, though, during the oil crisis of 1978, was that rear-wheel-drive cars would weigh a little more than the front-wheel-drive alternatives.

"There was a lot of competition for fuel economy numbers, so we said we would shoot for a car that was very modern and with a very,

very low drag coefficient," Lutz recalled. The Sierra did cost only $813 million to develop—a lot less than the $1 billion-plus Ford had spent two years before on a new Escort. But it had come at another kind of price to Ford—the beginning of a lengthy antagonism between Poling and Lutz that in time would cause Lutz to leave Ford. He would follow Lee Iacocca to Chrysler after Poling blocked his career path.

Still, Lutz's radical Sierra design tactic became a major influence in Ford long before the car went on sale. Lutz unveiled clay models in 1978 to an audience that included Petersen and Henry Ford II. Ever the showman, Lutz had two cars covered—one a traditionally shaped sedan and the second the aerodynamically lined car that would more or less become the Sierra. Henry Ford had major qualms about the more advanced design, the one Lutz wanted to do. The convincing job would take time. Lutz finally took matters into his own hands when the Deuce came to Europe for a "farewell tour" in 1979, the year before he would retire as chairman of the board. Henry was accompanied on the trip by Kathleen DuRoss, his companion at the time and eventually his third wife. As chairman of Ford of Europe, Lutz hosted as Henry and DuRoss visited dignitaries around Europe. They concluded the tour with a trip to the still-divided city of Berlin. The night before Henry and Lutz were to meet with the mayor of West Berlin, DuRoss decided to skip the formalities because she wanted to see East Berlin. Lutz's German wife of the time agreed to accompany her. Ford PR men quickly organized an elaborate series of movements at Checkpoint Charlie to get DuRoss through to the other side of the Iron Curtain.

After their Berlin visit the next day, Henry Ford and Lutz were scheduled to board a company plane in the afternoon to return to Ford's German headquarters in Cologne. "You'd better get back on time because I'm not waiting," Ford told the two ladies the night before. Henry II was always a punctual man. Not only was he never late for a meeting, he was almost always early. It was an obsession. The next day, DuRoss and Heide Lutz were late for the Ford plane and nearly had to find other transportation. Henry Ford ordered the pilot to take off the moment the two women arrived.

What was the rush?

Lutz had added a special trip to the company's design center in Merkenich, Germany, the next day. He wanted to show Henry Ford how the Sierra was coming along. And he wanted to prod the founder to sign off on the project once and for all.

The 61-year-old chairman was still highly skeptical, but Lutz won his approval. That September, the future Sierra was shown as a concept car at the Frankfurt auto show. That in turn freed Ford designers in North America to pick up on the new design themes.

Lutz remembers: "It wasn't that the Sierra came out and then everybody in North America said 'holy smokes'; but it was concurrent. Jack Telnack knew exactly what was going on in Europe, and when I was in the States I'd come and look at what was going on here. So it was transference of ideas. Henry Ford II finally said yes to the Sierra after months of 'I don't like it, I don't like round cars, it looks like it's out of a Jell-O mold' and so forth. The system was very tentative until we had him convinced that the Sierra was going to be OK. He said, 'well all right, this had better be good. I'm going to trust you, Bob, if you really think this is going to work,' and I said, 'Mr. Ford, I guarantee this is going to work. Every trend I look at tells me this is exactly where the industry is heading.' And he finally said 'yeah, go ahead,' and that sort of broke the logjam, and now everybody on the U.S. side felt safe." Another Ford executive at the time said that Henry Ford II was never wholly convinced, but the force of Lutz's personality was too much to resist. "He didn't say, 'we are all in this together,' he said 'we'll do it, but it's your ass if we fail.'"

When Henry Ford II retired in 1980, he had taken Bordinet with him, and Jack Telnack became Ford's head of design. Petersen, who had helped develop the Mustang, became president of the company in

1980. Now that he had real power and Bordinet was gone, Petersen was going to do something dramatic. He felt that something along the lines of the Lutz car he had seen in 1978 in Europe was the way to go. So together with Telnack, they pushed aerodynamics to the forefront in America, too.

First it was an egg-shaped Thunderbird that came out in 1983 followed by rounded-off versions of the new Ford Tempo and Mercury Topaz compact cars. Those cars received the same kind of lukewarm reaction in America that Lutz's Sierra had in Europe. At first, conservative dealers in the southern United States had trouble moving the odd-shaped new metal. But by the time the aerodynamic mid-sized Ford Taurus and Mercury Sable sedans arrived in the heart of the American passenger-car market in 1985, the public was accustomed to the new look. Ford had a huge hit. Caldwell and Petersen had bet the company on the Taurus and Sable. It would replace the un-lovely Fairmont in the Ford lineup—dubbed the "Squaremont" by some wags.

The designer of the Taurus was Ray Everts, one of the same designers who had helped conceive the Sierra. "Lutz was the prime mover of the Sierra, and the Sierra certainly influenced Ford's North American design direction," said an executive who was there at the time. Lutz recalls it vividly. "Whenever I was in the States, Jack Telnack and I would go talk about the '83 T-Bird, even though I was not responsible for North America, but Jack Telnack regularly showed me the car . So we kind of collaborated on those cars because it wasn't hard to see that was where the market was going."

Lutz moved to Ford's top international job in Dearborn in 1982, but had to return to Europe in 1984 to help sort out the problems caused in part by the slow-selling Sierra. He then returned to the United States again in 1985 to head Ford's truck operations. "After Lutz left, Ford got tentative in its design in Europe, less progressive," said a former Ford executive. "There was no continuity after the Sierra." But in America, the slippery-shaped Taurus was becoming the country's top-selling passenger car—that is, until the Honda Accord grabbed the lead in 1989. The Taurus was a bold stroke against the cube-like General Motors sedans, and it caused every carmaker in the world to rush to aero shapes. Lew Veraldi, the head of Ford's Team Taurus, had included several innovations in the car, but the cutting-edge design was the key. Meanwhile, Petersen was being hailed as a hero—his advancement to chairman that year with the retirement of Caldwell was assured. Yet his patronage of the aero look in America was in part a defensive move—an effort by Petersen to neutralize Lutz. If there was a star in the Ford Motor Company in the late 1970s, it was the flamboyant fighter-pilot chairman of Ford of Europe. Petersen, who had seen the Sierra prototype in 1978, knew that Lutz was about to startle and perhaps dazzle Europe with his car. If it became a big success, there would be no stopping the Swiss-American executive. Lutz would triumphantly return to America as Ford's new Lee Iacocca. Petersen was five years older, but the two men were headed for a showdown in Dearborn. Having watched Iacocca's career skyrocket with the Mustang, Petersen could foresee a similar turbo boost for Lutz, and he might well be presiding over a boxy old-style flop in America while Lutz became the company's standard-bearer for a more modern look.

Not only did Petersen want dramatic new styling, so did the new chairman and CEO, Phil Caldwell. It was a strange departure for Caldwell, who had a reputation in product circles for being deeply suspicious of change. But he showed a surprising level of support for the advanced designs coming out of Telnack's studio. Like Petersen, Caldwell didn't want to be cast as a throwback to the dull pre-Iacocca product days. The Sierra's struggles in the market were ironic. Had Caldwell and Petersen foreseen its slow sales start, they might not have been so quick to authorize the radical design changes in North America. Petersen and Caldwell deserve credit for putting Ford on the right design path, but Lutz was the agent of change. In 1998, as he prepared to retire from Chrysler, Lutz conceded that the Taurus was a gutsy move.

"I think things have to really be bad before people listen to guys like me," Lutz said. "The creativity of sensing trends entails risk." Many had expected Lutz to be planning the Taurus and Sable successors in Dearborn in the late 1980s, but he was at Chrysler by that time. "Then the bean counters came back and said these were unacceptable risks, and Ford went back to playing it safe," he said. Lutz says he would have never done the second-generation Taurus that appeared in 1993. "God, that second generation was aesthetically challenged. It basically destroyed the Taurus name. It was practically dead on arrival. The range came out after our Chrysler LH cars, and Ford had told the press, 'wait till you see the new Taurus.'"

Did Lutz deserve all the credit for Ford's company-saving shift to aerodynamic cars? One Ford executive from the era recalls that, "Lutz pushed Henry Ford hard for the aero cars. But Don Petersen did, too."

Lutz says: "Red Poling said my nefarious influence with Don Petersen had gotten them to do the Taurus and the Sable, and he said the Taurus and the Sable were going to be a big mistake, and that he— Red Poling [in charge of North American operations at the time]— said it was too late to stop, but that the car was going to be a disaster. They had just had them in a clinic in New England. And Red said 'Do you know what they like in New England?'

"'No, Red, I don't know what they like in New England.'

"'They like the Chrysler K-cars. That's what they like in New England.'

"'Well, God help them,' I said. 'I can't comment on the research, but I think the Taurus and the Sable are going to be tremendously successful.'

"'No, they're not,' Red said, 'and it's going to be your fault. I want you to remember that when the Ford Motor Company fails. I want you to know it was your fault for having talked Don Petersen into those cars.'"

The three-box four-door sedan became the dominant mode of personal transport in post-war America—right up through the early 1990s. It was the standard American rear-wheel-drive four-door, typified in the 1950s and 1960s by the Chevy Bel Air, Ford Galaxie, and Chrysler 300C. A basic three-box sedan had its station wagon version and convertible derivative, but no other real alternative.

In Europe, the small front-wheel-drive car was the particular genius of Sir Alec Issigonis, the creator of the BMC Mini in 1959. Giugiaro's first Golf in 1974 brought the evolution further, and their basic concepts survived in every small car produced in the world in the early 2000s. It took the innovative BMW to halt and reverse the trend. When the Bavarian company entered the small Golf class for the first time with the 1 series in 2004, it introduced a rear-wheel-drive car in an attempt to put driving pleasure into the premium sector of the class.

But the basic American sedan continued to soldier on. The last truly successful standard-sized sedans from a U.S. company were the 1985 Taurus and the 1992 Chrysler LH, the "cab-forward" model that arose from Bob Lutz's revitalized product development operation at Chrysler. After the Taurus, no medium-sized three-box passenger sedan from an American company has been the country's number-one-selling passenger car. That segment was taken over by Honda and Toyota, and Honda got there first with its Accord.

The Accord was the last Honda to bear the significant influence of Soichiro Honda himself. The same engineers who had worked with the founder on the CVCC engine and the original Civic had conceived and designed the first Accord in 1978. By 1989, the Accord was the best-selling model in the United States, and by the end of the century, the Accord and the Toyota Camry were the world's last dominant medium-size sedans. GM had a lock on the segment until its ill-fated GM10 project in the 1980s. Ford's second-generation Taurus was much less successful than the first. Only Lutz's LH sedans offered serious competition. Indeed, they proceeded to rule the middle of the American market in the 1990s.

Honda reinvented the mid-size sedan—the most popular American car segment—almost to the degree that Issigonis reinvented the small car. Honda improved the look, performance, and quality of the everyday sedans that General Motors, Ford, and Chrysler had grown fat on.

The fledgling Honda company frequently developed concepts that the much larger Toyota would capitalize on. Toyota's wildly successful Lexus luxury brand launched in 1988 was a replication of Honda's Acura experiment. And Toyota didn't really get into the Camry class in America until the Honda Accord had shown the way. The Accord and Camry were aimed at the heart of the U.S. market, and the only opposition that the American auto companies offered was the first Taurus and the Chrysler LH sedans.

Another reason traditional American family sedans floundered was the birth of the German sport sedan—the singular invention of Eberhard von Kuenheim's BMW, which put sports-car agility in a compact family sedan and then added luxury-car refinement. Von Kuenheim constructed a business around concepts that became the model for Mercedes-Benz, Jaguar, Volvo, Saab, Lexus, Infiniti, and numerous other wannabes. One of von Kuenheim's first acts after becoming chairman of BMW in 1970 was to lay out the product strategy based on three sedans—the 3, 5, and 7 series—one for every premium price range, with no unseemly platform sharing. Over time, von Kuenheim began to load the cars with some of the interior amenities of Cadillacs, Lincolns, and Jaguars, while sacrificing none of the autobahn-hardened performance that attracted drivers to BMW.

BMW was the model, but their model couldn't be duplicated. Toyota spent several billion dollars to develop its Lexus luxury division in the late 1980s, and Lexus was able to match the performance and, in the minds of many Americans at least, the élan of its target competitor—Mercedes-Benz. But Nissan's Infiniti luxury brand would never duplicate the sales or appeal of its target European competitor, BMW. Von Kuenheim's BMW was a far more difficult target than its competitor's imagined.

The minivan also helped kill the standard American sedan. Lee Iacocca wanted to build the minivan at Ford in the 1970s, but Henry Ford II refused to approve its development. At that time, Ford was working on a car program called "Erica" that would become the Ford Escort and would cost about $2 billion to develop.

"It was a huge investment in those days," said Ben Bidwell, who was then vice president for Ford's Car and Truck Group and later joined Iacocca at Chrysler. "It wasn't going to make any money, but we had to do it for corporate average fuel-economy purposes." Bidwell recalled to *Automotive News* a Memorial Day weekend when Henry II was visiting the company's design center. Bidwell was championing a program for a larger compact car called "Monica." Ford and Bidwell were the last people to leave the meeting. Ford said, "Ben, do you have a minute?" The two men got into Bidwell's Mercury Cougar because it had air conditioning. As they drove away, Ford told Bidwell that he was going to vote for the Erica program at the board meeting the next week, but not for the Monica program. "I just committed $2 billion of my family's money, and I don't want to go for another billion," he told Bidwell. "I don't want to put my family that deeply in hock." Henry Ford II was still funding major programs, in effect, out of his pocket, so the Monica was never made.

"Lee went over to Chrysler. Hal Sperlich was already there," said Bidwell. "Chrysler had the K-car, which was the perfect platform for what became the minivan. We (at Ford) were unable to do the minivan—which we called the Mini/Max—because it had to be low-floor front-wheel drive. The Escort wasn't big enough or wide enough. So in effect the Ford Mini/Max program was done at Chrysler because the platform existed there. Had we done the Monica, we would have had the platform to do what became the front-wheel-drive minivan."

For years, Sperlich worked on his concept at Ford. During an assignment in Europe in the early 1970s, he fell in love with the front-wheel-drive Fiat 127. His minivan concept had a flat floor, which required front-wheel drive. Sperlich says Iacocca was the most enthusiastic minivan supporter in the company, but Henry Ford II just didn't get it. "We called it the Mini/Max because it was a maximum package in minimum external dimensions," Sperlich said. But Henry Ford "was worried about betting the company, so he wasn't in any mood to spend any money. I don't think he was ever very enthusiastic about the concept. He just never got interested in it."

The question of who lost the minivan at Ford is still debated. J. D. Power once recalled that he argued for the van concept in the mid-1970s. He said the small van rated "poor" in an internal survey of the company's pickup and station-wagon owners, but that Power, a former Ford man who became the industry's best-known consultant, argued against the idea. He told Ford it should ask import car buyers about the van. Some of Henry Ford's defenders now say that there was too much research on behalf of the Mini/Max. It may be revisionism, but after his retirement, Henry Ford II told a Ford historian: "We got into a frightful habit in this company of relying too much on surveys. I'm not a big survey man. I think that if you are in the business you ought to know what the hell you want to do, and you can't rely on a survey to pull your bacon out of the frying pan." One former Ford executive says it came down to personalities. Henry Ford just didn't like Hal Sperlich, the public face of the minivan project at Ford. Sperlich simply rubbed Henry Ford the wrong way and continued to do so even after his friends and allies warned him against it.

Harold Sperlich began developing his minivan concept in 1971 while vice president of truck operations at Ford. He thought of a passenger van smaller than Ford's Econoline cargo van but one that could seat seven comfortably and was stylish enough to replace the typical sedan. "The whole question of creating a more space-efficient van that could be something that could replace the family car was really born during my stay at truck operations," Sperlich said in a 2003 interview. The garageable passenger van did not appear until 1983, but it accounted for almost one in every five passenger vehicles sold worldwide in 2000. The minivan became such standard fare in the United States that it became the object of ridicule, the car for American soccer moms. It was the least cool category of car in the world—even in China.

Any attempt to modernize the minivan, or take it upscale, or jazz up the design failed, from the tarted-up Chrysler Grand Caravan of 2001 to the radically designed Nissan Quest of 2003. The minivan was so secure in its place that it could not be budged. It just existed. Among the world's major car brands only BMW was strong enough to *avoid* having to offer a minivan to its customers.

When Lee Iacocca put Chrysler in the minivan business in 1983, he put the world in minivans. Europe's infrastructure wasn't right for the largish American-sized MPVs, yet several hundred thousand passenger vans a year were sold there under many brands by the end of the century. In 1996, the Renault Megane Scenic began a smaller minivan movement, more suitable for Europe—but its roots were in the Chrysler minivan.

Chrysler's concept was not entirely new. Many still maintained that the first true people carrier was the Volkswagen Microbus of the 1960s. And indeed, the U.S. generation that had spent much of its youth in VW vans was better prepared to accept the minivan 20 years later. When Sperlich came to Chrysler in 1977, he still had the idea of a minivan in his head and a lot of Ford research money behind it, but it took Lee Iacocca to get the concept on the road and make it a hit. The first minivan was introduced in 1984. Sitting in the back seat of his New Yorker limousine while traversing the freeways of Los Angeles in his retirement years, Iacocca felt a surge of pride with every monospace van he saw. Minivans were forever, and he was the man who made them happen.

Chrysler's concept was perfect. It had to be front-wheel drive so the floor could be flat. "You can skin it in plastic and change it every year if you want," Iacocca once said. "But you are not going to improve on it as a package." After the minivan's introduction, sales quickly grew to more than a million units a year, and almost half of those units were manufactured by Chrysler. Profits from minivans kept Chrysler in business. One executive who was close to the Deuce said, "I think if it had not been Sperlich arguing for it, he would have done it."

In 1985, Ford responded to Sperlich's front-wheel-drive Chrysler minivan with a rear-wheel-drive passenger van, the Aerostar. It sold a fraction of what Chrysler's did. GM also brought out a rear-wheel-drive minivan, the Astro. General Motors had also considered and rejected a front-wheel-drive minivan concept. Lloyd Reuss, who later became president of the company, said that among the dusty old prototypes locked away in GM's technical center was a vehicle very similar to the Chrysler concept. It too had been mooted by young engineers, but was shot down by the same kinds of forces that blocked the Mini/Max at Ford. Indeed, Iacocca broke into a broad smile when he had a look at the 1985 Chevrolet Astro and 1986 Ford Aerostar minivans on display at the Chicago Auto Show. These were Ford's and GM's answers to Chrysler's 1984 minivan. While Chrysler had based its van on the front-wheel-drive K-car platform used for the Dodge Aries and Plymouth Reliant, Chevy and Ford had built their minivans on rear-wheel-drive truck platforms.

The engineers and marketing types at Ford and GM thought that a truck-based vehicle was the way to go, because the extra toughness would be needed. But Iacocca and Sperlich were proven right. A car-based van with car-like ride, handling, and fuel economy was a clear winner over the rear-drive truck-like rivals.

Chrysler was given a head start in the segment that it has never surrendered—Chrysler has been the leading seller of minivans every year since its introduction. These were the vehicles that would maintain competitive balance in the world automotive industry, and they almost died on the vine—mechanical hulks, dreams of men who had no enablers, no Iacocca and no Lutz to make a difference.

An automotive Rip Van Winkle who awakened in 2000 after a 15-year nap and took to the streets would have been stunned by what he saw. The American backdrop was an army of off-road vehicles and minivans. It was the most striking radicalization of the roads since the disappearance of the horse. Spencer "Spen" King, who conceived the first Range Rover in the 1960s, is credited by many for having invented the modern sport utility vehicle. The first Jeep Grand Wagoneer in the early 1960s launched the concept in America. But the SUV didn't reach the U.S. mainstream until the 1987 Iacocca-led acquisition of American Motors by Chrysler—facilitating the renaissance of AMC's Jeep brand—and the introduction of the 1990 Ford Explorer. When Lutz returned from Europe in 1985, he took what was seen as a demotion, a dead-end senior-vice-president job running Ford's truck operations, a backwater in the corporation at the time. Ford executives say Lutz's former boss Red Poling shunted him into the position, settling a score after the two had clashed in Europe. No sooner was Lutz in the job than he began looking for a ticket out of Ford. Yet in his year at trucks, Lutz helped unleash the light truck revolution in America.

And what did it was the Explorer.

"We didn't call it the Explorer then, we called it the four-door Bronco II," said Lutz. "Originally it was just going to be the Bronco II we all remember—narrow and high, but with an extended wheelbase and two more doors, and it looked like it was born in a hallway. It was really this long, tall thin thing. I said, 'Look guys, this isn't going to work. If we're going to make this thing work, we've got to have a wider vehicle with more track width, and it's got to be demonstrably bigger than the Cherokee.'

"Everybody was panicking because the Cherokee was taking off and starting to sell really well, and there was this intense desire to have a four-door sport utility because that was the hot thing. I said, 'Let's really take our time on this; we have $400 million to spend.' That was all there was in the investment envelope, and I just had them work and work and work and work until we were able to get this largely unique vehicle. It carried over a lot of parts, but it was a wider vehicle than the Bronco II, and it did have the all-new front end, all-new styling. It wasn't called Explorer at that time, but it was the Explorer.

"When we had that full-size clay model of what was to be the Explorer, we put it into research, and it annihilated the Cherokee in research, so we knew that if we did the vehicle it was going be a home run. It was exactly the size that people wanted. Exactly," Lutz said.

In 1990, it seemed certain that the Japanese would be in full control of the auto industry by the end of the century. Japan's market share in the United States rose steadily and, led by Honda, Japanese assembly plants were springing up across the country.

Between 1980 and 1990, Japanese carmakers increased their share of the U.S. light vehicle market from 16 to 25 percent. What share would they have by 2000? Toyota was expected to pass not only Ford during the 1990s, but possibly even General Motors to become the best-selling automaker in the world. Then the Japanese economy began to teeter in August 1991. The first sign was a slight dip in sales of the new Toyota Corolla compared to the predecessor model the year before. It seemed a minor glitch at first. The new Corolla was priced a little higher because Toyota had added lots of standard equipment. But the slow start betrayed a larger problem. It was the first twitch of what would become a 12-year slide for what had been the most powerful economy in the world. Japan would fall behind its schedule for taking over the auto world.

What really happened to the Japanese automakers was not the strong yen, nor a weak domestic economy—it was minivans and SUVs, courtesy of Iacocca and Lutz. The Japanese were stymied, and the U.S. Big Three enjoyed a far more prosperous decade than anyone could have predicted in 1990.

The industry catchphrase in 1990 was "lean manufacturing, " the Toyota Production System. But the revival of American competitiveness in the decade had little to do with getting lean. All three U.S. companies continued to lag behind the Japanese in productivity and build quality. It was the huge sales of all those passenger trucks that made the difference, and the Japanese had largely missed out on the windfall.

It was perhaps only symbolic that the year after Soichiro Honda died, his company made its first major product mistake in America. Honda did a half-hearted job with its first minivan in 1992, and the vehicle sold poorly in the United States. Having launched Lexus in 1988, Toyota seemed unstoppable. Yet it failed with its first full-size pickup truck for the U.S. in 1993. And its Previa minivan, which was expected to run Chrysler's minivan off the road, was only a moderate success.

The American auto companies would manage to forestall the Japanese offensive for 15 years. Not until almost half way through the first decade of the twenty-first century did Toyota, Honda, Nissan, and other Japanese brands have a full range of competitive light trucks, SUVs, and minivans with which to challenge the Americans. The Japanese were so busy catching up, they fell behind the renewal schedule in Europe. When Japan and the European Union settled on an import quota in 1993, it seemed the EU was only delaying the inevitable. But 10 years later the Japanese could not even fulfill the allowable quotas. The SUVs and the minivans had knocked the Japanese off stride, and Iacocca was happy to take credit. "Jeep is the best brand in the world," Iacocca bragged in the early 1990s, "and no matter how good the Europeans and the Japanese are they haven't done anything like the minivan. It's a worldwide home run."

CHAPTER NINE

Personal Styles

The great men of the post-war auto industry each possessed a dynamism that inspired managers below them, but led to massive clashes with the bosses who ruled over them. Ferdinand Piëch battled every boss he ever had, even his uncle. Lee Iacocca aggravated Henry Ford II to no end. Bob Lutz got under the skin of nearly everyone he ever worked for, including Iacocca, Henry Ford II, and Eberhard von Kuenheim. Lutz always seemed to overshadow his superiors, which blocked his career path at several critical stages. His last two bosses, Chrysler Chairman Bob Eaton and General Motors CEO Rick Wagoner, simply learned to live with Lutz.

Each of the six had a huge personality, and none of them suffered from a lack of self-confidence. Each was a great communicator, though in vastly different ways. Each was capable of energizing entire companies—huge, cumbersome bureaucracies with tens of thousands of employees. At the end of the century, auto-industry CEOs were mimicking their styles. DaimlerChrysler Chairman Jürgen Schrempp patterned himself after Iacocca, who had—intentionally or not—styled himself after Henry Ford II and Soichiro Honda. In fact, while stationed in the United States in the 1980s, a young Schrempp finagled a meeting with Iacocca just to meet the master and absorb some of his charisma.

Bob Lutz's car-guy persona was the inspiration for every ranking executive in the industry—from Ford's Jacques Nasser to DaimlerChrysler's Wolfgang Bernhard. A half-dozen automotive CEOs who had worked for Eberhard von Kuenheim drew on elements of the great BMW leader's style, and Henry Ford II's philosopher-king style set the pattern for two U.S. presidents.

The six men changed the way CEOs in all businesses viewed themselves at the start of the twenty-first century. Soichiro Honda was the prototype for a generation of hotshot American computer billionaires. In the 1950s, most American car bosses were content to be known by their first two initials—R. S. McNamara, for example. Yet Ford's president 40 years after Robert McNamara was so image conscious that he ordered the media to spell his name "Jacques", rather than "Jac". By the end of the century, a strong personality was de rigueur among auto industry leaders; Nasser, Schrempp, and Nissan's Carlos Ghosn had the strongest. The thing that really empowered these men was the sheer strength of their personalities.

Soichiro Honda may have been the most natural leader the automobile industry has ever seen, a combination of Henry Ford I and Alfred Sloan Jr., the great organizer of General Motors in the 1920s. Honda possessed a certain ineffable quality—a personal ease that seemed to set him apart from almost everyone in Japanese society. He was a precursor to the moguls of the 1970s and 1980s, like Bill Gates and Steve Jobs—all of whom were influenced by Japanese methods, many of which are really more accurately defined as Honda's methods rather than Japan's.

Soichiro Honda had a kind of invisible management style. He never acted the part of the boss, yet he made most of the important decisions and kept his fast-growing company on a straight path. He never seemed to dictate strategy. The right strategy just seemed to follow his actions. He could bark orders with the best of them, but he'd also roll up his sleeves in the Honda R&D center and ask the young associates on the test bench what they were working on. Whether speaking to one or two people or addressing a large group, he was a boss without protocol, a charmer, as demanding as anyone the car business had ever seen, but with an ability to calm and enchant his workers. Honda believed in the power of youth and the common man. Workers who met him once spent the rest of their careers energized by the single encounter. His workers treated him like a god even though he never acted like one. Honda was fully human, with a titanic temper that caused employees to call him "thunder-san." He was also a world-class carouser, whose youthful indiscretions became part of his lore, but might have just as easily landed him in jail. It was typical of him that when the company was running out of money, Honda chose to announce he would enter the Isle of Man TT motorcycle race. It was as if he was unconcerned by the trouble swirling around him.

Hideo Sugiura, who later became chairman of Honda, remembers thinking that his boss had lost touch with reality, and he began to think of leaving the company. Like JFK announcing to America that we would land a man on the moon by the end of the 1960s, Honda electrified his employees with his boasts. Morale soared. Talk of Honda's TT challenge filled the air, and the unthinkable prospect of a Honda victory gave everyone at Honda a huge surge of pride. Honda's boast was a masterstroke.

Honda told his biographer, Sol Sanders: "I felt that a victory by technology, by brainpower, would surely bring great hope to the Japanese people, especially to younger Japanese." The common goal helped keep the company energized and afloat through one of its most difficult periods. And in 1961, he did indeed win the TT race.

Satoshi Okubo, Honda's chairman in the late 1980s, credited Soichiro Honda with what he called a free-structured individualism that is alien to old-style Japanese capitalism. He said the inspiration came directly from the founder. "He told us we should work for our-selves, not just for the company," Okubo recalled. "I thought that was fairly strange." This concern for individual initiative meant Honda was the first Japanese auto builder to blur the lines between engineering, styling, marketing, and other aspects of car development. Everyone got involved at every stage.

The industry's post–World War II leaders all shared a gift for cutting through clutter. In the case of Honda, it was like a wonder drug coursing through the veins of the corporate body. He could convey a simple message understood by everyone in the company, as well as suppliers, dealers, and customers. The Japanese tycoon made a deep impression on Iacocca when the two met in 1975. He had an open, public style, more like a popular politician than a cor-porate leader. "Honda is a genius," Iacocca recalled years later. "He is like old Henry Ford."

Iacocca was amazed that a man could build a massive auto com-pany, yet keep his feet so firmly planted on the ground. Iacocca knew plenty of powerful people, from Henry Ford II to Frank Sinatra, but never knew someone who had personally constructed an enterprise as vast as Honda. It charged the American with a new source of ambition.

Iacocca was the best communicator of them all; he even created a whole new style of business-speak during the Chrysler loan guarantee debate in the late 1970s and early 1980s.

Iacocca was a perfect impromptu speaker—able to encapsulate complicated issues into sound bites before sound bites were even invented. At the top of his game, he never used jargon. He had a fresh, down-to-earth metaphor for every situation that Chrysler or the auto industry faced. It was Iacocca who coined the phrase "uneven playing field" when talking about Japanese competition.

In an interview, Iacocca had talked about, "a new world that now includes a formidable rival, Japan, and a world where nobody else is playing by the rules of pure laissez-faire. . . . The field where this game is being played is not level. Instead it is strongly tilted in favor of Japan." Once, when asked if he was going to change the second-generation Chrysler minivan, he said, "No, no, no. I learned that from Mustang. When we have a winner, don't keelhaul the son of a bitch." But by the end of the century, every top car executive was using showy similes to underline a point. Iacocca smoked Ignacio Hoya cigars, which he waved at his underlings in meetings. He was a compelling figure—even for his superiors at the Ford Motor Company. "Whatever level you were in the company, he made you want to go out and sell a Ford to the first ten people you ran into in the street," said one Ford executive. "He was a natural at sales meetings," recalled William Clay Ford in his *Reminiscences,* an oral history project. "If he had a point to make, he could be a charmer. He could sell you anything, and back it up with his sales talk, logic, and facts. He reminded me a lot of Bob McNamara in his ability to retain facts, and in the way he could use them. He is an extraordinary salesman, an extraordinary talent." Iacocca was a businessman for the go-go 1960s. He was to his era of the automotive industry what Muhammad Ali was to boxing. He was bold, brassy, a braggart—a man who found a new way to articulate. He was a natural-born headline-grabber in an era in which most top executives of giant corporations were gray, almost invisible characters. Iacocca stood head-and-shoulders above the crowd of cheerless Detroit auto executives, and this was among the things that caused him to wear out his welcome with Henry Ford II.

In the giant faceless corporations that took shape in America, Europe, and Japan after World War II, personalities tended to be submerged. America's GI Bill allowed tens of thousands of returning veterans to go to college after the war, and the country's management ranks swelled with talent in the 1950s. They were older and more serious of purpose than previous generations of incoming managers. It was in those pre-individualist years that Iacocca began to make his mark at the Ford Motor Company. In Ford's button-down corporate culture, he stood out from the rest of the pack. Iacocca's communication skills allowed him to create a deep vein of loyalty in the company, and that was what enabled him to challenge Henry Ford II for ultimate authority in the 1970s.

This same personal charisma helped save Chrysler in the 1980s. No other American businessmen of the day could have rallied the country behind the Chrysler cause. Certainly not his Chrysler predecessors, Lynn Townsend or John Riccardo, nor GM's colorless Roger Smith and Ford's Phillip Caldwell. Lack of eloquence caused those other auto executives to fail to achieve grand dreams. Short, squeaky-voiced, tongue-tied Smith failed to change the GM culture in 10 years, though he put forth a visionary plan to do so. Smith restructured GM from top to bottom, made several bold acquisitions, and launched an all-new car division, Saturn. But he left everyone cold. In the 1990s, Ford chairman Alex Trotman tried to impose a massive global reorganization plan called Ford 2000, but the dour Scot didn't have the personal charisma to ram it through. The plan was comatose long before 2000 arrived. Trotman sought to centralize lines of authority, but nearly destroyed Ford in the process. It was a failure of leadership that left a giant corporation dazed and confused and headed for crisis.

Neither Smith nor Trotman was inspirational, which had almost everything to do with the failure of their visions. Like Soichiro Honda, Henry Ford II was mercurial with his topmost lieutenants, but a benevolent dictator to the rank and file. Albert Caspers, a German who became head of Ford of Europe, remembers how the Deuce once put him at ease. "The first time I met him, I was running Halewood (a plant in the United Kingdom) and he came to Halewood in a Gulfstream aircraft. I was 40 years old and very nervous. We were the worst Ford plant in terms of quality, labor relations, and cleanliness. The aircraft was coming to a standstill. I was standing on the tarmac. The gangway came down. I had my little speech prepared. But it went all different. Mr. Ford came out there and said,

'Hi Al, how you doing?' What can you say about that? I thought it was going to be very formal."

The Deuce's detail-savvy Whiz Kids were the inspiration for John F. Kennedy's youthful "best and brightest" cabinet and senior staff. But though Henry Ford II built a company of micromanagers, he himself helped to inspire a new style of American CEO, the kind typified by President Ronald Reagan. Henry Ford II turned delegation into an art form. But not in a lazy man's way. His almost instinctive understanding of the auto industry would baffle those who thought they knew it well enough to safely underestimate him. "He had a tremendous ability to concentrate," said a former Ford of Europe manager who frequently hosted Henry in the 1980s. "He could pick up the main points and drive through the essentials with a few questions. He could learn in half an hour what took others years. He had a great capacity to motivate. I was very much impressed."

Henry Ford II learned the art of getting to the point quickly as a 28-year-old who had to fix a giant company he knew almost nothing about. He became the most famous American businessman of his day—until supplanted by Iacocca in the 1980s. Presidents deferred to Henry II. First ladies seemed smitten, Lady Bird Johnson in particular. Washington politics bored him, but he moved comfortably in power-broker circles. He was more influential than Henry I during his grandfather's heyday. His style was to lay down a vision and have his executives work out the details. And his visions were often profound. With his German and British operations virtually at war with one another in June 1967, Henry sat both sides down in a room at the Plaza Athénée Hotel in Paris and ordered them to create a new pan-European business organization. Then he went off to watch his company's GT40s in the 24-hour race at Le Mans. The centralized Ford of Europe organization the executives established became the model for pan-European manufacturers of all kinds in the years that followed. "Henry quickly realized that the key to success was not to have all your capital used up in competing against yourself," said Bruce Blythe, a longtime aide and Ford executive. Henry Ford II never needed to sweat the details, he could see the big picture perfectly.

Ferdinand Piëch's veneer was cold and dry. In formal interviews he sometimes hesitated silently for minutes before answering a question. Often another question would be posed just as Piëch started his reply to the previous query. Said a former lieutenant: "He was certainly not a motivator. He used his tremendous power to get what he wanted. If you got in his way, you lost. He was Machiavellian." Piëch clashed with more underlings than the other five industry leaders combined. He either fired the underlings or forced them to quit in frustration. In his first three years as head of Volkswagen, Piëch got rid of more than 20 top managers. "The waste of human capital was shocking," said an executive who worked alongside Piëch at Audi. His method—whether by design or by nature—was to create an environment of fear. Some of it was by design. "He was tremendously secretive," said another executive. "He was always trying to find out what you were going to say before a meeting. He wanted to find something you might be unsure about and then attack you. A lot of very nice people suffered under Piëch. Many good people had to leave the group."

Piëch got off on such a bad foot with some VW executives that in late 1994 they sent an open letter to supervisory board Chairman Klaus Liesen. The executives charged that, "this company is run by a man with psychopathic traits." Liesen asked Piëch to ease up some. But for those who could survive his scalding management style, Piëch became a visionary, a prophet, almost saintly—a man entirely driven and principled by the ideal of automotive engineering perfection. He was almost Zen-like in his beliefs and was indeed fascinated by Asian cultures and psychology. "I was convinced that I could work for a Japanese firm and enjoy great times as an engineer," wrote Piëch in his autobiography. As with most thoughtful westerners in the industry,

Piëch too had his favorite, "Honda would have been my number one preference, and Toyota number two."

He seemed to mesmerize his lieutenants. Those who fell under Piëch's spell turned into zealots. It was as though by working for Ferdinand Piëch they were communicating with the spirit of Ferdinand Porsche.

He was a throwback to the dawn of the auto industry, to the European pioneers of the automobile and the automobile enterprise. Whereas American automotive pioneers such as Henry Ford and Ransom Olds rubbed the edges off their obsession with a certain folksy charm, the Europeans were often difficult, demanding, severe men who tormented those who worked alongside them. Piëch seemed as if he had been transplanted from the nineteenth century, as if he truly belonged in Cannstatt, having a late dinner in the shop with Gottlieb Daimler, Karl Benz, and Wilhelm Maybach. Piëch seemed to have more in common with Gustav Otto and Henry Royce than Jürgen Schrempp or Bernd Pischetsrieder.

Piëch brought a level of single-mindedness to the auto industry not seen since the days of the founders of the business. His eccentricities were tolerated not just because of who he was, but because of his talent. His brain seemed to buzz and crackle like an overhead power line. But in the end, he was weighed down with far too many yes-men. He had fired, exiled, or chased away too many talented executives, including his three successors as head of Audi—Franz-Josef Kortüm, Herbert Demel, and Franz-Josef Paefgen. In the process, Piëch had made the giant Volkswagen an extension of himself.

He seemed oblivious to controversy and the impact he might have on himself or the company. He created a huge political firestorm in 1993 when he lured away a General Motors purchasing executive named Ignacio Lopez who was accused of bringing GM secret documents with him. Piëch then rather awkwardly battled BMW for the rights to Rolls-Royce even though he knew he could never win the rights to the Rolls-Royce name. He managed to garner some of the worst public relations of any auto executive ever. In an era when Lee Iacocca could connect with millions of regular folk, Piëch seemed to have come from another planet. "He was difficult to work for," said one man who was fired by Piëch. "You had to be very certain of yourself. You could not bluff him. He suffered no fools. He was black and white, and in life there are a lot of grays."

Charisma took a different form in Europe than in America or Japan. Eberhard von Kuenheim's understated style was the opposite of men like Iacocca or Honda, but he formed deep bonds with his young executives, like Bob Lutz, Wolfgang Reitzle, and Bernd Pischetsrieder. Lutz's flamboyance seemed to borrow little from von Kuenheim's deadpan style, but he picked up a directness from the steely Prussian and much of the BMW boss's commanding presence. After he left BMW in 1974, Lutz's flair got him into trouble at button-down Ford. He clashed with the conservative world of Ford finance—namely his boss, Ford of Europe Chairman Harold "Red" Poling. "Bob was very passionate about cars, while Poling was very regimented, very cool, he might as well have been selling watermelons as cars," said an executive who worked with both.

A former Ford executive recalls: "Ford in the early 1970s was dominated by very practical people, Sam Toy (head of Ford of Britain) and Peter Weiher (head of Ford of Germany). Then you had the accountants and then all of a sudden you had Bob Lutz—flamboyant, an extrovert in a rather regimented company—you can imagine what kind of impact it made."

Lutz was physically imposing—even intimidating. He was 6 feet 4 inches tall and stood ramrod straight. He spoke with the gravelly voice of a drill sergeant, and everything about him seemed imposing. Subordinates couldn't help but snap to attention when he would appear. It was as though he had stepped out of the pages of Tom Wolfe's novel *The Right Stuff*.

Lutz would often use his great presence to make a point. "At Ford everything was analyzed 20 times," said a former executive. "Lutz was much more intuitive. He would just go into a room with a new product and all of the sudden enlighten a meeting." Lutz minced no words and used no jargon, plus he was funny and wise. The auto press hung on his words. Ford's CEO in the 1980s, Phil Caldwell, complained about the favorable attention Lutz was getting, and Lutz had to ask auto writers to stop printing so many stories about him. Henry Ford II enjoyed Lutz's company during his trips to Europe, but he also began to chafe when Lutz ran Ford of Europe and was the subject of so much hero worship.

When the always-punctual Ford once saw Lutz slip into a meeting late he reportedly said, "Well, here comes our movie star."

Lutz was indeed a star. He radiated authority. When Jürgen Schrempp wanted to pass the message in 1997 that he thought a merger with Chrysler ought to be pursued, he first sought out Lutz, who told him the guy he needed to speak to was Chrysler CEO Bob Eaton. "But you run the place don't you?" asked Schrempp, only half kidding.

Journalists loved to write about Lutz the car guy and his driving exploits. When he went to Ford in 1974, he inherited the Granada, a car unloved by Germany's enthusiast press. Lutz would drive Granadas to the limit, challenging BMW 5 series on the autobahn. But he would often leave the broken-down Fords at a remote autobahn exit.

"He was able to convince journalists that the Ford Granada, which had rather soft American road manners, was a better car than a BMW 5 series," recalled Rainer Nistl, Ford's motorsports publicist at the time. "Lutz challenged them to prove the contrary." In the process he made the Granada a success in Europe. Lutz knew that he unsettled those he worked for. He thought part of the problem was that he usually towered over bosses who didn't like his imposing physical stature. Plus, they didn't like it that he was a fighter jock and could speak several languages and always had beautiful wives. Lutz's troubles started with von Kuenheim and continued throughout the rest of his career—until GM Chairman Rick Wagoner, more than 20 years Lutz's junior, hired him in 2001, when Lutz was 69. "Realistically speaking, I don't pose a threat to Rick Wagoner," Lutz said.

Wagoner was probably the first superior who didn't feel the heat of Lutz. Even Eberhard von Kuenheim did.

"Von Kuenheim worried more about my public persona because we were about the same age. So there was this tension." Lutz and von Kuenheim in effect had been pitted against each other by Herbert Quandt.

"Quandt's plan was not necessarily to have von Kuenheim stay on for so long," said a longtime BMW executive. "He wanted to prepare an alternative, and this is why he hired Lutz. So there was a competition. If von Kuenheim had not been identified as being as good as he was, the alternative would have been Lutz. If he succeeded he didn't need an alternative. Well, he succeeded."

The resemblance between Lutz and baseball legend Ted Williams struck almost everyone who met Lutz and knew about Williams. The two U.S. Marine fighter pilots had a stunning similarity of style.

Williams and Lutz both believed in precision. In Williams' case, it was precision hitting, precision fly-casting; in both cases, it was precision flying and precision driving. Williams loved to drive cars and had a feathery touch at the wheel. His teammates said Williams could have been a race-car champion. Both men were variations on Chuck Yeager, the original pilot with the "right stuff" who broke the sound barrier. Most Bob Lutz types wound up running their own businesses. In the car industry they became dealers, not executives. The big corporations didn't suit them, wouldn't have them, wouldn't promote them. This type of man tended not to stick it out in corporate America. Both Lutz and Ted Williams were pretty lippy when they first came to prominence. Williams once said, "All I want out of life is that when I walk down the street folks will say, 'There goes the greatest hitter who ever lived.'" The desire was more than just ambition, but a sense of purpose and destiny.

When Bob Lutz arrived at Opel in 1964, Europe's veteran auto writers got a similar impression. He had a Ted Williams–like sense of urgency, as if Lutz were saying, "All I want out of life is that when I walk down the street folks will say, 'There goes the greatest auto executive who ever lived.'" And in the eyes of many, Bob Lutz *was* the greatest auto executive who ever lived. When Lutz retired from Chrysler in 1998, Peter Brown, the longtime editor of *Automotive News*, called him "the greatest auto executive of the past 25 years."

General Motors had never seen anyone like Lutz when he joined the company in 1963 in the New York Planning Office. His European upbringing and language skills quickly got him dispatched to Adam Opel. When he came back to General Motors in the twenty-first century, the first thing Lutz did was write a long memo for distribution among all of the company's engineers. He titled it "Strongly Held Beliefs." In it, Lutz codified 35 years of experience. Ted Williams had done something very similar just before coming out of retirement in 1969 to manage the Washington Senators—a move in itself as surprising as Lutz being pulled from retirement to take over product development at General Motors. Williams wrote, with John Underwood, a brief manual called *The Science of Hitting*, and it's considered the greatest instructional manual on hitting a baseball ever written.

Both Williams and Lutz talked too much. Neither could keep from saying exactly what was on their minds. Williams and Boston sportswriters were constantly at war. Lutz got along well with the automotive press, but he said things that rankled his superiors, especially Iacocca when they worked together at Chrysler. Williams' big mouth cost him two American League Most Valuable Player awards, the winner of which was selected by sportswriters. Lutz's big mouth cost him two CEO jobs.

At the end of their careers, the two top guns were viewed as oracles, the wisest old owls in their forests. And both were granted a golden twilight. Still hitting over .300 at age 42, Williams was called the best "old" hitter of the century. Lutz was still in action at age 72, the best old executive of two centuries.

Williams' fame was magnified by his last big league at-bat, a long four-bagger off Jack Fisher of the Baltimore Orioles, number 521 of his career.

As Lutz labored at General Motors in 2004, he too was intent on ending his own career with a home run.

CHAPTER TEN

Lutz Meets His Match

he test of a first-rate mind is the ability to hold two opposing ideas at the same time and still be able to function—so wrote F. Scott Fitzgerald. Creativity and order are very different from one another, but you need them both to be successful in the auto business. Henry Ford II had created the new order of business management in the post-war world but remained a fundamentally instinctive man—someone who "felt" things as well as he understood them and who acted on his feelings. Ford authorized and admired systems and the obsessive number crunching and analysis that Robert McNamara and his team performed on his behalf, but believed wholeheartedly in the power of the gut feeling, the intelligent hunch, especially when it came to cars.

When Robert McNamara left Ford to become U.S. secretary of defense in 1960, a month after being named the company's president, the official line was that Henry Ford II was deeply distraught. But one Ford executive, who spent many hours with Henry II late in his career, tells another story: "Henry Ford II didn't like McNamara because he couldn't get a look in. McNamara had all his numbers and arguments marshaled. You couldn't really discuss things with him."

Still, Henry Ford's ability to keep both creativity and order alive inside the Ford Motor Company allowed the firm to survive. Lee Iacocca had to thrive for as long as possible alongside his opposite corporate colleagues, McNamara and Edward Lundy. When Iacocca left Ford in 1978, he understood the importance of using both creativity and order to the company's best advantage, and he used this understanding to save the Chrysler Corporation from ruin.

A dynamic struggle was played out every day by armies of car guys versus armies of bean counters at Ford in the decades after Henry Ford II arrived, but none of the battles was more fascinating than the one that pitted Red Poling against Bob Lutz. It was an encounter between a man who represented Henry Ford II's left brain and another who personified the Deuce's right brain.

In the late 1970s, one was president of Ford of Europe and the other was his boss, the chairman of Ford of Europe. Their battles would have a deep influence on the future of the industry.

"Red and I got along extremely well on a personal level," said Lutz. "On a business level we disagreed because Red at the time was 100 percent numerate. He wanted data on everything."

Once, in the mid-1970s, the two men argued about how to raise prices in Germany. Lutz, who at the time ran Ford of Germany, argued that Ford could not increase the sticker price of its cars until a national wage agreement with the metalworkers union was finalized.

"I said, 'Red, we can't raise prices before we have the wage contracts settled with the IG Metall because it's just not done in Germany. You always wait until after the wage contract and then you use the excuse of the wage contract for raising prices. That's the way it's done in Germany, and that's the way the German government wants it.'"

Poling asked Lutz: "Well, how much is it going to cost us if we piss off the German government? I mean quantify that for me."

"I can't quantify it," Lutz said, "but I can tell you it's just not a healthy thing."

Poling responded, "I'll tell you what. I can quantify for you how much money we lose by delaying our pricing day by day. I can give you that in millions of dollars. But until you can show me how much it's going to cost us down the road by making the German government mad we're going to price."

"Well, I wouldn't do that," Lutz said.

"I don't care whether you do or not. You put down in numbers what it is going to cost to piss off the German government, and then we'll weigh your losses against my losses."

Lutz said, "Well, yours are totally predictable and mine aren't."

"That's exactly my point. We'll price," Poling fired back.

"We priced," Lutz recalls, "and we got all these negative headlines, and we took a big cut in our reputation, and ultimately the market share went back down. Was that the key reason? You don't know, but it was certainly a contributing reason for the decline of Ford market share in German."

Poling was incredibly numerate, an obsessive-compulsive product of the analysis culture. During a strike at Ford of Britain in the 1970s, Poling warned Lutz, by then his No. 2 at Ford of Europe, that the strike would cause Ford's plants on the continent to halt production.

"I have all the data here, I've got the supply of British-supplied materials to the German plants. I've got it all in detail. And the German plants are going to go down in 10 days."

"No they won't," Lutz said. "That's just the numbers you've been given, Red. But the German plants aren't going to go down in 10 days."

"What makes you so sure?" asked Poling, raising his voice an octave. "I get the information. I don't just go by 'I think' or 'I feel' or something like that. I go by hard numbers."

"Well, hard numbers often don't tell you the whole story," Lutz responded. "Hard numbers don't tell you that Ford employees are putting tooling parts in the trunks of their cars at the British plants, taking them over to Germany on the evening ferry so that we can keep making the parts on the continent, and your numbers don't tell you that the Valencia plant in Spain is switching over the whole production to 1.1-liter engines which are made in Spain and don't depend on the Dagenham engine plant, and your numbers don't factor in all the creativity of hundreds of people who are working on solutions to prevent the continental plants from going down due to the British strike."

Poling sat silently for a moment. Then he began again. "Ten days," Poling said. "Ten days, ten days and the continental plants are down."

"They will be operating in five weeks," Lutz said in retort.

Poling was getting angry. "Well, you just write that down," he ordered.

Lutz leaned over Poling's desk and wrote on Poling's reports, "Will be operating in five weeks."

Poling picked up the piece of paper. "OK, this goes right in my drawer," he said. "Right in my drawer. I'm keeping that there because I think that is exactly the type of behavior that is going to disqualify you from being my successor as chairman of Ford of Europe."

"Well, I'm sorry you see it that way, Red," Lutz said.

Five weeks later, everything on the continent was still booming.

"We didn't give a shit whether the British plants ever reopened or not," said Lutz. "One day I said to him, 'About that thing in your desk, Red.'"

Poling took it out and said to Lutz, "You turned out to be right, but you turned out to be right for the wrong reasons. See you had no way of knowing. This was the information."

Lutz and Poling once took the Myers-Briggs personality profile and came out as complete opposites. The psychologists said that it was amazing that these two men could even understand each other.

"In business he and I were absolutely at opposite ends of it, he would drive me crazy," Lutz said. Once Poling told Lutz that since Ford was not showing a profit on its French operations it should withdraw from the market. Ford was selling plenty of cars in France, but when all of the operating expenses that could be charged against doing business in the country were added up, Ford was breaking even at best.

"He said we don't have a fully accounted profit in France," recalled Lutz. "We were doing 100,000 units in France. I said 'No, we aren't making a fully accounted profit, but there is a huge contribution to fixed costs.'"

Poling said: "Well, if we don't make a net fully accounted profit in France, I'm not interested. We're not going to do business anywhere we don't make a fully accounted profit."

"Red, we're fully accounted breakeven—that means we've got 100,000 units soaking up $4,000 to $5,000 worth of fixed costs each," Lutz responded.

"I don't care about that," Poling said. "We've got to get out of France."

"Where are the absorbed fixed costs going to go?" Lutz asked. "It's going to be 100,000 units times $4,000—$400 million of fixed costs that are going to have to be absorbed somewhere else. So now that fixed costs get allocated over fewer units, so now the German ones are under water, so are you going to stop business in Germany? You can make the whole thing go away with some of these silly calculations.

"He was bent on teaching me to be anal, some of which took. I always respected that the business needs people like him. That I did learn."

But Poling had no use for Lutz's style.

Lutz said, "I appreciated his special skill of being able to take a whole book of numbers and flip through it and then say: 'There is a column in such and such a row that doesn't balance on page 14; the sums don't add up; get the guys to look at that.' It was absolutely amazing. But he had no appreciation for my special set of skills because they were not measurable. I think I was way more tolerant of his bias, which was toward the orderly world of quantification, than he was of my world of empathy and feeling—the ability to project, the ability to see the picture from partial information."

Poling was reflecting the very quantitative culture at Ford. In the late 1970s, most European carmakers offered a five-speed manual transmission. Lutz wanted one for the 1981 Escort. But Poling had the planners do an analysis on how much fuel a driver actually saved with a five-speed manual versus a four-speed manual. An exasperated Lutz gave the job to the planners, and in due course they came back with the answer Poling expected. The average European motorist drove about 90 percent of the time in the city, where the fifth gear is never engaged. So most people use a five-speed transmission as a four-speed transmission, and the few times they are out on the highway the fifth speed saves them only a small amount of fuel, which just doesn't compensate for the nonexistent cost savings in city driving.

"And therefore you are absolutely right, Mr. Poling, a five-speed transmission makes no sense whatsoever," said Lutz. "The only problem for us was it had become the going-in requirement for the customer. 'Does it have a five-speed gearbox?' If the dealer had to say no, then they weren't interested. And it was the same thing with diesel engines. He had the analysis done, and we and GM were both way smarter than the European companies in that we had it all figured out that nobody really needed a diesel because it would take the guy like 70,000 or 80,000 miles to amortize the price difference. But people don't look at it that way. They don't say, 'Gee, I paid $3,000 more for this diesel car, how many miles will I have to drive to amortize it?' They just see they are buying a car with an engine that gives them 25 percent better fuel economy; and by the way, the fuel is half the price. They don't do a gasoline-versus-diesel breakeven point slope of the line. People don't buy cars that way."

As long as Poling was still in charge—and he had a couple of months before he was due to transfer to a new position in the United States at the end of 1978—Ford's European engineers were not allowed to develop a diesel engine and were not allowed to work on a five-speed transmission. So Lutz had the guys work on the stuff on a skunkworks basis until he was officially anointed chairman of Ford of Europe in January 1979. When Lutz eventually became the Dearborn-based head of international operations, Poling would get his revenge by bouncing Lutz back to Europe in 1984, a time when Ford of Europe ran into trouble.

A Ford executive from the 1970s recalls that the Poling-Lutz fight was deeply personal.

"Poling saw Lutz as everything he wanted to be," said one former Ford executive. "He was funny, he knew how to choose the best cigar, best wine. He was dashing, debonair, all the things Poling wasn't."

Lutz said it took him 15 months to fix Ford of Europe after he returned for the second time. He was ready to go back to America in 1985 and claim his rightful place as head of international operations in Dearborn. "Now all the sudden here was Poling reneging," said Lutz.

Poling commissioned Ford's head of labor relations, Peter Pestillo, to apprise Lutz about his future at Ford. Pestillo told Lutz, "Let me just tell you how you are viewed within the Ford Motor Company. You are viewed as an upstart, maverick, swashbuckler. You don't operate on data, you operate on gut feel. We have to tell you we can't use your kind."

"Am I being fired?" Lutz asked.

"No," Pestillo said. "But we are injecting a sense of reality into your future expectations." Pestillo, a lawyer and no car guy, was a key Poling lieutenant—and trouble for Lutz.

"Pestillo was poisonous in the Lutz-Poling relationship because Pestillo saw himself as potentially facing off with Lutz for the CEO job," said a former Ford executive. "He would whisper in Poling's ear about Lutz. Pestillo thought he was a possible CEO."

Lutz could either take over the top job at Ford International again, he could stay in Europe, or he could take charge of U.S. truck operations.

But Poling let it be known that he wanted an executive named Phil Benton to head international and Lutz was dead set against remaining in Europe. So he took over trucks in the United States.

Then there was a fight over whether Lutz would be demoted to vice president or remain an executive vice president. Lutz hung on to the title. Poling then tried to get Lutz knocked off Ford's board of directors. "It consumes too much of your time," Poling told him.

Lutz answered, "I'm not going to come off the board unless Mr. Ford and the other board members and Don Petersen and so forth want me off." It was a painful period.

Could Lutz have weathered the storm?

"Red Poling now tells me 'You left just at the wrong time. You were rehabilitated in my eyes. You had done such a terrific job over in trucks. You got the business plan all straightened out—why'd you leave? You left right when it was all singing and dancing.'"

CHAPTER ELEVEN

Chrysler: Not Big Enough for Both of Them

In late 1989, Bob Lutz began to sense that he had something going at Chrysler. The press hadn't caught on yet, and neither had Wall Street. But Lutz and his devoted crew of engineers and designers—many of whom had come from the tiny American Motors Corporation—were beginning to make things happen.

They showed the outlandish Dodge Viper prototype at the Detroit Auto Show in January 1990, and everybody went crazy over the Corvette-fighting V-10–powered two-seat roadster. Lutz knew then that even if Chrysler ran out of money it could bring in investors and show them what he had in the pipeline. They would say: "We can't let this go to waste."

Meanwhile, Lutz was eyeing his competitors over at General Motors with a combination of envy and bravado. Lutz told Edmunds.com that he used to say to his Chrysler team, "Look guys, the bad news is the average guy at GM has 20 points of IQ on us. And the good news is that the average guy at GM has 20 points of IQ on us, because they're intellectual to a point where they will constantly study ramifications of things rather than acting. Whereas we're dumb enough to seize the obvious and we just go ahead and do it." At Chrysler, their seeming disadvantage over GM wasn't really a drawback because Lutz and his men realized that a less-than-perfect decision made quickly is better than a perfect decision made too late.

Lutz believed that most auto companies' product-development philosophy could be summarized as: "Let's go research everything and then try to develop a product out of this mass of research data." At Chrysler, he went the other way. His teams said, "Hey, we've got this great idea for an all-new product category that nobody has done yet, or an all-new styling philosophy." They did it with the first Ram pickup. They said, "Let's do it, and then research it and see who likes it and who hates it, why they like it, why they hate it, and we may have to make some modifications."

Lutz had been hired by Chrysler Chairman Lee Iacocca in June 1986. When he arrived, the first thing he did was sit down with the finance team and say, "Show me the business plan."

The finance team responded, "You're going to love it. It's rising levels of profitability, cash, and market share. We've still got our coupe to come out. We've got the large cars to come out. Everything is going to be great." Three years later, they were in deep trouble. Chrysler had been in this situation more times than it cared to remember. In its 70-year history it had had eight major financial crises.

The problem at Chrysler in those days was that Lutz and his boss, Chairman Lee Iacocca, didn't get along. The mutual antipathy and distrust was hardly concealed. At meetings and at press conferences where they appeared jointly, Iacocca would refer to his underling not as "Bob" or "Mr. Lutz" but simply as "Lutz." Lutz once called Iacocca a "doddering old fart." Lutz was strong enough to survive, but not deferential enough to get the final promotion. For all his talents, Lutz seemed to lack the kind of political astuteness usually associated with the executive suites of giant car corporations.

Iacocca, on the other hand, lived and breathed corporate intrigue.

"Iacocca on good days, he was fantastic," says Lutz now. "On bad days . . . you didn't want to know."

Iacocca was the hero-villain of Lutz's career. After Iacocca was fired by Henry Ford II in 1978, Lutz—then at Ford of Europe—wrote him a letter. Full of sincere good wishes, Lutz reckoned that it was one of the nicer letters Iacocca ever received. He felt instinctively that someday he and Iacocca—who moved to Chrysler just a couple of months later— would be of use to one another.

Lutz had moved triumphantly from the top job at Ford of Europe to Dearborn in 1983 to take over Ford's entire international operations. Ford of Europe then hit a rough patch; Lutz's new mid-size Sierra was off to a slow start, and the division was losing money. In Dearborn, Lutz was spending a lot of time engaged in heated transatlantic telephone conversations with Jim Cappalongo, his successor at Ford of Europe. It was when Cappalongo quit, blaming Lutz for his troubles, that Caldwell ordered Lutz back to Europe. Lutz felt that he was going back under a cloud. He was determined to get the place straightened out and demonstrate that the situation wasn't due to any lack of business acumen on *his* part. He gave it two years at Ford of Europe and, sure enough, turned the division completely around. That's when Lutz called Iacocca and said, "Hey, I've proved what I wanted to prove. I believe I have rehabilitated myself in the eyes of the Ford Motor Company hierarchy. I don't believe I'm ever going to make president or chairman here."

In the fullness of time, Lutz later thought about what he might have done. When he looked at the way succession stacked up and who left and who didn't, he felt he might have gone all the way at Ford. But Iacocca eventually made a firm offer, so Lutz went to Chrysler. One longtime Ford executive—one of the company's topmost officials in 2004—remained a Lutz loyalist nearly 20 years after Lutz had left. He believed Ford always had a gap in its senior management. It had several talented young executives in their early 40s, men like Premier Automotive Group and Ford of Europe boss Mark Fields, and product development chief Phil Martens. And it also had a lot of executives around age 60. The ones in between had largely been cleared out by the ill-fated Ford 2000 centralization strategy, which had consolidated power in Dearborn. The lack of depth in senior management ranks was a concern at Ford.

"Lutz would have been a great head of Ford Motor Company," said the executive. "If he had stayed, we would have ten Phil Martens instead of two Phil Martens. He would bring a whole lot of great people to Ford. With Lutz, Ford would have been more successful in the nineties. There would not have been the product drought if Lutz had been at the head."

Had Lutz stayed at Ford, Jacques Nasser, the Ford CEO who was fired in November 2001, would have inherited a stronger company and might himself have survived in his position. But instead, Lutz went to work for Lee Iacocca, eagerly anticipating Iacocca's retirement. Iacocca managed to stay on as Chrysler's chairman until he was 67, putting off his retirement twice, and only at the gentle insistence of the board of directors did he finally agree in late 1991 that it was time to go—once he had found a successor.

Lutz was Chrysler's chief operating officer and clear No. 2. He was the obvious choice but was uncrowned. Many years later, some who were at Chrysler at the time speculated that Iacocca anticipated a share raid by Kirk Kerkorian or perhaps another raider and harbored ambitions of using such a ploy to return to power. They say Iacocca believed that with Lutz as CEO it would be far more difficult. So Iacocca passed over his first lieutenant.

Lutz had done it to himself again. During his long career, he had managed to turn a succession of bosses—Eberhard von Kuenheim, Philip Caldwell, Red Poling, and now Lee Iacocca—against him.

Photo Gallery

FORD

A confident Henry Ford II in the early 1950s, as his turnaround at Ford Motor Company was beginning to look secure. *Ford Motor Company Limited*

Ford (left) took a liking to dashing and debonair Bob Lutz (right). Lutz took the boss on several tours of the company's European operations. *Bob Lutz*

The Deuce meets another monarch, Spain's Juan Carlos, while inaugurating Ford's new plant in Valencia, Spain, in 1976. *Ford Motor Company Limited*

Ford celebrates the opening of the assembly plant in Spain. *Ford Motor Company Limited*

Henry Ford II in 1987, a few months before his death at 70. *Ford Motor Company Limited*

HONDA

The young daredevil Soichiro Honda (above right), with younger brother Benjiro, after winning an auto race in Japan in 1936. Later that year, his racing career ended after a horrific crash just before the finish line of the All-Japan Speed Rally between Yokohama and Tokyo. *Honda Motor Company*

Honda working in one of his motorcycle plants in 1960. *Honda Motor Company*

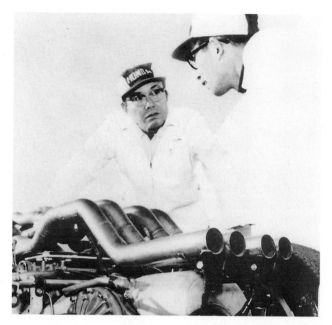

Honda (left) with a member of the F1 team in 1966. *Honda Motor Company*

Honda (left) in 1973 with long-time business partner Takeo Fujisawa, the man who oversaw the company's finances and marketing. *Honda Motor Company*

Honda with his wife Sachi at his 1989 induction into the Automotive Hall of Fame in Michigan. He had become, somewhat ironically, a goodwill ambassador for the Japanese auto industry. *Honda Motor Company*

Honda became an avid golfer late in life. While in Michigan for his Automotive Hall of Fame induction, he played a memorable round at the famous Oakland Hills Country Club near Detroit. *Honda Motor Company*

From left to right: Eberhard von Kuenheim, Bob Lutz, and Wilhelm Gieschen at a BMW Motorsport GmbH event in February 1973. Lutz launched BMW's Motorsport operation at von Kuenheim's bequest. *BMW AG*

Von Kuenheim in 1976. Things were beginning to click at the company he had taken control of five years earlier. *BMW AG*

The 1990 meeting of the Association des Constructeurs Européens Automobiles (ACEA) at BMW. From left to right: André Deleye and Pher Gyilenhammer (Volvo), Arno Bohn (Porsche), Wilfried Lochte (MAN), Lindsey Halstead (Ford), Aart van der Padt (DAF), Raymond Levy (Renaault), Giorgio Garuzzo (Fiat), Robert Eaton (GM), Carl Hahn (VW), Georg Kransund (Saab Scania), Edzard Reuter (Daimler Benz), and von Kuenheim. *BMW AG*

Von Kuenheim at the height of his glory in 1990. *BMW AG*

Wolfgang Reitzle at the peak of his powers at BMW in the early 1990s. At the time, Reitzle seemed certain to replace von Kuenheim as the company's CEO. *Automotive News*

Opposite, bottom: Von Kuenhiem (seated left) with South Carolina Governor Carroll Campbell at the 1992 ceremonies for BMW's agreement to build an assembly plant in Spartanburg, South Carolina. BMW's U.S. factory represented a landmark change in direction for German luxury carmakers. Present were current BMW Chairman Helmut Panke, standing fourth from left; then–U.S. President George H. W. Bush, sixth from left; and Bernd Pischetsrieder, later chairman of both BMW and VW, third from right. *BMW AG*

Right: Von Kuenheim in 1993, the year he retired as chairman of BMW's management board. *BMW AG*

IACOCCA

An irresistible force. Energetic, 33-year-old Lee Iacocca around the time he was named car marketing manager at the Ford Motor Company's Ford Division. *Ford Motor Company*

Lee Iacocca in October 1970, two months before Henry Ford II named the 46-year-old executive president of the Ford Motor Company. *Automotive News*

Iacocca in 1971. As Ford president, he told his managers to get their departments profitable in three years or sell them off. *Automotive News*

Iacocca as he appears on the cover of *Iacocca: An Autobiography*. *Anthony Lowe*

Iacocca relaxes during an interview late in his tenure at Chrysler. *Joe Wilssens, Automotive News*

Robert J. Eaton—the man Iacocca chose over Lutz. Iacocca called his selection of Eaton "the biggest mistake of my career." *Chrysler Corporation*

Eager to be an entrepreneur, Iacocca became a partner in an electric bicycle company after retiring from Chrysler. *E-Bike*

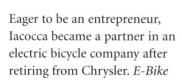

A young Bob Lutz while working at Opel in Germany in the early 1960s. *Adam Opel AG*

Right: Harold "Red" Poling, Lutz's nemesis in Europe during the 1970s. Poling would later became chairman of the Ford Motor Company— and block Lutz's further advancement in the company. *Ford Motor Company*

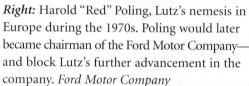

Lutz (right) at Opel with Tony Lapine—later head of product development at Porsche and the man Ferdinand Piëch unsuccessfully tried to bring to Audi. *Bob Lutz*

Lutz accompanied Henry Ford II on his "farewell tour" of Europe in 1979, his last visit as Chairman of the Ford Motor Company. Along the way, Lutz showed the Deuce the radical shape he proposed for Ford's next mid-market car in Europe—the 1982 Sierra. *Bob Lutz*

Iacocca (right) hired Lutz (left) at Chrysler, reviving Lutz's career. The two men often tangled. *Automotive News*

Lutz back at General Motors with GM Chairman Rick Wagoner. Wagoner, more than 20 years Lutz's junior, hired the legend in 2001 when Lutz was 69. No retired auto executive has ever been given such a gift. "Realistically speaking, I don't pose a threat to Rick Wagoner," Lutz said. *General Motors*

PIËCH

Ferdinand Piëch (right) and cousin Butzi Porsche in 1949 with their grandfather, the legendary Ferdinand Porsche. *Ferdinand Piëch collection*

Piëch receiving a "Goldenen Lenkrad" (Golden Steering Wheel) for the Audi 100 in the early 1980s. The award, handed out by the newspaper *Bild Am Sonntag,* is Germany's most prestigious automotive technical honor. *Volkswagen AG*

Piëch at Volkswagen: "He was a guy who moved the industry," said one colleague. *Volkswagen AG*

Piëch in Salzburg in 2002, shortly after his retirement from Volkwagen's management board. *Ferdinand Piëch collection*

Piëch (left) with Bernd Pischetsrieder, his successor as head of Volkswagen. Pischetsrieder also followed von Kuenheim at BMW. *Ferdinand Piëch collection*

Up until a certain point in his career, few doubted that Lutz would one day become the CEO of an auto company; except he kept getting the rug pulled out from under him by suspicious superiors. It happened again and again. His bosses would eventually grow irritated with the swashbuckling, movie-star-handsome one-time fighter pilot who raced cars, smoked Cuban cigars, and was constantly fêted in the press.

Lutz careened into one giant ego after another. Although Lutz and Henry Ford II appeared to get along, some of the Deuce's pals contend that Lutz reminded him a little of Lee Iacocca, and the Deuce didn't want another highly tuned ego in his midst.

Caldwell, Ford's CEO through most of the 1980s, was also irritated by Lutz's stardom and eventually ordered him to stop talking to the press. Lutz begged his reporter friends to stop writing about him, but it was too late. His career was damaged at Ford, and when he returned from Europe to Dearborn in 1985 the punishment was the job as head of U.S. truck operations.

Lutz had a personal magnetism that not only charmed the press, it inspired the extreme loyalty of younger colleagues. While at Chrysler in 1993, Lutz arrived at the Tokyo Motor Show with a military-style haircut that made him look like a Marine Corps commander. It was one of the hottest topics of the show—Bob Lutz's haircut. Soon Chrysler engineers began showing up for work with buzz cuts, not because Lutz had ordered it but because they followed their leader.

"When Lutz turned his head it was slowly, like a turret, not fast like a weasel," said one executive who worked with him years before at BMW. "The young men in the company studied him. But in the company of Lutz, some men didn't feel safe. He is potentially a dangerous man."

And Lutz couldn't be pushed around. There was his famous confrontation at Chrysler in 1991 with Richard Dauch, the hulking former Purdue University football player who was then Chrysler's manufacturing chief. After an argument, Dauch deliberately blocked Lutz's exit from a meeting. Lutz warned the massive ex-fullback that as a former Marine he was trained to kill. Lutz fired Dauch shortly thereafter.

Lutz had ample preparation for the fact that Iacocca wasn't going to anoint him as chairman. His expectations had been reduced to the level of, "I hope it's somebody I can live with."

One thing that played on Lutz' mind was, "Hey, wait a minute, the guys and I have put in so much effort to turning this thing around that I'm not going to quit and let somebody else take the credit."

In 1991, Lee Iacocca began inquiring among friends outside Chrysler about possible successors. As he grew older and more isolated, Iacocca found he knew fewer and fewer of the young executives who were making their marks at other auto companies. But as he asked around, one name kept coming up—Bob Eaton. The 52-year-old executive had built a terrific reputation as head of GM Europe.

Eaton had been very lucky in his career. On his watch at GM Europe, which began in July 1988, Eaton presided over an era of great success. While the parent company floundered in North America and Ford of Europe fell from profitability, GM Europe generated billions of dollars in profit, increased its sales and its market share, opened new markets, and vastly improved its labor relations.

But to many industry observers, Eaton was merely picking up where his predecessor, then–GM Vice Chairman John "Jack" Smith, left off. "If the table hadn't been set by Jack Smith, Bob Eaton would not have been able to dine," said Ken Levy, a GM Europe public relations executive in Zurich, Switzerland.

Eaton went to General Motors Europe after several years in charge of GM's advanced engineering team in Detroit. His colleagues in Europe painted a picture of an engineer who in his first operating job went out of his way to master details outside the product realm.

Yet he rode the coattails of a strong team of German engineers at Adam Opel, GM's German subsidiary. The Germans, with the assistance from Opel design chief Wayne Cherry, had developed a highly successful range of cars in the late 1980s and had put the company on a winning path.

If any one man was responsible for GM Europe's success in the late 1980s and early 1990s it was Opel's burly engineering and manufacturing czar, Friedrich "Fritz" Lohr, who had joined GM soon after World War II and was nearing retirement.

Lohr operated at Opel's technical development center in Rüsselsheim, Germany, and had all but ignored Bob Eaton down in Zurich. He sometimes didn't return his boss's phone calls and was often downright impertinent at meetings. Lohr had a marked preference for Eaton's predecessor, Jack Smith, and he didn't care who knew it. Before he retired in September 1991, Lohr took a shot at Eaton in an exit interview. "The money we earn today has nothing to do with the people currently running the business, absolutely not," he said.

It wasn't because he felt Eaton was just another American supervisor sent over from Detroit to clamp down on Opel's product spending. Eaton was himself an engineer, and a good one. But Lohr didn't believe Eaton was really an operations man. Eaton's one brush with running a business unit was GM's quirky acquisition in 1984 of Group Lotus, the tiny British sports-car maker and engineering consultancy built by the late legendary racing and sports-car impresario Colin Chapman.

Lotus was Eaton's baby. He wanted to use it as a skunk works for special GM performance cars. But the little Norfolk company proved to be difficult to manage and a personal defeat for Eaton. Eaton himself decided enough was enough and sold Lotus a few years later while he was in charge of GM Europe.

The one area where history would take the measure of Bob Eaton would be his handling of the Jaguar sweepstakes in 1989. Early that year, the British government announced plans to release the "golden share" it had long held in the great English marque. After years in the government's protective custody, Jaguar would be auctioned off. But the business was a mess. It was operating in old, decrepit plants that still showed the scars of World War II bombings. It was also building cars of embarrassingly poor quality—with doors that leaked, electrics that malfunctioned, and hydraulic systems that seized up in a heartbeat.

Jaguar's flamboyant CEO, John—later Sir John—Egan, opened the bidding by approaching General Motors, which had long coveted the brand built by the legendary Sir William Lyons. Egan had begun his career at GM's AC Delco division in the U.K. Most saw it as a foregone conclusion that GM would buy Jaguar and that Ford would take control of the other European car company up for grabs that autumn—Saab.

As GM Europe's president, the job of negotiating for Jaguar fell to Eaton. He carried on discussions with Egan and his team for nine long months in 1989, deciding ultimately that GM did not need or want full control. Instead it would go for a minority stake.

General Motors would inject fresh cash to help develop new models and upgrade the plants. But fundamentally it would let Jaguar be Jaguar, keeping it British and unadulterated.

Then in early autumn 1989, Ford joined the chase for Jaguar—a move that was no real surprise. Henry Ford II had long wanted to buy a British automobile company. Ford tried unsuccessfully to acquire Rover Group in 1986, and the Deuce had arranged for the acquisition of Aston Martin as one of his last acts before he died in 1987.

Eaton was suddenly pitted against Lindsey Halstead, the avuncular American head of Ford of Europe. He was supported by Bruce Blythe, then Henry's personal business adviser, who managed the relationships with the British merchant banks. While their respective headquarters back in Detroit watched and waited, the two men matched wits. Eaton was slow and cautious, Halstead bold and audacious. With Dearborn's backing, Halstead decided to spend whatever billions were necessary to buy the entire company, knowing that billions more would have to go into refurbishing the plants.

Eaton was aghast. He wanted to acquire no more than 30 percent of Jaguar and spend less than $400 million doing it.

Meanwhile, Ford was prepared to pay $2.5 billion for 100 percent ownership of Jaguar. Would GM respond?

Some inside General Motors thought Eaton should go for it—should counter Ford's offer and attempt to acquire Jaguar outright. But Eaton was not interested. "It's not worth it," he declared. "That amount is absolutely crazy."

Ford's bid caught General Motors by surprise. GM was still a week away from announcing its own plans—first to buy a 15 percent stake in Jaguar and then increase this to 29.9 percent. Egan later said that he had warned GM two weeks before that Ford would make a full bid.

Ford got Jaguar, but a few weeks later Eaton stunned the auto world by acquiring 50 percent of Saab. Unlike the high-profile Jaguar negotiations, GM's talks with Saab were handled in complete secrecy. Only once did word threaten to get out—when a business reporter spotted Saab-Scania's top PR executive, Kai Hammerich, in the Zurich airport. A fast-thinking Hammerich explained that he was returning to Sweden from a ski trip in the Swiss Alps.

Meanwhile, Fiat executives thought they had Saab sewn up on the very December day that the GM deal was made public. Swedish journalists assembled for a press conference in Trollhattan, Sweden, expecting to hear that Fiat had acquired Saab. They were stunned when Bob Eaton strode into the room.

GM paid $400 million to buy half of Saab, while Ford was presumed to have wildly overspent to obtain Jaguar. At the same time, Eaton's GM Europe kept totting up profits, while GM in North America was sliding into an abyss. Eaton's personal stock soared. He had taken on the aura of a brilliant high-stakes operator.

In later years, the wisdom of Eaton's actions in those frantic few weeks in late 1989 came under question. Ford had spent hundreds of millions more to buy Jaguar—five times Jaguar's net asset value. But

Jaguar slowly began to pay off for Ford, while GM struggled unsuccessfully for years to fix Saab, with its less potent brand identity.

Eaton understood the limits to his abilities and was openly modest about his qualities and the role in his career played by luck. When a friend asked him in 1991 what he would do to fix the mess that GM's North American operations had become, Eaton said bluntly, "There's nothing I could do. There's nothing anyone could do."

Lutz had grown older and wiser by the time Bob Eaton became his boss in 1992. At this stage of his life and career, Lutz decided to accept his fate—he would never make CEO. There was just something about him that kept the top job out of reach. He was too flamboyant, too outspoken, made too many enemies, got too much attention, stepped on too many toes. Too often he questioned the judgment of his superiors. He was his own worst enemy.

Lutz, who turned 60 in 1992, was eight years Eaton's senior. It was time to submit. "Sometimes what you want is not what you need," Lutz said.

Lutz had achieved such a uniquely powerful position as the No. 2 eminence at Chrysler that he didn't really need to be the CEO. He could all but ignore Bob Eaton and continue building Chrysler in his own image. Only now he could do it without Lee Iacocca looking over his shoulder.

Lutz already commanded the intense loyalty of his troops. He would take the company where it needed to go whether he was chief executive or not—almost as if Eaton weren't there. Anyone whose opinion he really cared about and whose support he really needed was already with him.

Steve Harris was a public-relations executive who began his career at General Motors in 1972 and wound up working at American Motors in the 1980s. He was at AMC in 1987 when Chrysler bought the company from Renault. Harris promptly ascended the PR ranks at Chrysler and by 1990 was the company's top spokesperson.

When Eaton was brought in over Lutz, the auto world sat back and waited for the sparks to fly. Keeping them from igniting a crisis of confidence at Chrysler was Harris' job.

One of two things was expected to happen. Lutz would quit, taking hordes of loyal followers with him. Or else he would work tirelessly, Iacocca-like, to undermine his new boss. Only the latter was not really Bob Lutz's style. Not that he was such a nice guy—he simply thought too much of his own abilities to believe he needed to resort to shenanigans. He always believed that his talent would win out. Infighting wasn't his way.

Harris knew enough to exploit Lutz's esprit de corps and to present the two Bobs as mutual admirers and best of friends. He all but ordered his two bosses to play along. He urged the Bobs to be cordial to one another—in public and as much as humanly possible in private. As Chrysler's fortunes soared in the mid-1990s with the success of the Jeep line, the Neon subcompact, and the LH, it became the triumph of "the two Bobs."

In fact, being president and COO of Chrysler under a guy like Bob Eaton turned out to be the best job Lutz ever had. If Eaton had been a dogmatic control freak who wanted to do everything himself, things wouldn't have been nearly as much fun for Lutz.

With Iacocca it was different. Lutz had profound business disagreements with Iacocca about the company's diversification strategy. Lutz felt Chrysler should focus on the automobile business. But he also knew in his heart that he had been unnecessarily provocative and at times disrespectful and probably guilty of a cardinal sin, which was to not show solidarity with the officially appointed leader.

Lutz and Eaton appeared to have come to terms, and they set ground rules for peaceful coexistence. The word from inside the company was that Eaton had agreed to let Bob Lutz set Chrysler's product agenda and see it through. Lutz promised not to second-guess Eaton on strategic matters, if he could help it. The irony was that Eaton was the true engineer and Lutz the marketing and operations man, not the other way around.

Eaton joined Chrysler with the understanding that he would become chairman when Iacocca retired at the end of 1992.

After Eaton's arrival, he and Lutz would get together about once a week for a dinner at the swank Townsend Hotel in Birmingham, Michigan, the leafy Detroit suburb. They would be seated away from prying eyes in a more or less private setting.

"We'd just chat on how the company was going and how we were planning to run it and so forth," Lutz recalled. "At the time I found myself wishing that he had said, 'Yeah, you're right, this is working pretty well, why don't you just keep looking after that and I'll do the broad, strategic things.' That in fact is not what he said. What he said was, 'Well, I'm a pretty hands-on guy myself. I come out of engineering. My specialty is product. I think I'm pretty damn good at product. I also believe I know a lot about manufacturing from my time reworking the manufacturing in Europe, and I would like to become quite heavily involved in all of the product and manufacturing decisions.'

"Initially I was kind of disappointed and thought to myself, 'I wonder how this is going to work.' But, you know what, after a couple of weeks, maybe months, it all just settled out. I think he got the impression that the thing had a lot of momentum and was going in the right direction. We included him as much as he wanted to be included. We'd take him on the ride and drives and obviously gave him frequent styling reviews, but I'd say he never tried to really directly interfere. So from that standpoint it was it was very good.

"He got into manufacturing a little more than perhaps a chairman would who has a chief operating officer underneath him. I let [Chrysler manufacturing chief] Denny Pawley deal with that. I said,

'Look Dennis, the boss likes manufacturing. He thinks he was very good at manufacturing, just deal directly with him on manufacturing questions.' I had no problem with that at all."

Eaton had been forced to cede vast amounts of control to Lutz. He had heard all the stories about Lutz. Stories had been handed down from the old Opel hands at GM Europe, and Eaton had been fully briefed on the clashes Lutz had had with Iacocca. Eaton, not one for confrontations, wanted to avoid such conflicts.

Indeed, the "two Bobs" seemed to get along famously. But in 1998, as Lutz neared retirement, he finally began to let off some steam. At the right time in the right mood in the right place, he would unleash his true feelings about Eaton and his contributions to Chrysler's resurgence. So accustomed were people to the story of the "the two Bobs" that they could hardly believe their ears.

The resentment was understandable. Lutz had performed a miracle at Chrysler in the late 1980s and early 1990s and, it could be argued, lost his last chance of becoming the CEO of an auto company because of it. He had inherited a product-development system that was a mess in a company that could not survive without an unfailing series of product successes. He was not the only miracle worker at Chrysler in those days—not by a long shot. But he was the catalyst, and at the height of his powers.

Chrysler followed the Viper with the LH sedans, a pair of full-size models that were as important to Chrysler as the 1985 Taurus was to Ford. To get it done, Lutz had to call upon all his experience and all the genius he had been exposed to from the men he had worked under—even the ones he fought with.

Lutz had absorbed the brand-building tenets of Eberhard von Kuenheim during three impressionable years at BMW almost 20 years earlier. He was instructed in von Kuenheim's method of giving engineers their head to develop cars that customers might not know they wanted until they saw and drove them.

Lutz needed the marketing savoir-faire and risk-averse nature that his current boss, Iacocca, had demonstrated earlier in his career at Ford and in his early days at Chrysler.

Lutz needed the cost discipline he.had learned at Ford—not without some pain—from Red Poling, who had himself learned from Henry Ford II's original Whiz Kids. And he would need the golden touch of Soichiro Honda.

According to one account, it was the ex–Ford executive Hal Sperlich who in 1987 suggested to another former Ford executive, Chrysler vice-chairman Gerry Greenwald, that the company ought to conduct a study of the Honda Motor Company's highly successful methods for developing new products.

Honda was the most lavishly praised company in the auto industry in the 1980s. In 1990, the year after the Honda Accord took over as the top-selling car in the United States, Chrysler even created an advertising campaign that compared itself to Honda.

The campaign, which broke in May 1990, trumpeted the news that some potential car buyers prefer Chrysler's cars to Honda's. In the ads, Iacocca detailed the superiority of Chrysler's products. The campaign was headlined "Meet the Americans that Beat the Hondas."

But what was really going on at Chrysler at the time was that the company was restructuring itself on the Honda model. A couple of years earlier, a Chrysler study team had worked for five months studying every scrap of information it could find on how Honda developed its new cars so speedily and successfully.

Honda was more highly regarded than Toyota, which only became the standard-bearer of the industry after the 1990 book *The Machine that Changed the World* by James P. Womack, et al., summarized the laws of lean production.

The idea of benchmarking Honda was a typical Ford Whiz Kids approach, the kind of thing Bob McNamara and the young Henry Ford

II would have gleefully done in the 1950s—had there then been a Honda to examine.

Chrysler's study team uncovered the system that was founded on the principles that Soichiro Honda preached—the system that downplayed the importance of hierarchy and bureaucracy, relied on "youthful spirit," and rotated engineers through many different jobs rather than pigeonholing them for life.

At its core, the Honda system stood for teamwork of the kind that sprang from the company's motorcycle and Formula One racing teams and then from the engineering task force that developed the CVCC engine.

Honda employees were encouraged to experiment and make mistakes. At the end of his career, Honda had said: "Looking back, on my work, I feel that I have made nothing but mistakes, a series of failures, a series of regrets. But I am proud of an accomplishment. Although I made one mistake after another, my mistakes or failures were never due to the same reason. I never made the same mistake twice and I always tried my hardest and succeeded in improving my efforts."

At Honda, developing a new car was based on the principle of platform teams. The general parameters of a new model were set, then the platform team, with its project leader, had the authority to take care of business with a minimum of meddling from higher-ups. The project leader also had a power base for rebuttal when top executives didn't like what they saw.

Most automakers studied Honda to one degree or another. But Chrysler put what it learned about Honda into action, and the man who did it was Bob Lutz.

Chrysler created its own platform teams that brought together engineering, design, production, accounting, and marketing. The goal was to speed development of new models—an area where American automakers lagged far behind the Japanese—and eliminate the indecision and confusion of top-down development programs and senior-executive second-guessing.

In early 1988, the Chrysler team that studied Honda presented its findings to Miller and Greenwald, who thought the results presented a worthwhile opportunity. If Chrysler were to adopt the Honda platform-team system, Lee Iacocca would be placed in the difficult position of having to give up much of his authority.

But Iacocca did sign off on the platform-team proposal. He reserved the right to meddle, but he handed over much of the power he had fought for a lifetime to attain in this one bold move.

Though he believed in the late 1980s that Japanese carmakers were not playing fair, Iacocca would not prevent Chrysler from benefiting from Honda's genius. The second Soichiro Honda lesson Iacocca applied at this crucial moment in his career was the importance of giving his younger managers more control.

After Chrysler's acquisition of American Motors in 1987, Iacocca had decided to keep the American Motors engineering team intact— a move that Lutz praised. The AMC team was already handling Jeep, so Iacocca put it in charge of Chrysler's pickup trucks as well.

Before the takeover, the AMC unit had managed to achieve so much with so little that Chrysler executives wanted to learn how they had done it. Keeping the AMC guys together would help them understand.

One of the reasons turned out to be François Castaing, the Renault executive who, like Ferdinand Piëch at Audi and the CVCC engineers at Honda, had formed their work habits in the intense atmosphere of race-car engineering. Through the 1970s, Castaing had been in charge of Renault's Formula One team. It was a small, cross-functional engineering platform team, with everybody involved in everybody else's business.

"From his post in the engineering department, he was the human linchpin who helped us to turn the lessons of the Honda Study into action," Lutz once wrote.

Chrysler's engineering department had been a series of silos: body engineering, chassis, powertrain, electrical. Castaing and Lutz disassembled the component-specific engineering groups and formed units that were responsible not just for components, but for a whole vehicle.

But empowering Castaing and the AMC team created a lot of resentment among Chrysler's proud engineering corps. Among the theories advanced for why Lutz didn't became CEO of Chrysler was the bad blood created within the entrenched engineering community when so much authority was given to Castaing, the alleged carpetbagger from AMC. Iacocca got dozens of anonymous letters from old hands in Chrysler's engineering department complaining about what Lutz and Castaing were doing.

Many years later, one anonymous Chrysler engineer's view of history was expressed in a letter to the industry publication *Automotive News*:

"Bob Lutz, who came from Ford, and the AMC refugees landed at Chrysler at about the same time. In order to avoid the fate Bunkie Knudsen experienced when he went to Ford from GM, Lutz and Castaing formed a sweetheart alliance. They started bad-mouthing Iacocca, purging the company of many Chrysler veterans and replacing them with their allies. . . .

"On that fateful day a few years ago, with Castaing meeting with his pals, the announcement came in that Bob Eaton would replace Iacocca. You could hear the chins hitting the floor. The meeting turned into a wake. Their boy, Bob Lutz, had lost in his bid for CEO."

Along with Honda and Castaing, there was another influence for Chrysler's platform teams. Lutz had created one—20 years before, shortly after he had joined BMW.

"I had an epiphany at one point. When François started talking about platform teams and describing the concept and I thought 'that's what I did at BMW in motorcycles when I got there.'"

When Lutz arrived at BMW in 1971, sales of motorcycles had all but collapsed because of the competition from Japanese companies. As he got to know the company, he found that no one had responsibility for the motorcycle business. Engineering had a little piece of the bikes, as well as manufacturing, design, sales and marketing. But Lutz couldn't figure out who pulled it altogether.

"That was the problem," said Lutz. "No one did. It just sort of ran itself and was always reactive, and it had run to the point where we really wanted to shut it down."

Lutz went to see von Kuenheim and asked the BMW boss if he could pull all the motorcycle guys from the various departments together once a week for half a day at a time. He wanted to outline a future strategy, including the kinds of new models BMW should be developing and producing.

Von Kuenheim gave his OK, so long as Lutz didn't forget that his day job was head of sales and marketing for BMW cars.

The meetings started, and BMW developed the R90S, a King Kong bike that hearkened back to the post–World War II 600-cc BMW bike. The new bike transformed the fortunes of BMW motorcycles.

"It occurred to me I had created a platform team for motorcycles," Lutz said. "So I understood what the concept was that François wanted and we pursued it."

But the platform team concept made it possible for Chrysler to develop the products that powered the company's miracle of the 1990s.

The LH large-sedan project was the test-bed for the platform strategy. Very quietly, Chrysler split up the big engineering house into platform teams. The LH team was the first one. Then it had the advanced group and the future small-car platform, for the vehicle that became the 1993 Neon.

The groups acted like autonomous automobile companies. They had full accountability for managing the allocated investment, meeting variable cost targets, and meeting all the quality and vehicle performance targets.

Lutz also installed methods for making sure that each platform team didn't rush off and reinvent the windshield-wiper motor, for example.

The important commodity buys stayed with the same selected buyers. But they had broad latitude. Chrysler didn't tell its LH group how much of the total vehicle cost to allocate to the interiors, for instance. Under the old system, the company broke costs down and said the team could spend, for example, $200 on the front suspension, $150 on the rear suspension. Now they had an over-all objective.

The LH program had been around for years and was a problem. The old-line Chrysler engineering group had developed a program that was spinning out of control as they made plans to load it with the latest technology trends.

After Lutz made Castaing head of Chrysler engineering, the Frenchman stopped the LH program in its tracks. Lutz then set rules for the program—timing, investment, cost targets, design layout (it would be a concept called "cab-forward"), and the LH mission—"not to be all things to all people, but to be highly affordable family sedans that hit the sweet spots in terms of features the way the best Japanese and European cars had been doing for years," Lutz wrote.

Lutz then had the idea of combining the resolute finance side of the auto industry with genuine car-guy mentality.

Tom Sidlik, who many years later would become the top purchasing executive at the combined DaimlerChrysler, had started his career in Ford finance.

Lutz asked Sidlik to implement a system of product costing right out of Robert McNamara's playbook—the "red-book" system of product costing.

In his autobiography, Lutz wrote, "Thanks simply to the fact that our finance people and our product people were now on the same team, we were finally able to start estimating with precision what the absolute cost of a part or system should be."

The LH, which debuted in September 1992, was one of the industry's landmark cars, like the Honda Civic CVCC and the first Ford Taurus.

An essential part of the Chrysler miracle was the company's enlightened and collaborative approach to managing its supply chain—something previously unheard of amid the history of contentious relations between U.S. auto companies and their parts suppliers.

Chrysler's Supplier Cost Reduction Effort (SCORE) program was founded on the principle that cost sharing was a key element in building trust and better relationships between carmakers and suppliers. The idea was to establish partnerships with suppliers and develop a common mindset.

These partnerships were based on shared cost and technical information. The big difference was that at Chrysler, under the SCORE program, the supplier decided how much of its annual cost savings it wanted to keep and how much it wanted to pass along to Chrysler in the form of lower prices. Meanwhile, General Motors and Ford were demanding that any cost reductions achieved by its vendors be handed over in full.

These improved relations enabled Chrysler to work closely with its suppliers to co-develop features that would otherwise have been unavailable to the No. 3 U.S. carmaker. This symbiotic relationship between manufacturer and supplier was similar to the cooperative supplier relations encouraged by Eberhard von Kuenheim—a system that enabled BMW to match technology with Mercedes-Benz.

BMW had to rely on its suppliers, and so did Chrysler in the late 1980s and early 1990s. But they were both following a concept handed down from Soichiro Honda.

"The SCORE program had Honda written all over it," said David Nelson, Honda of America Manufacturing's longtime head of purchasing. No carmaker in the world has a closer bond with its suppliers, and

Soichiro Honda was the reason why. When Honda decided to begin building cars in 1962, the first thing he did was make a trek to Japan's major automotive suppliers.

The founder and his team of young engineers had designed a chain-driven convertible sports car, the 500-cc S500. It was a kind of a four-wheel motorcycle.

"It was an extraordinary engineering achievement," said Nelson.

But Japan's existing auto suppliers wouldn't agree to supply the parts for it. They all but ignored Honda because they weren't interested in doing business with a tiny motorcycle firm that wanted to compete with their customers. They were committed to Japan's established car companies.

Soichiro Honda could find no one to make the components he needed to build his cars, so he had little choice but to go to the little companies that made parts for his motorcycles and ask them to make automobile parts. They agreed to supply Honda with the parts he needed, and 40 years later those motorcycle suppliers are still supplying Honda with automobile parts.

Nelson went to see some of these suppliers in Japan in 1988, not long after he joined Honda at its manufacturing operations in Ohio.

"They were so proud of the kind of relationship they had with Mr. Honda," he said.

One was the stamping company KTH. The founder, Hiroshi Takao, who had started his business to supply Soichiro Honda in the 1950s, still worked there when Nelson paid his visit.

"Quite a lot of those entrepreneurs had no formal education," said Nelson. "One was Takao. The man had a ninth grade education. . . . I went to see the plant. It was 60,000 square foot and had seven people working there (in 1988). It was so automated I couldn't believe it. Everything was automated beyond your imagination."

Nelson saw the same type of thing at many other tiny Honda suppliers in Japan. The inventiveness was almost unbelievable. He recalled seeing a plastics company where the dies changed automatically. He'd never seen such a thing before.

"These suppliers were specific and unique to Honda," Nelson said. "And they had a kind of free spirit that had permeated through the entire supplier chain, just like they did in the racing programs.

"The relationship Mr. Honda had with Mr. Takao was like a brother. It was intimate. At Honda's suppliers over there, you walked into their lobby and they sold Honda cars or motorcycles or whatever. It was a very tight relationship."

Nelson said that about 75 such suppliers came to Ohio from Japan. These were the companies that made things that Honda couldn't buy in America.

"They could make things better than the companies in America," he said. "Whether it was the close tolerances on a rocker arm, or a crankshaft or an engine part, it was extraordinary."

The same suppliers followed Honda to its other international operations, from Canada to Swindon, England. Susan Insley, one of Honda of America Manufacturing's top executives, was struck by how small these companies were. "These companies were like mom-and-pop businesses," she said. "They were family owned. At that time there was a lot of talk about keiretsu, but Honda couldn't get into the keiretsus. They were shut out. If Mr. Honda was going to get into the industry, he had to work with these very small companies. They quite literally grew up with Honda.

"These are the companies that came to Ohio in the 1980s with no guarantees that they would get 100 percent of the business," said Insley. "It was a tremendous gamble for them. For many of these companies their American operations became their biggest operations.

"Those Honda suppliers were a kind of miracle. They made their way in America. They had great faith in Mr. Honda and in the Honda Company," Insley said.

Nelson said, "There was a special feeling between Honda and its suppliers that went beyond that of Toyota and Nissan. It was deeper than Toyota and Nissan." There were big differences in those days between Honda and Toyota—a huge cultural gap. "Toyota was established," said Nelson. "They were so formal. You couldn't use the word *formal* to describe Honda."

Neither could you at Chrysler in the early 1990s. In the auto industry, one miracle begets another.

CHAPTER TWELVE

The Style of Lutz

O n Friday mornings during the summer of 2002, top executives of General Motors gathered at the corporation's ultra-secretive design center in Warren, Michigan—16 miles from GM's headquarters in downtown Detroit. There, under a massive styling dome, the biggest bosses of the world's biggest industrial company would engage in what they called the "walkaround."

They spent the morning circling the production vehicles and concept cars in GM's pipeline, posing questions to stylists and engineers and bouncing reactions off one another. Fridays at the design center had become a ritual, the place executives went to see and be seen in the new General Motors. With each passing week that summer, more and more of the company's honchos would starttheir Fridays in Warren, even nontechnical executives like chief financial officer John Devine.

Often, the executives and engineers who were gathered would hear the roar of an approaching helicopter. It was none other than Bob Lutz, the 70-year-old flyboy vice chairman. Lutz liked to commute to work in his McDonnell Douglas MD500 E jet helicopter to avoid the traffic jams between his home in Ann Arbor, west of Detroit, and the tech center.

Lutz loved a grand entrance. At GM's proving grounds in Milford, Michigan, he would often do a couple of screaming, low-level passes in his Czech-made Aero-Vodochody L-39 ZO Albatros fighter jet before setting plane down on the grounds and walking up to a group of astounded engineers and test drivers. Wayne Cherry, GM's vice president for design, would laugh when he heard the buzz of Lutz's copter at the tech center. He knew the group would be in for a stimulating morning.

It didn't matter who was there—even if GM Chairman Rick Wagoner was part of the Friday walkaround. Lutz stole every scene he was in. The energy focused and the action tightened whenever Lutz clicked into the frame.

It had always been that way with Bob Lutz. Twenty years earlier, when Lutz ran Ford of Europe and his American bosses came to visit, the European press treated the U.S. big shots as though they were Lutz subordinates. Former Ford President Donald Petersen recalled once being asked by a German journalist if he worked for Lutz. Petersen got a chuckle out of it, but most of Lutz's superiors didn't like standing in the younger man's shadow.

The Friday walkaround was one of Lutz's ideas. In GM's old system, top management didn't get in the game early enough and consistently enough. Senior officials delegated decisions. One bad result of keeping top executives out of the loop was that sometimes they would see a car nearing production and couldn't tolerate it. Lutz had rejected what he regarded as an awful redesign of the Buick Regal, thus delaying the renewal of the car to the 2005 model year from the 2004 model year.

Before Lutz, top management delayed a 2002 redesign of the Chevrolet Cavalier and Pontiac Sunfire after rejecting the styling. The delay cost GM two years. Lutz determined that when the top executives were in on the decision from the start, that kind of delay couldn't happen.

Lutz had fixed it so that no longer would product development mysteriously move through countless steps in a faceless system where dozens of people could slow the process but few could say yes. Now product decisions were being made by flesh-and-blood people, with Lutz at the center.

The Friday walkarounds were just one sign of the transformation that occurred after Lutz joined General Motors on September 1, 2001. And he arrived not a moment too soon. By Christmas 2000, morale among product engineers and designers had sunk to a dangerous new low. A recession had taken hold in the United States economy, and GM was cutting back. The company's engineers felt the brunt of it.

A senior GM electrical engineer named John Wilson (not his real name) kept an e-mail journal that captured the times: "We are getting ready for the Christmas shutdown here, and they just came through and told all the secretaries that their jobs were being eliminated as of January 16. I sometimes wonder if the bean counters who are running this place have any hearts at all. The girls are all standing in the halls crying.

"The company is going to a basket weave, converging all the engineering groups in a lean uniform org chart. I don't see how they are going to be lean around here and still manage all that it takes to do a vehicle program from napkin to production. And they want us to do it in 18 months down from 24. I just did a 24-month program and it was a blur and the design that was released suffered from it. Lots of the other engineers have signs in their offices of a sinking ship and they call it convergence charting. So I've been looking around for a new job just in case."

Three months later, Wilson was called into his boss's office.

"The company has told me that I will be laid off at the end of next week," Wilson wrote. "It's what I predicted would happen. Everyone is crashing and burning. It's wild. It's a good time to get out of the auto engineering field. I see nothing but bad times ahead for the bean-counting idiots. The rock bottom is coming up fast. The workload on the poor guys who are left is staggering and will surely cause recalls and poor-quality cars.

"You can't introduce eighteen-month vehicle-development times and new engineering training requirements—like now all engineers have to take a six-month computer drafting class—at the same time that their workload has tripled. Then after they complete that, they are expected to make all the 3D math design changes themselves. On top of that, they are getting rid of the drafting department, so there's no checkers.

"I am sure it looks all good to guys like Wagoner, but he could not design a shoestring. Anyway, I wanted to quit doing this crap and take a race-engineering job. I was too scared before, but now I have to. So here I go."

It turned out that Wilson didn't go because his boss got him a job at one of the suppliers on the project. In fact, he was given the exact same job on the same model program—but he was employed instead by the supplier. He didn't even have to change his office. He worked three times as hard for the same pay.

A couple of months later, Wilson wrote: "GM is still looking at making all kinds of stupid little cuts instead of thinking about quality. Now their big buzzword is module. The plan now is to have the suppliers do all the engineering of these modules and make the suppliers recall-responsible. GM wants to just assemble these modules and sell the vehicle. When I say modules I mean, like, door assemblies totally built up, with glass wiring, everything, all assembled and they just bolt it to the car. Same thing with instrument panel assemblies, chassis, wheel and tire, etc.

"All I know is that it means there is wholesale dumping of engineers—most like me going to the supplier. That way, GM can be run by non-engineering-type people and leave the thinking to the suppliers, along with the risk. That's pretty good thinking for a non-engineering brain."

Such was the mood among GM engineers in January 2001, about the time Lutz, then the retired COO of Chrysler, took part as an after-dinner speaker at the *Automotive News* World Congress in Detroit. Many in the audience that night thought Lutz came across for the first time as an old man. He had once called Iacocca a "doddering old fart." Now he was looking and sounding like one himself.

Lutz was now 69. After retiring from Chrysler, he had taken over as chairman of Exide Technologies, a maker of automotive batteries, and he used his forum that night to talk at tedious length about the battery business, which left many in the audience fidgety. True, Lutz was now in the battery business, but that is not what people wanted to hear him talk about. Friends and longtime admirers shifted nervously in their seats as Lutz hammered home his point about the bright future of the "humble battery." They fingered their wine glasses and traced circles on the white table linen with their dessert spoons.

But when Lutz began to talk about design the audience grew attentive. He began his speech by attacking many of the exotic concept cars that had debuted the week before at the Detroit Auto Show down the street.

"Ugly cars, no matter what the market, don't sell," Lutz told the audience. "As a sort of elder statesman in this business, I feel almost an obligation to the industry to say that I'm concerned about a lot of the concept cars we're seeing lately. Many of them are all-out weird. It's as if the designers are no longer designing for the public, but rather for each other, trying to be evermore off-the-wall than the competition.

"It reminds me of the height of the abstract-art boom in the 1960s and 1970s, when you viewed one blue circle and one line on a canvas, and then had to read a two-page description of what all the artist meant.

"There are concepts over across the street [at the Detroit Auto Show] that look like a whole family of angry kitchen appliances: demented toasters, furious bread machines, and vengeful trash compactors.

Then there are the assemblages of mere steel tubes, leather, and plastic—they look like exercise machines. And worse yet, a lot of these concepts all seem to be drowning in a sea of sameness: high beltlines, tiny windows, flat fronts, rhomboidal headlights, and slab sides. Auto companies that fall in love with this stuff do so, I submit, at their peril: Jack-o'-lantern styling may get photographed at show time, but if it sells, it'd be a miracle."

Lutz was all but formally declared a has-been that night. The following evening, Trevor Creed, Chrysler's British-born head of design, was an after-dinner speaker at the same meeting. Gently, but firmly, Creed rebutted his former boss, implying that Lutz's assault on modern car design—including offerings by Chrysler at the Detroit show—were evidence that the auto business had finally passed Bob Lutz by.

But Lutz's powerful words that night seemed to put him back on the map. Indeed, his remarks resonated with GM chief executive Rick Wagoner. Wagoner was a lanky Harvard MBA who had come up through GM's renowned New York treasurer's office, the real powerhouse and main executive breeding grounds of the corporation. He moved to Detroit from GM Brazil in 1992 as GM's chief financial officer, his career ignited by the coup d'état that brought down GM Chairman Robert Stempel that autumn.

Wagoner was steeped in the ways of a half-century of GM number crunchers. But he was different, too. Soon after inheriting the CEO mantle from his mentor Jack Smith in 2000, Wagoner began to ponder how to reinvigorate vehicle development at General Motors, how to get GM's product planners and engineers to conceive and build cars and trucks that got the blood pumping.

To Rick Wagoner, Bob Lutz was making sense that evening at the Renaissance Center. Wagoner began to think that Lutz—or at least a younger version of Lutz—was just what GM needed in its top executive tier.

At the time, one could have easily named the chief car guy at almost any automaker in the world—the most visible and passionate and influential product enthusiast. At Ford, it was a young Welshman named Richard Parry-Jones or perhaps ex-BMW executive Wolfgang Reitzle, the dashing German who ran the Premier Automotive Group, Ford's luxury-car division that included Jaguar and Volvo.

Former engineers were in charge of several European and Japanese auto companies. But GM's top car guy? Well, you couldn't name one. GM's product bosses were not enthusiasts, they were bureaucrats, all but lost in a sea of brand managers and bean counters. And it seemed to matter. GM's lack of product sensibility had been costing it market share for 20 years.

The corporation had hordes of engineers and designers, good ones, some of the best, but they were directionless. GM was run by accountants, the men who in 1993 had stepped in—out of necessity— to stop the bleeding and save the company from ruin, wresting the power away from a pair of engineers, Bob Stempel and Lloyd Reuss.

Those senior executives who weren't accountants were marketing specialists, mostly recruited by the John Smale, GM's non-executive chairman and the former CEO of consumer products giant Proctor & Gamble.

Even when GM attempted to be courageous and forward-looking in the late 1990s, the resulting products were hopelessly off target. The Pontiac Aztek, a compact sport utility vehicle that debuted in early 2001, was about as unsightly a car as the industry had seen since GM's bulbous Chevrolet Caprice of a decade earlier.

General Motors design had been in a 30-year slump. Not since the 1966 Oldsmobile Toronado had a new GM car won the heartfelt praise of motoring enthusiasts. There were a few minor styling hits along the way—the late 1980s Pontiac Grand Am and the short-lived Pontiac Fiero in 1984. But GM had been systematically out-designed by other carmakers for decades.

The Aztek played a big part in bringing Bob Lutz to General Motors. It was the kind of monstrosity Lutz had castigated the industry for a few months earlier. Yet Wagoner and GM North America boss Ron Zarella, a marketing specialist who had been recruited by Smale from eyeglass maker Bausch & Lomb, both believed in the Aztek. It boasted innovative interior packaging and allegedly "cutting-edge" design. In fact, it looked like "a tape measure housing on wheels," according to one writer.

Wagoner and Zarella believed the Aztek would be the next big thing. They even fast-tracked the car—expedited its development, hoping to get what they thought was an obvious winner to market as soon as possible.

Harsh criticism of the Aztek hastened Zarella's departure from GM in late 2001 and convinced Wagoner to question his own personal taste—it was so obviously out of sync with what North American consumers wanted.

Wagoner resolved to put someone who knew cars into a position of real power. He was untroubled by talk that corporate raider Carl Icahn was eying General Motors. Wagoner knew GM didn't need and wasn't threatened by Icahn; it had proved to Wall Street that it could restore financial discipline. What GM needed was a paranormal product genius. So, in June 2001, Wagoner decided to seek advice from the very man he wished to replicate. He invited Lutz to dinner.

Lutz had retired from Chrysler in the autumn of 1998, just as the DaimlerChrysler merger was being consummated. He had gone out a hero—Detroit's most respected auto man since Iacocca was at the height of his powers. But whereas Iacocca was a man of the people; a folk hero, Lutz was also a hero to the relatively small community of Detroit insiders. Among the town's automotive cognoscenti, he was far more highly esteemed than Iacocca.

Lutz was the ultimate car guy, so deeply devoted to all things automotive that he even spurned Detroit's favorite off-hours pastime—golf. But he wasn't an engineer. The supreme leader of all car guys was a marketing man. Early in his career, Lutz had run the sales-and-marketing operations at Opel and then BMW. But he proved a popular industry axiom: engineers sometimes didn't get it and sometimes couldn't be trusted to have the uncomplicated sensibilities of a pure car lover.

For many engineers, cars were impersonal technical challenges, not living, breathing creatures as Lutz saw them. American chief engineers, with few exceptions, could not have envisioned the Dodge Viper, the first true U.S. muscle car since the 1960s.

Lutz loved cars, but more importantly seemed to understand why others loved them. He had a sixth sense for how regular people reacted to what they saw on the street. It was a knack, like a record producer who couldn't read music, but knew a hit when he heard one. He also had a knack for making the automotive press see things his way.

At 69, Lutz may have seemed over-the-hill to some, but Rick Wagoner thought differently. Sitting in a private dining room at a swank local restaurant, the two men talked at length. Lutz, feeling the anguish of being an outsider, told Wagoner what to do and what not to do—as he had railed at the industry conference a few months before. Finally, Wagoner put forth the idea that he had been toying with for a couple of weeks.

"How do you feel, Bob? Would you be up to joining us?"

Lutz did indeed feel up to it, but he wanted to be more than a paid advisor. He wanted real power—with responsibility for GM's vast product plan—just as he had had at Chrysler. That felt right to Wagoner. The real Bob Lutz would do until the imitation came along.

A few days after Lutz joined General Motors, he wrote a memo that went out to all of the company's senior engineers and designers. Titled "Strongly Held Beliefs," it summarized Lutz's approach to product development—and to design in particular. It amounted to a manifesto on behalf of the corporation's much-maligned designers and engineers.

"As one of you said to me the other day, Design is being 'corporate-criteria-ed' to death," Lutz wrote. "By the time the myriad research-driven 'best-in-class' package, the carryover architecture, the manufacturing wants, the non-stone-chip rocker placement, the carryover sunroof module, and on and on, are loaded in, and the whole thing is given to Design with the words, 'Here, wrap this for us,' the ship sailing toward that dreaded destination, 'Lackluster,' has already left the dock."

Lutz told his engineers: "We don't want anarchy, but we do need more of a 'Who says?' attitude. None of us is infallible. But arguing for what you believe to be the right course is the key to moving forward. In our business, taking no risk is to accept the certainty of long-term failure. Even Aztek, in this sense, is noble!"

From the beginning, Lutz delighted the troops—the engineers and the design staff.

When Lutz came to GM he had been given the chance to climb once more into the cockpit. He was living the dream of every auto executive who, upon retiring at or near the top, took the shocking descent to a life of normalcy they hadn't known in decades.

Many plotted ways to return. Iacocca, von Kuenheim—even the men whose names were on the building, Henry Ford II and Soichiro Honda—could not fully let go. Only Bob Lutz managed to claw all the way back, and three years after he retired. He had been given the greatest gift.

One senior Ford executive said the loss of Lutz hurt more than the departure of Iacocca. "Lutz was a real game changer. I'm worried about all the good people Lutz is attracting to GM. The real impact of Lutz isn't felt today, it will be felt years from now."

CHAPTER THIRTEEN

Consolidation of
the Industry

Jean-Martin Folz had never worked in the car business before joining PSA/Peugeot-Citroën as the company's heir apparent in the spring of 1996. It was an appointment typical of France's auto industry and often the subject of criticism among the cognoscenti, but it also gave French car bosses a unique perspective on the way things were.

When the 50-year-old engineer was named PSA's top man the following year, replacing the flamboyant Jacques Calvet, the industry was the verge of a major shakeup—a sudden lurch into buying and selling and merging of car companies. PSA seemed to be ripe for such a game. It was a likely merger partner for its rival countryman, Renault, or the Italian Fiat—the weak man of Europe—or a rising Japanese company. But Folz soon concluded that mergers and acquisitions weren't right for PSA or the Peugeot family that still controlled the company.

Folz had worked for many different sellers of commodity goods during his career; in his previous job he ran a French sugar conglomerate. Here was a man who understood commodities and didn't believe that an automobile was one. It was a strikingly original position for a non-car guy, trained at France's elite École Polytechnique. Most hadn't counted on Folz to take such a view. But he didn't accept what had become automotive industry doctrine—that by 2000 there would be only about six car groups in the world, and any company not part of those six could not possibly survive.

It was a lesson Folz had learned by studying the career of Eberhard von Kuenheim of BMW, another non-auto man thrust into the leadership of a car company by a controlling family. That the auto industry would inevitably consolidate was the gospel according to Lee Iacocca, conceived more than 20 years earlier. Iacocca envisioned a global auto industry at the beginning of the twenty-first century that was made up of a few giant surviving car manufacturers. He didn't see much of a future for small, independent auto companies. He expected big mergers and buyouts to occur. That, more or less, is what happened.

In fact, Iacocca had not only predicted the outcome, he helped set it in motion. He put the industry on a course that led to the merger mania at the end of the century. Iacocca was long retired when the DaimlerChrysler merger was announced in May 1998, but it was really his deal—he had dreamed it. His vision of the future was a logical extension of the thinking of Henry Ford II, his old boss.

But von Kuenheim at BMW and Soichiro Honda saw things differently. They believed independent auto companies should—and would—survive on the strength of attractive products and superior technology. So did Ferdinand Piëch, who fought to keep his family's Porsche sports-car company independent and made only minor acquisitions during his decade as head of Europe's largest auto group. He never once contemplated the kind of merger Iacocca had long envisioned for Volkswagen and Chrysler. Instead, that kind of vision was left to empire builders like DaimlerChrysler Chairman Jürgen Schrempp.

There were two automotive worlds at the turn of the century. One consisted of groups that had merged or had acquired other companies. The other was made up of companies that had not.

The former represented the philosophy of Iacocca and Henry Ford II and the latter the beliefs of Honda and von Kuenheim. Against all odds and most considered opinion about the future of the industry, the independent companies were winning the day. The healthiest vehicle manufacturers in the world at the end of the century were the ones that had resisted major merger. They were PSA/Peugeot-Citroën, Toyota, Honda, BMW, and Porsche. The companies that jumped impulsively into mergers and acquisitions in the late 1990s were struggling. And their problems mainly resulted from the deals they had done.

Henry Ford II was the incubator of the primal urge to consolidate the automotive industry. He didn't believe small independents could survive because he had watched them fall by the wayside his entire life. In 1952, he had attempted to put Ford's sales back in front of Chevrolet's in the United States by unleashing a price war. During that price war, Hudson, Nash, Packard, and Studebaker were either killed off or merged into oblivion because they couldn't slash prices enough to compete and remain in business as independents.

When Henry II looked around for companies to buy in the 1960s, he considered acquiring Honda. He also had an infatuation with owning fabled European marques. In 1963, he thought he had bought Ferrari. Twenty-five years later, Ford almost acquired Alfa Romeo, only to have Fiat step in at the last moment. He tried to merge Ford of Europe with Fiat in 1985, with Bob Lutz leading the Ford negotiators. Talks dragged on for months before the two sides gave up. And Ford never missed an opportunity to ask von Kuenheim to sell the Bavarian company to him. The year before Henry Ford II died, the Ford Motor Company tried to buy Britain's Rover Group. But a popular outcry against an American takeover caused the deal to collapse. Ford was the market leader in the U.K. and didn't need a popular uprising. A month after Henry died, the Ford Motor Company finally got control of one of his target companies and bought 50 percent of Aston

Martin, the tiny British exotic sports-car company. A year later, Ford made the biggest acquisition in its history when it splurged $2.5 billion on Jaguar.

Henry Ford II had liked Aston Martin's Lagonda sedan. After the agreement with Aston, Ford's wife, Kathy, bought her husband a Bentley, thinking it was a Lagonda, an honest mistake. She bought the wrong car from the wrong company.

Lee Iacocca had a more strategic philosophy about industry consolidation. When it came to mergers and alliances he was a geopolitical thinker. While at Ford in the 1960s, Iacocca wanted the company to acquire Honda. Iacocca felt it was an up-and-coming brand that could guide young buyers into Ford products. The deal would have changed the face of the industry, had he managed to pull it off.

"Several times I've wanted to buy Honda," Iacocca said wistfully late in his career. He had been drawn to the company almost like a moth to a flame, and his fascination for it led to the spat with Henry Ford, which led to the final falling out. Iacocca had even convened a meeting on the subject. He told Henry Ford, Ford's finance director Ed Lundy, and the other powerful Ford finance executives: "I want to buy a toy-car company, and then Schwinn bicycles, and then Honda (which then made mostly motorcycles) so I can get customers from the time they are in kiddie cars up until they are buying Cadillacs." He was voted down. Ford's bureaucrats thought motorcycles were unsafe, and might even be banned. It was a classic Ford-style confrontation between inspiration and straight-line thinking.

But Iacocca's quest for global alliances didn't end there. He became the progenitor of the idea of the global automobile company. Although Iacocca spent his entire career in North America, he was intrigued by the growing international scope of the industry and saw opportunity for taking initiatives within it. Iacocca reasoned that the worldwide auto industry, with its horde of independent companies, many of them propped up by national governments, would consolidate into as few as a half-dozen major players. There would be General Motors; Ford; the Japanese, which he dubbed "Japan, Inc."; a similar "Germany, Inc."; possibly a French-based group; and a couple of companies that would be made up of the rest. Iacocca and Sperlich began to talk seriously about putting together one of the groups. Iacocca saw it as a consortium made up of Chrysler; American Motors, which was then controlled by Renault; one of the lesser Japanese makes; and possibly Volkswagen. It was an intellectual exercise Iacocca could indulge after being dismissed by Ford. Sitting quietly in "Lido's Lounge," the faux bar in his Bloomfield Hills, Michigan, home, Iacocca was thinking strategically.

Here was a guy who had just come from running Ford Motor Company and still had the competitive electrons racing in his brain—and he smelled a whiff of the future. Iacocca had more intellectual horsepower than all the academics studying the future of the auto industry in all the universities throughout the country, combined. He even arranged for his friend John Gutfreund, chairman of the investment bank Salomon Brothers, to research the project. A few months later, when Iacocca became CEO of Chrysler Corporation, he would move one step further toward his master plan for "Global Motors."

One of the first things Iacocca did was to try to arrange a troika with Nissan and Volkswagen. His theory was that a modern carmaker needed U.S. distribution, European technology, and the manufacturing discipline and quality of the Japanese. "It would have been a helluva conglomerate," he once said, "but it didn't work. For one thing, we lost $1 billion in 1979 at the time we were negotiating with Volkswagen. They thought we were going down the tubes."

But Iacocca had in effect forecast the way the industry would go.

In the late 1980s, he predicted, "There should be some consolidation in Europe. France's Renault and Peugeot should be one company.

Volkswagen, Mercedes, BMW, and Porsche could be another one—and a formidable one, I might add."

In the spring of 1981, Iacocca had another idea. He began exploring the possibility of a merger of Ford and Chrysler. He called it "a last ditch plan, an idea that sounded preposterous on the surface, but actually made a lot of sense." Iacocca felt Ford could use the front-wheel-drive K-car platform Chrysler was then developing. He also figured that joining the two companies would provide synergies and efficiencies that would add $1 billion to the bottom line of both companies. That would save Chrysler, and make Ford a genuine No. 2 to General Motors. Iacocca even said he would step aside to avoid a conflict with Henry Ford II—after 12 months. The deal would have almost certainly invited antitrust action, but Iacocca said he had already vetted the deal with some key legislators on Capitol Hill. But the merger never got off the ground. Iacocca's old Ford nemesis, Philip Caldwell, now chairman of Ford, refused to give the idea a serious hearing.

When Renault began to falter in the mid-1980s, Iacocca was by then presiding over a much stronger Chrysler, and he was able to buy American Motors Corporation from the French automaker in 1987. That was the first step in the eventual reconfiguration of the global auto industry. With AMC, Chrysler suddenly had the wherewithal to become a true challenger to General Motors and Ford. And in the process, Iacocca had picked up quite a sweet plum in AMC's Jeep brand.

If there was any auto executive in the world who knew what to do with a brand like Jeep it was Iacocca. In fact, Jeep had always been a central tenet in his Global Motors scheming of nine years earlier. Iacocca felt that the Jeep off-road-vehicle brand represented as strong a consumer brand as Coca-Cola or Disney. So Iacocca focused heavily on Jeep and in the process helped to launch the sport utility vehicle revolution in the United States.

Meanwhile, Iacocca had another great idea. In 1988, Iacocca and Allied Signal Chairman Edward Hennessy talked about mounting a

$40 billion bid for General Motors. This was pure Iacocca bravado, and, as with the Ford-Chrysler merger and several other ideas, he was dead serious. But antitrust problems got in the way. "It would have been easier to buy Greece," he said.

Still, Iacocca had touched off the consolidation frenzy—not only by acquiring American Motors, but by having saved Chrysler and thus preserving a beachhead for Daimler-Benz when the time came. He carried the Ford mentality from mid-century, a religious belief in economies of scale and Henry Ford II's lifelong obsession with being as big as General Motors.

Iacocca's last big dream was to merge Chrysler with Fiat—thereby adding the European operations that Chrysler lacked, but which Ford and GM had aplenty. It was to be his holy grail, the culmination of his years of thinking about global automotive matchmaking. Negotiations with Fiat started in 1989 and carried on for more than a year before collapsing in late 1990. Chrysler's fortunes had begun to ebb again, and the two sides couldn't see eye-to-eye on how to structure the deal.

There was also opposition inside Chrysler. Lutz, Iacocca's No. 2, thought it was a bad idea and would say so to anyone who would listen. He celebrated openly when the negotiations ended. It may even have been that period of opposition that cost Lutz the CEO job. But the consolidation movement was afoot. Within a decade, a chain of events that would lead to the DaimlerChrysler merger would forever alter the landscape of the automotive industry.

The tantalizing May 1998 deal for Chrysler Corporation to merge with Daimler-Benz was the first stage of Lee Iacocca's dream realized, and it electrified every auto executive in the world. CEOs had a sinking feeling that they could easily be left behind and that this could end up as their career epitaph. Daimler-Benz boss Jürgen Schrempp and Chrysler Chairman Bob Eaton—Iacocca's successor—had pulled a fast one on the rest of the automotive world. And once Schrempp had Chrysler, he immediately looked to acquire a Japanese automaker—just as Iacocca had prescribed. While Schrempp's minions wrestled with the practical details of bringing Daimler-Benz and Chrysler together, he pursued Nissan.

Negotiations between Daimler-Chrysler and Nissan carried on for almost a year, and Schrempp was finally voted down by his own board in March 1999. Within days, Nissan had another partner—the same Renault that nine years earlier had sold American Motors. The French company had recovered nicely in the interim without the burden of AMC.

Takeover fever remained intense. After failing to acquire Nissan, DaimlerChrysler went recklessly into a far less prudent deal in early 2000—control of the troubled Mitsubishi Motors.

Ford meanwhile bought Rover's Land Rover division, which most industry executives considered the only worthwhile part of the Rover group, which BMW lost patience with and happily sold. The Rover passenger-car business was cut loose and went to an independent management buy-out with little hope of long-term survival. Fiat, which had been struggling for a decade, was next in line for acquisition by DaimlerChrysler. Although the deal seemed inevitable, Fiat patriarch Gianni Agnelli ultimately decided not to sell to Schrempp and the Germans.

Agnelli was comfortable with General Motors as an alliance partner, however. GM feared being left out of the consolidation sweepstakes and in 2000 bought 20 percent of Fiat's automotive division. GM also saddled itself with a "put option," an agreement that Fiat's owners could use some day to force GM to buy the entire company. In the meantime, Ford had acquired Volvo Car Corporation from the Volvo Group in 1999, leaving BMW and Porsche as Europe's only independent brands. From the view of 2004, only the Renault-Nissan deal had worked out as planned. Indeed, under the sure hand of Carlos Ghosn, the deal worked out so well that the recovered Nissan grew in value many times greater than that of its parent company, Renault.

Meanwhile, Schrempp's "Welt AG," the German version of "Global Motors," had turned into a value-destruction machine. Chrysler was underperforming in the highly competitive North American market, and Mitsubishi was losing out in Japan. In April 2004, DaimlerChrysler decided it would invest no more money in Mitsubishi and soon after sold its 10 percent stake in South Korea's Hyundai Motor Company. Iacocca's vision as executed by Jürgen Schrempp had failed.

Jacques Nasser, the Ford CEO who had engineered the takeover of Volvo and Land Rover, was long gone by that time. Most critics felt that Nasser had lost sight of Ford's basic business while acquiring other companies, such as Kwikfit, the tire and exhaust business in the U.K., which cost $1.6 billion. Meanwhile, other problems cropped up at Ford's newly combined companies. For one thing, no one really knew how to manage the multiple brands that were being piled up in groups. Ford threw Volvo and Land Rover into a new division with Aston Martin, Jaguar, and Lincoln, presuming that there would be synergies.

The first instinct of the new multiple-brand owners was to protect them—to resist putting Jaguar parts in Volvos or Land Rover parts in the Lincoln Navigator. But if you couldn't capitalize on the economies to be gained from platform and parts sharing, where were the synergies? Soon the entire Premier Automotive Group was struggling. Jaguar had only begun to turn the corner in the mid-1990s when things went sour again. In 2002, Jaguar lost $500 million. Jaguar's X-type— targeted to compete against BMW's 3 series—was failing in part because the car-buying public understood that the small Jaguar was largely based on the less-expensive Ford Mondeo. Platform and parts sharing between the Mondeo and the X-type was just the kind of economy of scale that mergers and acquisitions were supposed to deliver. But at Jaguar it was hurting acceptance of the X-type.

And Volvo, the strongest Ford acquisition, was chafing as it tried to maintain a degree of independence within the Ford world. After its failed merger with Renault in the early-1990s, Volvo sought other partners to give it financial muscle, so it welcomed Ford's 1999 bid. But the Ford and Volvo business cultures were at odds. "Volvo is unbelievably overstaffed compared with Ford," said a Ford insider in 2003. "They are making money, but it's not a very good return on investment."

A frustrated Volvo official countered, "We just don't have enough people to feed them. They may know how to run a Ford company, but they don't know how to run a Volvo company."

Volvo's Swedish ways were nothing like the Whiz Kids–inspired U.S. military–style executive hierarchy at Ford. "We have a different business climate in Sweden," said a former Volvo official. "It's not so hierarchic. People are more open to debate and question things a lot further down the line and deeper into the organization. There's a very strong empowerment of the way people act, take decisions, and implement decisions."

There was a culture clash at DaimlerChrysler, too. American and German executives had trouble getting along. The new partners didn't do many things in the same way, and the differences threatened to undermine the giant merger. The Germans were irked by the Americans' unstructured style, while Americans thought the Germans were too rigid and formal. But the differences were sometimes more than just a matter of style. "Each side thought its components or methods were the best," said a senior product-development executive in Stuttgart.

An early example was when German and American engineers discussed the production costs of a Mercedes-Benz E-class seat in 1999. "They told us that the Chrysler 300M seat cost a fraction of the price and that we should use either Chrysler seat components or come up with suggestions on how to reduce the cost of our seat significantly," said a Mercedes-Benz designer. "Our engineers were completely beside themselves. Then our benchmarking department acquired a 300M seat and stripped it down." The Mercedes specialists were appalled by what they found. "The seat did not meet any Mercedes-Benz standards," said the designer. "If we purchased this kind of seat component we would refuse to pay more than half of what the Americans pay their suppliers."

What had been billed as a "merger of equals" quickly became an outright takeover by the Germans. The top American managers were soon cleared out. That led to a thinning of Mercedes top management—a typical problem for the newly consolidated groups. Mercedes sent two of its top executives to Chrysler: Dieter Zetsche and Wolfgang Bernhard. It then sent several more to Mitsubishi. Similarly, Ford began dispatching manufacturing and marketing specialists to Land Rover and Volvo. Renault Chairman Louis Schweitzer transferred some of his finest young executives to Nissan, including his very best—operations chief Carlos Ghosn. Still, the inevitability of industry consolidation was unchallenged. Those who argued against it—men like Jean-Martin Folz of PSA, Porsche AG patriarch Ferry Porsche, and the disciples of Soichiro Honda were drowned out.

Folz could not see why his two brands, Automobiles Peugeot and Automobiles Citroën, would have to be absorbed into a larger group or merged with Renault or Fiat or be acquired by DaimlerChrysler or any of a number of other scenarios put forward. Analysts thought Folz was kidding himself. Nine months after he took over as CEO, Daimler-Benz merged with Chrysler. That's the way the industry was going. But Peugeot had been down that road before. It acquired Citroën in the late 1960s and absorbed Chrysler's European operations in the early 1980s. The two deals had almost killed Peugeot and left bitter memories inside the company. It took several years for the combined Peugeot-Citroën to right itself.

Indeed, by the early 2000s, PSA was the hottest carmaker in Europe. In the first four years of the decade, it gained four points of market share, the largest rise of any single brand since Ford of Europe under Bob Lutz in the late 1970s.

So it was. At the turn of the century, the most successful auto companies in the world were the independent ones, the ones that had sidestepped the consolidation frenzy. BMW was a cash-generating juggernaut, and tiny Porsche boasted the highest profit margins in the world. In Japan, the most successful companies, Toyota and Honda, were also the ones that had avoided merger entanglements. Ford and DaimlerChrysler, which tangled itself up whenever possible, struggled. General Motors bought a 20 percent stake in Fiat Auto in 2000, regretted it regularly as Fiat piled up the losses, but sat out most of the acquisition game. GM began to have one of its most successful stretches in decades. In fact, for a while, GM's only concern was Fiat.

As soon as Lee Iacocca felt flush again at Chrysler—some time in 1985—he called von Kuenheim. "Don't sell without talking to me first," he told von Kuenheim, conscious that Ford and GM would both give their eyeteeth for ownership.

The Quandts wouldn't sell BMW, but by the early 1990s they did, however, begin to feel the uncontrollable urge to merge. Honda had a minority stake in Rover Group and had been supplying the British company with vehicle platforms and engines. But true to the philosophy of Soichiro Honda—and a commitment made to Rover's owner, British Aerospace—Honda vowed never to seek outright ownership of the company unless Rover wanted to be taken over. Thus Honda Chairman Nobuhiko Kawamoto was stunned and deeply angered when BMW abruptly acquired Rover from British Aerospace in January 1994 without so much as a reference to him.

BMW had bought the company without Honda having a chance to match the bid. BMW had refused to be acquired, but it was ready to run another company—or so it thought. In the end, BMW's seven-year stewardship of Rover cost nearly $5 billion. The BMW brand itself remained strong though, and almost immediately after unloading Rover in 2000, BMW was back. Its sales and profits rose dramatically. There were seven automakers around the world larger than BMW in

2004, but none stronger. Archrival Mercedes-Benz continued to rake in profits, but much of it was needed to underwrite losses at Chrysler and Mitsubishi.

Porsche went into serious decline in the late 1980s. The dollar had weakened against the deutsche mark—undercutting sales volume and profits in the company's crucial United States market. An American named Peter Schutz was Porsche's CEO at the time. When Ferry Porsche asked Schutz in 1988 what to do if the company's fortunes declined further, the CEO replied, "Then you should sell the company." Ferry was disappointed and hurt.

Ferdinand Piëch, Ferry's nephew, decided to increase his influence, and the two decided that Schutz had to be fired for even suggesting that the company be sold. Porsche, the world's smallest global automaker, recovered in the 1990s. It zoomed to the top of the profitability pyramid by mid-decade, just four years after it seemed ready to collapse. Such transformations can happen in the auto industry—and do regularly.

While striving to keep his family's company independent, Piëch went on a small buying spree of his own as chairman of Volkswagen AG in the 1990s. He acquired Rolls-Royce Motor Cars, but he could retain only the Bentley brand because BMW bought the Rolls-Royce name in a separate deal with British aerospace giant Rolls-Royce plc. He also bought Italy's Ferrari-chaser, Lamborghini, just as he had bought the remnants of the Bugatti brand in 1998, but he resisted any broad mergers or acquisitions for Volkswagen. Having achieved strong brand acceptance in the U.S., Japan, and China, there was little imperative to buy market entry, and the access to a cheap labor supply had been achieved with the fire-sale purchase of both Skoda in the Czech Republic and SEAT in Spain.

Piëch's addition of Lamborghini to the supercar stable was effectively picking up an Iacocca castoff. The Chrysler chairman snatched up the morsel as a dessert course to the 1987 main meal of American

Motors. Lamborghini's executives of the day came to see it more as a lifestyle decision by the flamboyant American rather than a sound business deal. The flavor to his $25-million purchase came when this son of Italian immigrants immediately bought a Tuscan vineyard and enrolled in Italian language school.

David Jolliffe and Tony Willard in their 2004 book, *Lamborghini— Forty Years* wrote: "Chrysler's failure to deliver the promise it offered to Lamborghini, its workforce, owners and other enthusiasts was lamentable." Bob Eaton, when running Chrysler, knew that after seven years of chaos, the investment was a lost cause and sold Lamborghini to a financial consortium in 1994. Piëch came calling four years later.

The companies that remained independent meanwhile were rolling out hit cars and trucks and accumulating the extra profits per unit that dwarfed the savings derived from common platforms.

This was the philosophical dividing line in the early part of the twenty-first century—whether to adopt the philosophy of Iacocca, Henry Ford II, and the Whiz Kids by relying on economies of scale and back-office synergies to lower costs, or follow von Kuenheim's and Honda's focus on individual enterprise.

But as things stood, the five main independents sold more cars at higher transaction prices, returned greater shareholder value, cooked up more engineering innovations, invented and succeeded with more new vehicle concepts, and built greater brand loyalty than the merger-burdened heavyweights. Maximizing synergies and merging dissimilar corporate cultures took so many resources and so much energy that the heavyweights had little left over for forward-thinking creativity. Except for the several independents, the automotive industry's great push for consolidation has been killing much of the entrepreneurship and uniqueness that have been the lifeblood of the business since its inception.

Saab is a good example. A few weeks after losing Jaguar to Ford in 1988, General Motors acquired the small Swedish carmaker. Saab had been one of the brightest success stories of the 1980s—stumbling onto a rich clientele in the American market, and pushing its sales up to 48,000 in 1987 before the collapse of the dollar against European currencies caused sales to reverse.

Saab, the aircraft maker, began building cars in Sweden soon after World War II, experimenting with design concepts, squeaking by in the 1950s and 1960s, then hitting on something big in the 1970s with its turbocharged engines.

By the 1980s, Saab was not far behind BMW in U.S. sales, having built a brand identity that was powerful, but not easy to explain—certainly not by GM executives, anyway. At his first press conference after GM bought 50 percent and assumed management control of Saab, the new American CEO, David Herman, was stumped when a Swedish reporter asked him to describe Saab's brand character. In fact, GM spent the next 12 years trying to define Saab and develop cars that would allow the company to sell more than the mere 120,000 it sold in 1987, but has not topped since. The old Saab hands in Sweden complained about the way things had unfolded under GM. Saab cars had become less distinctive, and many believed Saab would have been better off on its own all those years.

The problem was the industry's relentless drive to own, to think of cars in the way Ford Whiz Kid Bob McNamara did—as commodities to be "costed-out" and number-crunched. This drive to own has resulted in the trivialization of the automobile and of the new wave of principles to arrive in the industry at the turn or the century. It took ex–sugar salesman Jean-Martin Folz to recognize it for what it was.

CHAPTER FOURTEEN

The Power of Youth

T he power of youth got things moving again after World War
II. The men who built the modern business did so in large
measure because of their high threshold for risk. And chief
among the risks they accepted was handing responsibility to men who
were young and impatient and unrepentant—men like themselves.

They shifted the natural order of things by moving away from the
emphasis on seniority that had begun to dominate European and
American corporate practice in the two decades before World War II.
The global demographic upheaval created new opportunities for businessmen who understood the fresh dynamics of the era. Men with
young eyes and ears figured things out first. They were far less disoriented by the great mid-century trauma of war. Most of industrial Japan
stuck to its pre-war age-based hierarchy. The notable exception was the
still juvenile Honda Motor Company, the motorcycle upstart that official Japan didn't need, didn't want, and wouldn't help.

The six men believed in meritocracy—the virtue of talent, the
notion of having the best and most qualified person in every job. Each
had handled massive responsibility at a young age and so had done
their part to pull down the age barriers in the auto industry. Henry

Ford II was 27 when he took command and control of his grandfather's company. Soichiro Honda ran his own successful mechanical repair shop in Hamamatsu, Japan, when he was 22, and a successful automotive supplier when he was just over 30. When he started his new company out of the rubble of the war, Honda was forced to rely on inexperienced men.

Later, the Honda company was a redoubt for young misfits who wanted to advance fast or who simply felt the need to involve themselves in something out of the ordinary, such as race-car engineering or overseas marketing or dreamy research. They didn't want to rise slowly with the waves of contemporaries at Toyota or Nissan. Some had nowhere else to turn because their educational pedigree left no place for them in Japan's industrial mainstream. But most who went to work for Soichiro Honda did so because of the things they burned to do—and could do nowhere else. It was the same thing that drove young Americans in the 1980s to the computer start-ups that reworked the American economy rather than enlist in established corporations with their hierarchies and career waiting periods.

Soichiro Honda retained a lifelong belief in the passion of youth, though as he grew older, the young lions in his company would challenge and disturb—just as the young lions of Ford would challenge the aging Henry Ford II, and the young turks at Chrysler challenged Lee Iacocca. At Honda, it happened as the company became established and began to attract the kind of elite educated engineers who had shunned the company in its early years.

Youth took precedence for all six men because they were all hungry—hungry for success, impatient for change. By accident and design, each created youth cultures in their companies. Youth equaled energy and power. Age was lethargy and power.

Ferdinand Piëch assembled rebel bands of young engineers and technicians and test drivers at Porsche in the 1960s and Audi in the 1970s. Bob Lutz was 30 before he entered the auto industry. He graduated late from high school and then spent nine years as a fighter pilot in the U.S. Marine Corps. But after joining General Motors in 1963 he was impatient for action. He barrel-rolled through a succession of jobs and companies—GM's Adam Opel AG in Europe, then BMW, then Ford.

CEOs under age 50 were as unconventional in post-war Germany as they were in Japan. Yet in 1970, Herbert Quandt installed 41-year-old Eberhard von Kuenheim as head of BMW. Von Kuenheim's chief rival, sales-and-marketing boss Paul Hahnemann, dismissed the new man as an "apprentice." Von Kuenheim began to surround himself with even younger executives—so much so that it upset his colleagues on the BMW management board. Lutz, for one, thought von Kuenheim spent too much time consulting his twenty-something staff.

Lutz felt von Kuenheim was circumventing him and his counterparts on the board. He suspected that von Kuenheim saw him as a rival. But long after Lutz had left BMW, von Kuenheim kept his method of working with an eager and ambitious young staff. Not only did von Kuenheim empower his fledgling experts, his kitchen cabinet as some called it, he drew strength from them. The young *assistanten* came from Germany's best business schools. Most came from good German families, too, as von Kuenheim had. Meeting every Monday morning with his aides-de-camp, von Kuenheim felt he could keep close tabs on the inner workings of BMW. And it was from these ranks of brilliant young lieutenants that Wolfgang Reitzle and Bernd Pischetsrieder emerged, as well as several other young executives who would dominate the European auto industry years later.

Wolfgang Reitzle, engineer extraordinaire, was the shining example of von Kuenheim's BMW youth movement. He was the wunderkind of German industry in the 1980s. He dazzled the boss with his analyses of the model lineup at a time when BMW was going through something of a product-identity crisis. He had all the impatience of youth and displayed the kind of energy von Kuenheim felt BMW needed.

The early responsibility handed to the six men set them apart from everyone else. It endowed them with a sense or purpose and mission and destiny. Iacocca set an exact schedule for his rise up the Ford corporate ladder. He kept a chart of dates on his bedside table showing when he thought he was due to reach another rung on the corporate ladder, according to Peter Wyden in *The Unknown Iacocca*. He felt thwarted when he became a Ford vice president after his 36th birthday, not at 35, the deadline he had set.

In a giant industry in which success was usually parceled out in small doses, in which executives took small steps up the corporate ladder, Honda, Ford, Iacocca, von Kuenheim, Lutz, and Piëch had power bequeathed to them early. They brought with them, in their orbits, other capable young men, creating new talent pools in old organizations. That led to conflicts and inner turmoil with older, established executives, but it also unleashed tremendous tension and energy. The youth cultures created the kind of natural conflict that Soichiro Honda had predicted and, in fact, counted on. There were other young guns in the post-war auto industry, men like John DeLorean of General Motors. But whereas DeLorean's youthful striving at GM was beaten out of him by the Kremlin-like organization, the youth culture Henry Ford II had created at Ford allowed DeLorean's counterpart and contemporary—Lee Iacocca—to thrive. Iacocca was 47 when he was named president of Ford. At the same age, DeLorean was about to be booted out by the graybeards at GM.

Much later, Iacocca's Chrysler turnaround team included finance wizards in their 30s who put together the company's loan guarantee package and then got it approved by the United States government. Honda's youth culture was the most striking of all. When Honda retired in the fall of 1973, he named Kiyoshi Kawashima president at

47, a mere pup by Japanese CEO standards. In Japan, company directors were rarely under 50.

At Honda, youthful responsibility was part of the plan from the beginning—completely against the grain of the typical Japanese company—then and now. In 1981, the average age of the project team that developed the Japanese-market Honda City was 27. Soichiro Honda knew that the tension that arose from the gap between generations was a source of power, much like one of his engines, and he was bright enough to harness it. He once said, "Youngsters will think that things must be changed and the older generation will be critical of young people, always. The generation gap is nothing to be surprised at. It is only too natural that there exist insurmountable differences between the two." This was radical thinking in Japan. But it was the lifeblood of the Honda Motor Company and the key to its uniqueness.

The men who led Honda's company in the 1980s and 1990s—the ones who had learned at the feet of the founder—sometimes being chewed up, sometimes being gently encouraged—were a different breed from their counterparts at the other Japanese automakers. You could even see it in their faces. They were more animated, less guarded, less formal, funnier. Each was somehow boyish, as Soichiro Honda had been. It never left them. Men like Irimajiri and Nobuhiko Kawamoto and Yoshihide Munekuni and Hiroyuki Yoshino always grinned—even late in their careers when they felt the great weight of supreme responsibility. As they aged, they never forgot their youth.

"Titles and age were of very little importance to Mr. Honda," said Susan Insley, a senior vice president of Honda of America Manufacturing in Marysville, Ohio. "That was a big influence at Honda. At a meeting any subordinate could rise and say something." It was no coincidence that Honda's products—beginning with its Super Cub in 1958—became connected with young consumers, especially in the United States. Indeed, Honda's youth power in the early 1960s was the lubricant that gave it immediate name recognition as a carmaker.

Soichiro Honda knew all of this instinctively because he had never really had a boss. He had never been part of a hierarchy. His words were doctrine.

"One thing I never say is, 'Young people nowadays. . . .' After all, the same thing was said about me when I was young. The younger generations are naturally more advanced. Although I already have reached the age of having to think of the landing of my life, a person gets a better feeling when he is pulling back on the control stick to lift the airplane. What I am trying to do is to help the younger people fly safely. So my message to young people is this: 'Have your own purpose in life, hold your control stick tight, and fly high.'"

Honda may have been thinking of his final "landing," but he never seemed to age. Dave Nelson, Honda of America's purchasing boss from 1987 through 1997, remembers playing golf with the great man at the famous Oakland Hills Golf Club in Birmingham, Michigan, in 1986. Honda was 80. The company's Japanese executives had expected that getting their leader on the course would be a snap. But at the hallowed Oakland Hills—the home of the famous 1951 U.S. Open and the 2004 Ryder Cup matches—the club management calmly informed the Japanese men that the famous industrialist would have to find a member to host him if he wanted to play a round at Oakland Hills.

The call went out among Honda's American organization. "They called me at home because they figured if anyone knew a member it would be a purchasing guy," said Nelson. Nelson called his friends Bruce Brown, the head of sales and marketing at Goodyear, and Ron Cutler, head of sales at TRW, both of whom were members.

Two foursomes went off the first tee on a miserable day of rain and wind. "He had perseverance," remembers Nelson. "It was cold and windy and he was 80 and he was frail. He was out there swinging and swinging. He beat me, although he didn't always hit from where his ball landed. Let's just say he bent the rules a little. But it was the most impressive thing I've ever seen. He enjoyed it so much. He didn't slow down. He was serious about the golf, but was funny about everything else. It was all in Japanese and sometimes the translation was not so funny—but he was popping off and cracking jokes all the way."

The first wave of Japanese executives Honda sent to America to launch manufacturing operations in Ohio in the 1980s had been many of the same bright young men Soichiro Honda had cultivated at Honda R&D in the 1960s. They had all worked on the racing programs and were members of the small task force of young engineers who developed the low-emission, high-efficiency CVCC engine. The engineers called themselves the "all-or-nothing" team. In the 1980s, they regaled the Americans new to Honda with tales of the man whose name was on the building. "They loved to tell the stories, and we heard all of them," said Nelson. "They were all the leaders of all the key teams as young men—racing, CVCC."

In particular they heard the story about Shoichiro Irimajiri being booted around the R&D offices by Mr. Honda in 1965 after his design mistake had forced Honda out of the British Grand Prix. "I remember Iri telling us that Mr. Honda was a fireball, a complete fireball," said Insley. "Mr. Honda told Iri: 'I hate college graduates. They think everything is in a book.' Iri told that story to all the young graduates in the 1980s. It was meant to convey a lesson. All of them, Iri, Yoshino, would tell the stories. Mr. Honda had a temper, but they loved him and admired him."

Irimajiri graduated in 1963 from the prestigious Tokyo University College of Engineering, the MIT of Japan, and he was one of the first engineers from an elite school to join Honda. He had worked on the racing teams and the Clean Automobile Engine project. In the 1980s the company chose Irimajiri to be president of Honda of America Manufacturing, setting up the first Japanese auto assembly plant in the United States, in Marysville, Ohio. He was the shining star of his generation of Honda engineers

"My dream in childhood was to design jet fighters," said Irimajiri. "I went to Tokyo University and studied aeronautical engineering, and I enjoyed it. But at the end of university I found that we could not develop a jet fighter by ourselves in Japan because of the conditions that Japanese industry had to obey. I was very disappointed. I needed to find something similar." Only Honda, Yamaha, and Suzuki among Japanese motorcycle manufacturers were involved in racing at the time, and Honda was making a big push.

"I read in 1961 or 1962 that Honda had won a Grand Prix motorcycle race, and that excited me," Irimajiri said. The young engineer might have ended up at Toyota or Nissan, but he was deeply impressed by some of the engineers he met at Honda. One was Yoshio Nakamura, who controlled Honda's Formula One racing team in the 1960s. Another was Akira Sono, a 1961 graduate of Tokyo University, who worked for Honda R&D. "So, instead of designing jet fighters, I decided to go Honda to develop racing machines."

There was another enticement for an adventurous young graduate of Tokyo University who didn't want to follow the traditional slow-going Japanese career path. "I was informed that Mr. Honda was a very, very extraordinary person," he said. "That's why I joined Honda." But the first time he met Honda, about a month after entering the company, Irimajiri was unimpressed.

"He was small and looked like an ordinary person. I expected him to be very, very special looking, and he was not. But his eyesight was very sharp, and he was very energetic."

Two years after starting at Honda, Irimajiri incurred the wrath of the founder. Irimajiri was on the racing team, and to his surprise he discovered that Soichiro Honda was not some Olympian figure whose name was on the building but who was otherwise invisible to the company's workers.

"Although I was just a young engineer, Mr. Honda constantly would look over my shoulder and ask me questions about my drawings.

'What is this?' and 'What is your intention for this drawing?' he would ask. Although he had no formal training, he immediately would point out defects in my design. He would comment, 'It looks too weak' or 'that looks too heavy.' While in the beginning I'd think he was mistaken, after I recalculated I'd find out that he was right," Irimajiri said.

Each week during the Grand Prix racing season, Irimajiri had to prepare a new engine for competition. During the British Grand Prix disaster, the Honda car was sidelined with a burned piston. After the loss, the engine was sent back to Honda R&D for study, and Soichiro Honda personally supervised the teardown of the engine.

"Who designed this burned piston?" he barked. Irimajiri admitted that he had. Honda ordered the young engineer to bring him the original drawing for the piston and the one depicting his own alteration. Irimajiri laid out the drawings, and Honda began to review them. Honda quickly spotted changes that Irimajiri made to the racing pistons. "Why did you make these changes?" he asked the engineer.

Irimajiri answered that he had been able to substantially reduce the weight of the piston. "I believed my design was carefully backed up by various calculations and evaluations of past data," Irimajiri said. "So I confidently explained my theory to him—and he exploded."

Honda screamed at Irimajiri, "Who do you think you're talking to? I designed and made that! And I have years of experience in the piston manufacturing business." Irimajiri tried to respond while Honda grew angrier by the minute, yelling, "You! Stupid! No wonder the piston gets burned. You have changed the thickness here." Irimajiri argued back. He claimed that his design change had nothing to do with the overheating, which sent Honda through the roof.

The boss had an explosive temper, but the incident had its roots in Iri's youthful arrogance. "I had graduated from a first-rate university and was told that Mr. Honda had graduated only from elementary school. I thought I needed to educate Mr. Honda, and so I would talk to him about theory."

The older man would have none of it.

"If you think college academics are everything, you are totally wrong," Honda told Irimajiri. "You will be useless here at Honda unless you spend more time being on the spot for many years to come." Irimajiri was forced, burned-out piston in hand, to apologize for his mistake to every person in the machining and casting shops who had worked on the part. Honda followed him around the Honda R&D offices as he said he was sorry.

The anecdote has often been told inside Honda with a kind of light all's-well-that-ends-well spin. But it was a serious moment—not only in the career of the young man but in the life of the older man. Soichiro Honda had wanted Irimajiri fired.

"He definitely said, 'You have to retire from the company,'" Irimajiri said. "He said, 'You have to leave this company.' But I had great confidence that I would do a good job for this company. I was not nervous, and I rejected the idea of quitting."

The aging Honda had always been bombastic and was given to dramatic flashes of anger. But he was beginning to show signs of age—of irritation and impatience with his young staff, not unlike the late-career behavior of Henry Ford II and Iacocca and Piëch. Honda was becoming set in his ways. The challenge by Irimajiri, the well-schooled engineer who had questioned one of the company's basic engine designs, was a landmark occasion.

"He said several times that I had to leave, and I said I would not," said Irimajiri. "He called my boss, the head of Honda R&D, and said, 'fire this guy.' But my boss was so nice and he had had lots of experience with that kind of thing. He said to Mr. Honda, 'Wait a minute. I'll talk to him.'" Irimajiri survived the firestorm of abuse. He had nearly been sacrificed on behalf of all young stallions who would later challenge the supremacy of the founder on more important matters. "Mr. Honda would get so angry and say lots of dirty words. But when he calmed down he began to recover his confidence in young people, and he started to give more power to young engineers." It was a turning point for Honda and his company and its attitude about younger staff.

The Clean Automobile Engine team that Irimajiri joined a few years later was led by the 39-year-old Tadashi Kume. The all-or-nothing team seemed to work around the clock, fully immersed in the job of developing a low-emissions powerplant. The group also included future Honda president Nobuhiko Kawamoto; Yasuhiro Sato, who would eventually lead a major Japanese auto supplier; Hiroyuki Yoshino, who replaced Irimajiri in Ohio and would later become Honda's president; and Takeo Fukui, another future Honda CEO.

Irimajiri was named head of the project, and in 1973 was sent to Dearborn with a small team of still younger Japanese engineers to go to work in Ford's powertrain labs. Irimajiri and his men stayed for half a year. Their job was to convert the Ford's 5.7-liter powerplant into a CVCC engine. One day in Dearborn, Irimajiri was called in by the general manager of the Ford tech center and asked if he had a Japanese flag. "I was told that Mr. Honda was coming to visit Mr. Iacocca." The flag was needed for a welcome ceremony. While in Dearborn, Honda went to see his CVCC project team, which was installed at the E.E.E. building in Ford's engineering complex. "I remember when Mr. Honda came to our office most of the top executives of Ford were surrounding him," Irimajiri said. "But he broke away and came up to me and said: 'You are working hard on the CVCC project.' I said yes. He said it was a big job, and then he asked all of us: 'Do you need some money?' And we said yes, and he gave us all $100 traveler's checks. He just signed them over.

"He had lots of interest in the CVCC project. It was one of the most important issues for him. There was a lot of competition to meet the Muskie law—two-stroke, diesel, powercharger, thermal reactor, lean burn, catalytic converter, direct injection, gas turbine. Everybody was working to find which system was best for the future.

"Because of his nature he had a huge, huge personal interest in investigating all of those engine systems. I still strongly remember the rotary engine from Mazda. That performance shocked the consumer. It was very powerful and very small. By using a heat reactor with the rotary some thought it might be possible to meet the Muskie regulations. Even Honda had a lot of engineers, including me, who thought we needed to test the rotary engine.

"But Mr. Honda was very clear. He said the shape of the combustion chamber of the rotary engines was such that the engineers couldn't continue to improve fuel consumption. It was a very clear statement. I didn't know if it was true or not. I was 32 or 33 years old. But 10 or 20 years later I found that Mr. Honda was right. He could sense the future," Irimajiri said.

In the late 1960s, Irimajiri had been co-project leader on a plan for developing an air-cooled engine.

"That was a product of Mr. Honda's dream of an air-cooled passenger-car engine," he said. "The concept was weight savings. He thought that even a water-cooled engine must be cooled with air from radiator. So why do you need water? Why not cool the engine directly by the air. That was his theory.

"There were lots of air-cooled engines in the world, but they were noisy. His theory was that you needed to speed up air flow by making a high-pressure fan or duct.

"We found we could develop a high performance air-cooled engine, but all the materials, the rubber gaskets and such, needed to be very, very expensive because they had to survive. So the engine was very expensive, and it wasn't feasible. The company had already decided to mass produce that kind of engine, and we lost lots of money selling that kind of car."

Meanwhile, Honda's air-cooled H1300 coupe had been a failure in the marketplace, and when Mr. Honda insisted on air cooling for what would become the CVCC engine, his young engineers, led by Kume, rebelled.

"There was a huge argument," said Irimajiri. "Why did we have to develop and manufacture that kind of very expensive engine? It was not a technical issue, it was a business issue." Kume was so enraged by Honda's obstinacy that he quit the company. Many years later, after he had become president of the company, Kume invited several Honda of America executives to a tea ceremony at his home in Tokyo. He told them all the story of how he left the company in anger. Kume said that after he walked out he kept expecting someone at Honda R&D to call him back. He thought it would take a couple of days or maybe a week. But three months went by and no one called. Finally, Kume wandered back, cap in hand.

Meanwhile, Takeo Fujisawa, Soichiro's longtime partner and the head of all non-technical operations in the company, tried to change Honda's mind about air cooling. Fujisawa came to the young engineers and told them to make a detailed study of why the H1300 failed to make money. "At the end of the day the conclusion was very simple," said Irimajiri. "The car was a business failure because the H1300 was air-cooled.

"So the conclusion was very clear. We had to change our strategy. To make a real business success, a water-cooled [engine] was much more adequate. The younger engineers made a very persuasive argument."

Soichiro Honda finally gave in. It was a turning point for the company. "Mr. Honda had been too strong," said Irimajiri. "He had been coordinating all the initiatives of the company, and it was very hard to guide the company."

Soichiro Honda had lost the debate with the younger generation. He was shamed enough to decide to retire as president of the company he had built—but only after the water-cooled CVCC engine project was completed. He was 67 years old and still had lots of energy and ideas. But he would yield to the youth movement in his company. "Honda CEOs did not stay until their 70s or 80s," said Susan Insley. "They always retired early. That was the pattern that Honda-san set. That was his lead. They took a step back."

If Mr. Honda had stayed another 10 or 15 years, the next generation would have been discouraged. There would have been a knock-on effect. The young Honda managers of the 1980s would not have been in control, and it would have been a much different company, not quite the one that took the world by storm.

Insley remembers the Honda she worked for in the 1980s and early 1990s was very, very young in age and in spirit.

"The greatest gift Mr. Honda gave was his philosophy," she said. "It permeated every Honda division, every office, every plant in every country. He wanted to give back to society."

Kume, who quit in anger and then came back to become president of the company, saw the episode as a crucible for Honda and his company. "If young people don't rebel against their seniors there is no progress," he said.

Twenty-seven-year-old Henry Ford II surrounded himself with a slew of young World War II officers who quickly and energetically righted the chaotic Ford Motor Company. And it was the Whiz Kids who gave the old family firm a shot of enthusiasm and adrenalin, but they were pretty full of themselves. They were good, and they knew it, and they poked their noses into every aspect of Ford company life. One of the most prominent Whiz Kids, Jack Reith, remarked at a meeting with several veteran executives: "In my 13 months in the auto business," he said, "I have never seen anything like this."

Iacocca was the youngest vice president in Ford history, and he brought with him a cadre of gifted contemporaries. Iacocca understood the changing American demographics and was eager to exploit the trend of giving responsibility to and empowering younger staff and management.

Iacocca's longtime associate Hal Sperlich once recalled: "Kennedy was president. A young president. It was like youth was taking over. Iacocca brought a youthful energy and perspective in a world that was starting to go youthful. I was the car guy, the product-planning type, and he and I immediately hooked up because he wanted very badly to make his mark with some new product. So he turned to me, and that's how the Mustang happened."

One of Iacocca's first acts was to set up a marketing team to study the shifting age population trends in the country and make recommendations about what that meant for the car business. Soon Iacocca and his generation of sales and product specialists delivered the Mustang to a waiting American youth market. The first Mustang was built on March 9, 1964, and it was an immediate hit.

In 1985, Iacocca was flush with personal success and feeling just this side of infallible. One thing he decided during those robust economy years—between the recessions that began and ended the decade in America—was that cash-rich Chrysler could move upscale by building a classy car together with his old friend, Maserati chieftain Alejandro De Tomaso. They would build a car called the Chrysler TC by Maserati.

Iacocca was a brilliant marketing strategist, though sometimes in an old-fashioned way. He resorted to badge engineering or using famous names to perfume a product that wasn't very noble. He once took a Mercury Monarch and made it into a Lincoln Versailles by festooning it with a padded-vinyl and snakeskin-grain body side molding. But he was a great schemer and always exhorted the troops to achieve more with less. It was what he had done as a young man with the Mustang.

The Chrysler TC by Maserati was going to change the way the world looked at Chrysler, Iacocca thought. It would be designed and built by Maserati in Italy, using Chrysler mechanicals—basically a LeBaron convertible platform. When Lutz arrived from Ford in 1985, the project was in the product program, fully funded, but was heavily delayed because of serious problems in Italy. Lutz and Iacocca's other side men, including Gerry Greenwald and Hal Sperlich, were recommending that the project be dropped.

But Iacocca wouldn't have it. He thought this was a masterful chess move, Chrysler linking up with a famous Italian name. The car was going to be great. "The most beautiful thing to come from Italy since my mother," Iacocca said.

The Maserati episode was to become Iacocca's salutary lesson. Just as Honda had to fire a loyal and trustworthy colleague before admitting that the successful instincts of youth had deserted him, Iacocca too needed a difficult lesson.

While Iacocca saw a beautiful new Italian sports car, the world saw the Maserati for exactly what it was, a LeBaron convertible with the useful section—the rear seats—cut out of the middle and with different front and rear end styling. The whole thing had been put together with what could only be called marginal quality. The assembler, De Tomaso, was not one of the world's great car builders when it came to quality and reliability. So the car became a hopeless flop in America. And it cost some people their careers, like poor Joe Campana, Chrysler's overweight sales and marketing boss. Campana was in charge of the Chrysler brand, which included the Chrysler TC by Maserati, and he was under huge pressure to sell the things. The cars had finally started coming off the boat in droves, and the first dozen or so went really well at charity auctions and among the Hollywood Rat Pack and other Friends of Lee.

But after that, things got tough. Joe Campana did what he had to do. He gave away $5,000 per car to get the dealers to take them, and the dealers passed the savings on to the customer. Inevitably, about a month later, some friend of Iacocca called and said, "Hey, Lee you told me this thing was going to be hotter than a two-dollar pistol and that people would be standing in line for them, but an acquaintance of mine just bought one, same one as mine, and he told me the dealer gave him $5,000 off. What's going on here?" Iacocca got Joe Campana into his office and said, "I just had this call from this guy. What the hell is the truth?" And Joe broke down and said, "Lee, I didn't know how to tell you, but we can't move these things, so I've been trying quietly to get them into the market with some discounts." Iacocca went ballistic. He called Lutz in and ordered him to "get rid of Campana." That was the end of Campana's career. But it was also an epiphany for Iacocca. He seemed to sense that he no longer had the knack, and he was the kind of guy who had always lived off his knack.

Iacocca met twice with Soichiro Honda in the two years after Honda retired. He wanted to understand why a man would ease off the throttle at an age when he still had energy and ability and ambition. But Honda had left the company in the hands of younger people and would simply preside as the "supreme advisor" over the empire he founded. Iacocca seemed to come to a similar conclusion. He would become "supreme advisor" of Chrysler, the company he had saved. By doing so, Iacocca allowed the Lutz-led Chrysler miracle of the late 1980s and early 1990s to occur.

Lutz remembers: "He never said it, it was never anything said overtly. He never called me and said, 'Hey maybe I don't get it anymore. It was just all of a sudden he just stepped into the background and let the combination of Tom Gale, François Castaing, and myself basically run the product program."

For Honda and Iacocca, bowing out was among the most difficult and crucial decisions of their careers. But to preserve energy and imagination in their companies, they had to let go. And as a final testament to their greatness, they did. Henry Ford II also knew when it was time for him to leave. In his post retirement-interview with Ford historian David Lewis, Ford said: "I had to get out. I didn't have any choice. I had to get out. I was dragging. I was not doing anybody any good, including myself."

Soichiro Honda held on to the energy of youth long after he left day-to-day responsibility behind. He spent three days at Honda's Ohio factories in 1989, when he came to America to be installed in the Automotive Hall of Fame. Hiroyuki Yoshino was in charge of the Ohio factory at the time. "It was the only time I ever saw Yoshino worried," said Susan Insley. "He was worried about how to control Honda. We couldn't keep him in the golf cart as they drove him around the plant. He wanted to shake hands with everyone. A man who was 80 signed autographs for everyone—on thousands of Honda hats. He shook hands with thousands and thousands of associates."

Bob Simcox, one of the auto plant managers, finally remarked to the old man, "Mr. Honda, you have so much energy and enthusiasm."

Honda told him, "That is my job. I must inspire my people—and it should be your job too."

CHAPTER FIFTEEN

Unstoppable Globalization

B MW shifted into hyperdrive when Eberhard von Kuenheim took control of the company in 1970 and gave it an international focus. "We were very provincial," said von Kuenheim. "We were not a European company, we were not even a German company. We were a Bavarian company."

For better or worse, von Kuenheim, Henry Ford II, and Soichiro Honda, in their different ways, were responsible for the internationalism of the automobile industry at the end of the twentieth century. Because of them—late in the century—auto companies and their executives began to think and act globally, though sometimes to their considerable detriment. If nothing else, the three men proved that internationalism was more than a program initiative, it was a talent. Each conceived of an automotive world without borders—but none more so than Soichiro Honda, and none was more successful than Honda.

The Ford Motor Company already had a footprint around the world when Henry II took over in 1945. The original Henry Ford had seen to that. But the company was not managed as a global organization. Henry II came to believe that the far-flung elements of his empire

257

had to think and act as one, though he first needed to get the assorted Ford duchies in Europe to pull together first.

With help from a young Bob Lutz, von Kuenheim recast the provincial BMW as a worldwide exporter that owned and controlled its national distributors around the globe. In that way, it became the first automaker to have a tight rein on the management of its brand in every corner of the world. But Soichiro Honda came to internationalism in a different way. His company was tiny and all but shut out of Japanese industrial society. He needed the rest of the world so he could survive.

Honda had no right to think his company could succeed in foreign lands. But he plunged his firm into America and Europe and throughout the rest of Asia, starting with motorcycles, and following up a decade or so later with cars. And he did it with more than just marketing chutzpah, he did it with technology and true enterprise. The Honda name became as far-reaching as the great American consumer brands—Coca-Cola and McDonald's and Kodak and Ford. Iacocca's Global Motors was the intellectual underpinning of the DaimlerChrysler merger and thus the current shape of the industry. But that idea, too, came from Soichiro Honda. Not because Honda was buying and merging companies, but because Iacocca observed in Honda the possibilities of global partnerships. Iacocca knew that a Japanese company such as Honda had much to offer an American company such as Ford. Soichiro Honda inspired others inside the Ford Motor Company to try to create cars that would appeal to drivers everywhere—and save hundreds of millions of dollars in development costs in the process. That was the Ford bean counters' idea of a world car.

Soichiro Honda had a different idea. He thought of the diversity of the world's drivers first and the business synergies second. Honda and his company created the world's second world car after the Volkswagen Beetle—the 1975 Civic. Ford spent the next 25 years trying to build and sell a world car of its own, setting off on some quixotic adventures in the process. Mr. Honda was seeking a global market, while the Ford finance team was looking for a wider area over which to spread costs. The Honda way succeeded. Ford's way failed. When Soichiro Honda declared in 1954 that he wanted his little motorcycle manufacturer to be a global company, he was partly mimicking the actions of his hero, Henry Ford I. The first Henry Ford was not only selling cars in Europe a few years after starting his company, he was building them there, too. Honda wanted his company to exist outside the borders of Japan. It was partly because he was a visionary and partly because his young company had no other choice.

The Honda Motor Company was unwelcome at home in Japan— where the established companies were pampered and protected by the country's Ministry of Trade and Industry. Honda had to find its own way, like an orphan, surviving on street smarts. The same thing happened all over again in the early 1960s, when Honda decided he wanted to produce automobiles, too. He had to investigate opportunities in world markets.

When Honda emerged as the most respected car brand in America in the mid-1980s, people in Japan could hardly believe it. Honda was a fine middle-of-the-pack brand in the domestic market. But in Tokyo it was difficult to comprehend how successful the little company was becoming overseas. It was like Americans who enjoyed Jerry Lewis but couldn't understand why he was such a show business legend in France. Soichiro Honda always took a global approach to his company.

The company's international doctrine was put forth in 1954. Even though this little company was in Japan, it's founder's vision knew no geographic boundaries. Mr. Honda said the company's headquarters should not be in Japan, but in a satellite hovering over the earth. Cedrick Shimo, former vice president of Honda International Trading, Inc., told author Robert Shook that survival absolutely depends on

259

global thinking. Late entry into the automobile industry made it difficult to compete against the already established automobile manufacturers in Japan.

"We had no choice but to look at the entire world as our marketplace, and it was this thinking that motivated us to establish a manufacturing plant in the United States." Not only did Soichiro Honda want his company selling cars outside Japan, he boldly proclaimed in the 1960s that he wanted to make a world car—a car that would appeal to car buyers in countries anywhere in the world. It was more than an idle boast, or brave talk. It was a dedication to a cause not unlike Honda's fanciful prediction in 1954 that a Honda motorcycle would someday win the Tourist Trophy motorcycle race on the Isle of Man.

To achieve the world car, Honda did something the auto men of Detroit and Stuttgart and Paris and Wolfsburg and Turin never thought of doing before. He sent his staff out in the wide world to find out what drivers in foreign lands wanted and needed in a car.

The little Honda company succeeded as an exporter because its executives never thought of it as exporting. Soichiro Honda saw the world as one large domestic market.

Honda put together two groups of engineers who crisscrossed the globe, studying how people interacted with their vehicles. One team focused on the United States and the other on Europe. Teams of engineers from Honda R&D spent over a year in foreign countries, paying close attention not only to the cars being built and sold overseas, but to the local road networks and the size of parking spaces at European houses and American shopping centers. They studied the effect of traffic roundabouts in France; the long stretches of straight, flat driving in America; the autobahn speeds of Germany; and the twisty country lanes of England.

They wanted to know how fast Germans drove and how much British drivers used the brakes. They wanted to know how Americans and Italians packed their families into their cars.

Years of study were poured into the first true Honda automobile—
the first world car—the Civic.

Ford's world-car strivings partly grew out of the fact that the
company always needed to do more with less. It never had the kind of
resources that General Motors could command. But it also had a
brand—the blue Ford oval—that was recognized everywhere in the
world—in Europe and Asia as well as North America. General
Motors didn't have that. It seemed only logical that Ford should build
blue-oval-badged cars that could appeal to customers everywhere.
That made some sense to Henry Ford II, one of American industry's
true globalists to emerge from World War II, and it made spectacular
sense to the studious young finance men Henry II hired soon after
the war.

But until the example of Soichiro Honda in the 1970s, Ford didn't
know how to proceed. In the late 1950s, Ford executive Robert
McNamara saw the beauty of the business case for cars that sold in
multiple markets. He had planned to bring Ford of Germany's
Cardinal to the United States in the early 1960s and launch it into the
American small-car wars. Lee Iacocca killed the plan seemingly within
minutes after McNamara left Ford to become U.S. defense secretary in
the autumn of 1960.

The cramped little Cardinal was all wrong for America, Iacocca
decided. Still, some Ford cars from England had made their way to
American shores. In the cornfields of Ohio, you can still find English-
made Ford Anglias from the 1950s. Ford's North American operations
had considered building Ford of Europe's 1976 Fiesta, the company's
first front-wheel-drive car, in the United States, too. Iacocca, by then
president of the company, was on board this time and contributed
his short-lived Honda engine idea. In later years, Ford tried repeat-
edly to develop a true world car. The 1980 Escort for Europe shared
a name and an approximate size with the Escort launched almost
simultaneously in America. It was supposed to have been a shared

world-car platform, but the two Escorts literally wound up sharing almost nothing.

That failure to find any commonality was regarded as a failure of will inside Ford. Throughout the mid-1980s, Ford's executives kept trying. Or at least they kept theorizing about cars that would service both America and Europe. Ford expected the second-generation Taurus mid-sized sedan in 1992 to be built on the same platform as the new European Scorpio sedan. But that world-car project was dropped because the European and American product planners couldn't agree on the key elements of a single car. For one thing, the Europeans wanted rear-wheel drive and the Americans by then demanded front-wheel drive.

One world car did get built—as its name suggests. Ford spent over $6 billion to bring out the successor to Lutz's mid-sized European Sierra—the 1992 Mondeo. The platform was also used to manufacture the Ford Contour and Mercury Mystique derivatives for the United States. The Mondeo fared OK in Europe, but the U.S. cars were disappointing sellers. Interior dimensions that suited Europeans perfectly left Americans feeling pinched.

Ford devised other world-car programs on paper. It was a business theory, something the Whiz Kids would have forced through if it had been at all possible. In fact, it was the young managers who learned at the feet of the Whiz Kids who later in their careers sponsored one world-car concept after another at Ford in the 1980s and 1990s. Those projects didn't come from the product-development teams or the metal-moving guys—the Iacocca gang and its descendents. They came from the business analysts and the theoreticians.

"Why couldn't Ford do what Honda did?" the bean counters asked. It was after sitting with Honda in 1975 in Tokyo that Lee Iacocca dreamed up Global Motors. But his idea was about European, American, and Japanese companies banding together, not world cars. He had pushed for a front-wheel-drive Fiesta for the United States, but didn't really believe you could mass-produce one car for the world. History, by and large, proved him right. And he learned it firsthand when he tried to turn Chrysler's American minivan into a global vehicle in the 1980s and 1990s.

Bob Lutz had something of a world-car craving himself when he was at Ford. While in charge of Ford of Europe, he wanted to get his European Sierra into the U.S. market—at least the high-performance version of the car. The Sierra arrived in the United States in 1985 as the Merkur XR4Ti, a hot turbocharged version of the basic medium-range Sierra with two outrageous spoilers. Lutz had a feeling for world cars. He had been partly responsible for the globalization of one of the most global brands of all at BMW. The Merkur XR4Ti and the Merkur Scorpio that followed were attempts by Ford to cash in on the German import sensation that BMW inspired in the United States in the 1980s. But the two cars were marketed half-heartedly in America and lasted only a short while.

Years later, after following Iacocca to Chrysler, Lutz had another go at a world car. He very nearly succeeded against all odds.

Lutz was convinced that he could build in the United States a small car that would steal some market share from Japanese companies around the world, including in Japan. He poured Honda methodology into the project, using a Honda-style platform team and Honda-style simplicity. The car was Chrysler's 1994 Neon, and it was to be Lutz's grand finale in the small-car world. He had already returned Honda's and Toyota's fire in the mid-sized sedan wars with his 1992 LH twins, the Chrysler Concorde and Dodge Intrepid. Now it was time to do it in the subcompact segment. This time he was going to teach Toyota and Honda about cost, about sensible engineering of cars.

Chrysler had spent $1.3 billion and 31 months developing the Neon as a high-volume import-fighter, and gave it a splashy $80-million marketing sendoff in January 1994. It was an immediate hit in the United States. But how would it do overseas against Japanese competition? In the end, it didn't have much impact in the European and Japanese markets. It is very difficult to turn independently owned retail networks into a humming distribution machine for a single car from an unproven provider in a distant land.

Once again, uninspired marketing was at least partly to blame. But the Neon was the most successful Big Three effort in the subcompact segment in the United States since the subcompact segment got its name. And it frightened the Japanese, especially Toyota. Toyota engineers couldn't wait to get its hand on Lutz's small car in the spring of 1994. When they did, they tore it down bolt by bolt in Japan to see what made the subcompact so economical to build. Along with their suppliers, they picked over the Neon's carcass at a special presentation on April 25, 1994 at Toyota's corporate headquarters complex in Toyota City. Then, after taking their close-up look, they sat down and wrote engineering critiques that soon saw the light of day. They said the Neon reflected a level of manufacturing savvy and designed-in cost savings that was "unprecedented" for an American car.

But in a put-down reminiscent of what Big Three engineers were saying about Japanese cars in the 1970s, the Toyota engineers said the Neon matched the quality and fit and finish of a first-stage Toyota prototype—a car still several stages away from production and far from ready for the marketplace. The Neon "got by with the minimum level of quality," according to the Toyota findings. The thoroughness of Toyota's critique of the Neon had not been seen at Toyota City since the company's engineers tore down several Mercedes models in the 1980s while developing the Lexus LS 400.

At the supplier *tenji kai*, or "autopsy," thousands of disassembled Neon parts were laid out for inspection in a large exhibition hall. Executives and engineers from the 240 companies invited—often as many as three representatives from a single company—walked through, stopping to make notes or consult with Toyota engineers.

The idea was for suppliers to find out things for themselves, to touch and feel, rather than sitting through a seminar at which Toyota told them its conclusions. However, such an event was rare at Toyota. "They look at a lot of cars, but they don't turn every one into a study session," said a supplier executive at the time. "The Neon was deemed to be of enough interest to do it. After all, this was the Japan-fighter."

Toyota's review was not an entirely negative indictment of the Neon. The main feature of Lutz's car was its cost competitiveness, according to the Toyota examiners. "Japanese car manufacturers tend to use the highest quality for all parts," the report said. "The fact that the Neon can get away with the minimum is good." Toyota engineers lavished praise on the Neon for its overall simplification, the integration of components, the purchasing of full systems from single sources, and the reduction in the number of parts. They cited the extensive use of plastic in areas such as the engine bay and transmission and the wide use of low-cost steel.

"The drastically simplified parts structure is evident from the beginning of the design," Toyota noted. Lutz's engineers were complimented for finding several ways to reduce machining and paint-processing steps, such as a simplified system for punching holes in sheet metal from one side only, rather than from multiple angles. The analysis praised the wisdom of not painting the muffler, front bumper reinforcement, fuel tank, and metal fuel-tank band.

Indeed, not painting things that people don't see was considered a stroke of brilliance. Chrysler didn't paint the Neon's gas tank, while at Toyota all fuel tanks—even on the smallest car, the Starlet—got a coat of anti-corrosion paint. "In a large way, this was a matter of realizing that 'Hey, there may be a simpler way of doing things, an easier way,'" said a Japanese parts-company executive who took part in the tenji kai. "If the item is non-functional and nobody sees it, then maybe we don't need the usual Toyota method. It can be a way to cut costs."

But as Toyota engineers tore apart Chrysler's Neon small car, they also damned it with faint praise. The low-cost sedan, which sold for $10,000 to $14,000, was cleverly designed, nicely styled, and attractively priced—but the Japanese engineers emphatically concluded that the Neon's quality was not up to Toyota's standards. And they claimed that inadequate power in high gear in cars equipped with automatic transmission was a level of performance "not sufficient for a 2.0-liter car." They recorded excessive vibration and engine noise, inadequate braking power according to Toyota's standards, and varying paint thicknesses from hood to skirt.

Nissan President Yoshifumi Tsuji said at the time that Nissan was learning several lessons from the Neon. He called it a clever example of how to reduce costs by better design. "We have a lot to learn on reducing parts," Tsuji said. "Where we would have five parts to make up a component, the Neon has three. Where we would use five bolts, the Neon body side was designed so cleverly, it needs only three bolts. They have done an excellent job." But it was not all praise from the Nissan president. "In some parts, they took a risky approach in terms of body protection and quality durability," said Tsuji. "We don't want to imitate that." Chrysler executives thought that Toyota and other Japanese automakers were so worried by Neon that they're trying to poison public perception of it.

Lutz's right-hand man, François Castaing, Chrysler's vice president of vehicle engineering said at the time: "Why would Toyota leak something like that? If your cars are overpriced, because they are over cost, and you are trying to explain to your dealers why you are losing your competitiveness, well, the easy way out for them is to imply that their standard is right, and everybody else's is substandard."

Neon sales were running so strong that Chrysler had delayed adding a two-door Neon so it could catch up on orders for four-door models. And for the first time, the Japanese were taking a Detroit car and benchmarking it and saying maybe this is the car they should imitate.

Chrysler executives admitted that the engine was noisy and that the Neon got two coats of paint compared to three on Toyota models. But they said they used corrosion-resistant galvanized steel and dipped the body in a phosphate bath for additional protection before painting. So only two coats of paint were needed, helping keep Neon's price down. And Chrysler disputed Toyota's claim that the Neon had weak brakes. They noted that every car sold had to meet a federal standard to assure consumers of the security of good brakes.

Lutz went ballistic when the benchmarking critique was published. "It is hardly news that Toyota, Nissan and Honda, et al., do not like the Neon," he wrote at the time in a letter to the editor of *Automotive News.* "Toyota has now, perhaps inadvertently, joined the other two in taking public swipes at our vehicle. "Why? Because it is the first serious, visible, highly acclaimed and highly successful small-car challenge to the Japanese. It demonstrates that, given a sharply focused product vision and teamwork both within the company and with outside suppliers, the United States can compete with the best in the world.

"Further, the Japanese industry, and Toyota in particular, are faced with monumental cost pressures, partly exchange-rate induced, but partly due to what Toyota itself refers to as 'wasteful quality,' i.e., the over-engineering and over-specifying that the customer never sees, never feels, and never experiences in any way except in the price he or she pays for the vehicle.

"Messrs. Eiji and Tatsuro Toyoda (the brothers who ran Toyota) have stated publicly that cost reduction must now be pursued with the same vigor as that applied to quality improvement in the prior decade. And they are absolutely right. Small wonder, then, that the Neon gets benchmarked. The Neon is exactly what the market wants: high real quality in the things that matter, great styling, superb performance, roominess, safety and . . . low price. Small wonder, furthermore, that alarmed competitors say, "Nice, but . . . " to buy time until they can work their own costs down. That will probably have to await the next new-product generation."

Ten years later, Lutz seemed no less perturbed that Toyota had leaked criticism of his car. "That was pretty outrageous," he recalled. "It is not usual that a competitor will tear down a vehicle and then sort of call in the press and say you can't believe what a piece of crap this is. However, they did it, and that did not help obviously.

"Unquestionably, Toyota learned stuff from tearing down our vehicle. Everybody approaches the tradeoffs a little bit differently. No company is so smart that it gets all of it right all of the time."

Honda included. But its first foray into U.S. manufacturing was pretty much as good as it could be. It was the first Japanese company to build a car assembly plant in the United States. In 1978, it had started by building a motorcycle plant in Marysville, Ohio. It opened its car factory in Marysville in 1982. And the car factory was pure Honda resourcefulness and enterprise.

"It was a very new experience for everybody at Honda," said Shoichiro Irimajiri, who was head of Honda of America Manufacturing from 1984 until 1989. "We thought it was the only way for us at Honda in America to survive, to be successful."

Before it launched its U.S. car factory, Honda studied the international operations of companies around the world once again. "To do the best in the United States we learned about the history of companies worldwide which had succeeded or failed in their international operations," said Irimajiri. The conclusion was that Honda's American manufacturing operations had to be a virtually freestanding operation—a local company rather than merely an extension of Honda in Japan.

"To be a real world company we had to create a kind of independent power in the United States," he said. "If the U.S. had to rely on the Japanese operations forever it would fail. From the beginning of my career in the States, we were very clear we were going to be an independent, self-reliant company. We knew we needed to sell 500,000 to one million units. We needed parts suppliers' assistance. We needed R&D. We needed an engine production plant. That was the ultimate goal. It was for us a simple operation."

The Marysville factory was built long after Soichiro Honda retired, but the founder played a major role in the decision to assemble cars in the United States. "He was retired but was kind of a symbolic figure," said Irimajiri. Every critical decision was reported to him."

Almost every Japanese carmaker followed Honda in building cars in North America. First Nissan, then Toyota, Mitsubishi, Subaru, Isuzu, and Suzuki. By 2004, almost four million cars were built by Japanese companies in America. Eventually the German prestige brands came, too—von Kuenheim's BMW first, and then Mercedes. BMW wasn't the first German automaker to build an assembly plant in America when it set up in Spartanburg, South Carolina, in the mid-1990s, however. Volkswagen had built a plant in Westmoreland, Pennsylvania, 20 years earlier. But it was the first time a Germany luxury brand had done so.

That Honda was first of the Japanese to build a U.S. plant should have surprised no one. Honda was first with everything—with a clean-engine program, a luxury-car division, and collaborative supplier relations. Whatever it was, Honda would get there first—and globalism was no exception. Honda's view of the world kept evolving, so while Ford kept trying to build world cars, Honda had reversed course. By the early 1990s, the Accord models for Europe and the United States were designed for their local markets. So was the Civic. The cars were close in size and concept, but they weren't built on the same platforms. This approach was an aspect of Honda's method of globalization that Ford and others had missed altogether. Honda had begun tailoring cars for local markets because the companies had studied the local markets so closely. In 1994, Ford launched Ford 2000—its concept of centralized management of global operations. In so doing, Ford was mimicking an outdated form of Honda internationalism.

By 1994, Honda had retained enough commonality to save a little money on its multi-national cars, but the precise differences in styling, performance, and vehicle dynamics had to be fitted to individual markets. This is why Irimajiri believed so strongly in the independence of his American operations in Ohio.

The recession of the early 1990s set the auto industry off on a Honda-inspired global wild-goose chase. Going international was believed to be the key to efficiency and to sidestepping national economic downturns. But the auto world had misunderstood Honda and its global push. Indeed, when the global recession came to an end, many of the misguided strategies to which it gave rise did not. In the recession, auto companies learned discipline. They got leaner and began hoarding cash. They also got tough with suppliers. Some adopted brutal tactics learned from Inaki Lopez, the former General Motors and Volkswagen purchasing boss.

The Lopez squeeze on suppliers—the antithesis of Soichiro Honda's and Eberhard von Kuenheim's beliefs and practices—hurt quality at GM and VW, both of which employed him, and eventually limited the performance of each company. But the worst idea that came out of the slump was the decision to go global at any cost. Hit hard at home, car groups sought shelter from downturns by spreading out geographically. They rushed into emerging markets on the theory that mature markets cycle up and down while new markets go up forever.

The mid-1990s were years of sheer expansionism, of setting up plants and partnerships in faraway places. Yet most global forays either failed miserably or were at best disappointing. Even worse, they centralized distant empires to create one-stop global management. Neither idea worked. Emerging markets were more volatile than mature markets. And being global just meant carmakers had nowhere to hide. The modern world has one economy. Everything was connected. North America, Europe, and Asia couldn't be quarantined.

270

Groups such as DaimlerChrysler, with its new association with Mitsubishi, got hit in three places worldwide, not just one, when markets lapsed in the early 2000s.

Sales of Fiat's Project 178 world car—the Palio family of vehicles aimed at the world's emerging markets—were about half of what Fiat hoped for. The Palio's markets collapsed soon after the strategy unfolded.

Executives from Mercedes-Benz and Chrysler crisscrossed Asia in the mid-1990s looking for partners. Years later, they had little or nothing to show for all those air miles. Meanwhile, the new global management structures caused companies to lose customer focus. In 1995, Ford of Europe's inward-looking organization was dismantled in the name of Ford 2000—doing more damage in about 18 months of neglect than the company was able to undo in five years. Ford 2000 was the most prominent global strategy, though GM also organized for world conquest.

GM's international focus led to a couple of moderately successful manufacturing joint ventures in Asia and Eastern Europe. But the company diverted resources from Germany—its most important non–U.S. market, a mistake from which it took several years to recover. Ford fell asleep in Europe during that time. "The (Renault) Twingo was a wake-up call for us," said then–Ford CEO Jacques Nasser in 1996 when he introduced the Kia.

After that, Ford has had a number of wake-up calls in Europe: the Renault Scenic small minivan and the rise of the diesel engine to name but two. Decision makers were in Dearborn, and they were busy thinking globally, not locally. PSA/Peugeot-Citroën and Renault came out of the recession of the 1990s with a different focus. They couldn't afford to go global, so they went local—and listened more closely to their customers. They picked up the market share that Ford and GM lost in Europe.

Why did those global strategies fail?

By the turn of the twenty-first century, the auto industry was outgrowing its world-car phase. The signs were everywhere. General Motors had put Europe in charge of developing the platform on which the next Opel/Vauxhall Astra would be based. Ford had changed its worldwide "small- and medium-vehicle center" *in* Europe into a product-development center *for* Europe.

"We missed not having a hand on the pulse," said David Thursfield, who had taken over in 2000 as the new president of Ford of Europe. DaimlerChrysler needed a new small-car strategy because the Neon flopped outside North America.

Mid-market cars had to be developed where they were sold. You couldn't send teams from Germany into the United States to help Americans design European derivatives. You couldn't turn a European car into an American car by simply installing a cup holder and an automatic shifter. You couldn't transform an American car into a European car by retrofitting diesels. You couldn't "tune" cars to local tastes. You couldn't put a regional hat on them. America was full of crossover vehicles that wouldn't cross over the Atlantic. What was cozy in Europe was cramped in America. Good packaging in America was a waste of space in Europe. Flexible seating in Europe was impractical in the U.S. Europe's refined V-6 power left Americans hungry for more oomph.

There were vast differences between the European and North American markets. That was why Ford lost its way in Europe in the 1990s and why Fiat, Peugeot, Renault, and Rover withdrew from the North American market. It was why VW collapsed in the U.S. just as its Golf was redefining the middle of the market in Europe.

A difference of tastes in Europe and North America was the reason the new Beetle conquered America but was a mere curiosity in Europe. Volkswagen's three-box Jetta outsold the Golf hatchback by seven-to-one in the U.S., while in Europe it was the exact opposite. Minivan sales, a fixture in America, peaked at a little over 300,000 in Europe. Compact minivans emerged instead. GM's Calibra sports coupe completely crushed Ford's Probe in Europe. The Probe was designed and built in the U.S.—that was why.

The evidence was everywhere. Other examples of European/North American differences in automotive tastes include:

• Wolfgang Reitzle cancelled plans to sell the Lincoln in Europe almost immediately after joining Ford from BMW in 1999.

• Mercedes-Benz's U.S. executives fought hard to keep the A-class small car out of America.

• Lexus was a minor factor in Europe.

• Nissan's Infiniti luxury brand didn't exist in Europe.

• Citroën didn't exist in the U.S.

• Nissan could sell its upscale Maximas in America, but not in Europe.

• Ford's Scorpio and Sierra failed as German luxury imports in America in the 1980s.

• Each new effort to sell Cadillacs and Chevrolets in Europe came to nothing.

• Omega-based Cateras looked sad on Cadillac dealer lots in America.

• GM's Opel Vectra floundered in the U.S. as did the Saturn SL in Europe.

But inward-looking product strategies succeeded. Ford designed the huge Expedition SUV for the American heartland. Renault created the Scenic for the cities and villages of Europe. And there was no other way to do it. Global cars forced compromises—the one thing modern customers will not accept.

CHAPTER SIXTEEN

Reitzle: Seventh Out of Six

I t wasn't always such a good idea to be sucked into the orbit of the top men. Many young executives of extraordinary potential allowed themselves to be drawn close to the center of power, only to be thrown out for minor or imagined sins, or simply to prove the authority of absolute power.

A prime example—very possibly the prime example in the recent history of the auto industry—was Dr. Wolfgang Reitzle, who found himself caught in the vortex of both von Kuenheim and Piëch. Those experiences were formative and destructive in equal measure. Together, they derailed the career of a brilliant young executive who was the natural successor to his two German countrymen.

Had Reitzle found the strength or encouragement to stay at Ford and move up from the Premier Auto Group to the main game, he would have found himself in the interesting position of competing head to head with the very senior man in charge of product strategy at General Motors, that graduate of the BMW management school, Bob Lutz.

For more than a decade, a time when BMW was in ascension, Reitzle was second only to von Kuenheim in importance at the Four

Cylinder Tower. Reitzle was portrayed to be a boy genius, and he was. Reitzle was a wizard, a conjurer of classic cars. With his Errol Flynn moustache and Italian suits, he was a dashing, charismatic figure whose potential seemed limitless. Like Lutz, Wolfgang Reitzle was born to be the chief executive of an auto company. And like Lutz, the only kind of company he would run as CEO was a supplier—a supplier on the fringes of the industry at that. In 2002, at age 53, Reitzle finally became the boss, but at a company that made forklifts, not fashionable cars.

After leaving the Ford Motor Company's Premier Automotive Group—the holding company for Ford's array of prestige vehicle brands—Reitzle returned to Germany to head Linde AG. It was more than a little sad. Both von Kuenheim and Piëch were to blame for the end of his career in cars. In 1990, when Reitzle was 41, there seemed little doubt that he would become chairman of BMW's management board three years hence, when von Kuenheim was scheduled to retire. The only possible challenger was BMW's crafty finance director, Volker Doppelfeld. Still, it had to be Reitzle, the sharpest young mind in the car business.

He was born in Ulm, Germany, in 1949 on the border of Bavaria and Baden-Württemberg and joined BMW in 1976. Reitzle was a manufacturing engineer straight out of Munich Technical University, and he was at BMW during the company's transformation from a wobbly Mercedes pretender to the world's purest automotive brand. Reitzle had much to do with the transformation. But he never got the big payoff—the top job at BMW. Although he became known as a product ace, he spent the early part of his career reconfiguring the way BMW built cars. He introduced new methods to improve quality and efficiency, including designing and running the company's first pilot assembly lines to prepare new models for production. His roots were in manufacturing and tooling, which helped cement an early bond with von Kuenheim, the machine-tool man. But Reitzle's personal flamboyance could not have been more different from von Kuenheim's sense of proper presentation. Reitzle's choice of suits alone managed to create a whole look for the company.

At any major auto show in the late 1980s and early 1990s, the men from Munich were more stylishly dressed than their counterparts at other companies. At VW they favored checked sports coats. At Mercedes they wore mostly conservatively cut blue suits. The Brits favored London banker pinstripes. But the BMW executives often wore shiny gray, sharply lapelled, narrow-waisted, double-breasted suits that looked as sleek as BMW cars. Partly it was von Kuenheim's sense of a unified corporate culture, but mostly it was a reflection of Reitzle's own fashion sense. He had substance to go with his style and was astoundingly vigorous, a bundle of nervous energy, his eyes ever darting, his hands always in motion—lighting a cigarette, signaling an underling, drawing a diagram to explain a concept. Reitzle always seemed impatient and distracted, yet had a knack for never making others feel marginal. He seemed able to listen intently to several people at once. He was a man of action, never stopping.

During late-night business dinners at restaurants, Reitzle would frequently reach for his cell phone and call a secretary or an assistant to issue some instruction for the following morning, or possibly order them to drive to the office, pick up a document, and bring it to the restaurant so he could use it to make a point. He was also a golf fanatic, rare for a German. One of the great moments of Reitzle's life was being admitted as a member to the Augusta National Golf Club in Augusta, Georgia, home of the Masters tournament. Acceptance as a member depended not on his high BMW position or his close friendship with two-time Masters champion Bernhard Langer, but just on his being Wolfgang Reitzle, a star in his own heaven. He recalled the day the letter from Augusta National arrived at his office in Munich informing him that he was in. Reitzle was afraid to open it. What if they had turned him down?

His career moved at a breathtaking pace in the 1980s. His first appearance on the global stage was the 1986 introduction of the newest BMW 7 series. Armies of press were flown in from around the world to see and drive the new big BMW. A cocksure 37-year-old Reitzle stood in front of them and talked extemporaneously about the car for which he had led the development. It was the kind of self-assurance that had dazzled those inside BMW for years. Speaking English with a high-pitched, clipped Bavarian accent, he conveyed such boyish enthusiasm that he almost overshadowed the car. Reitzle, like Bob Lutz, took a holistic approach to the auto industry. He could discuss the power of the brand as well as any consumer marketing guru, and he could talk about fabrication techniques, machine repair, quality checking, and materials ordering. He was famous for being able to drive a prototype a short distance and tell the chassis engineers what was wrong with the suspension and handling and spell out precise fixes.

And did Reitzle know style. He would round up his team and take them to fashion shows in Milan, drumming a culture of creativity into his designers and engineers. Reitzle was a product of the BMW system, of von Kuenheim's system, which was established to chase Mercedes-Benz and respond to the technology challenge of Ferdinand Piëch at Audi. And he was a strategic business thinker, who in the end proved to be right about BMW's misguided decision to buy Rover and its equally mistaken decision to take a hands-off role in running it. Von Kuenheim talked endlessly about *comment,* the French word that means "how," but was used by von Kuenheim to signify how BMW people should comport themselves. He was always saying that something "didn't fit to the *comment,*" says a former BMW manager. But Reitzle got away with being different.

"Reitzle and von Kuenheim were completely, completely different," said a colleague. Reitzle's golf obsession didn't fit von Kuenheim's idea of BMW. And Reitzle was far more publicly visible than von

Kuenheim. But von Kuenheim knew the young executive was tremendously valuable to BMW, so Reitzle got special treatment.

If there were ever two men destined to wind up as heads of great automobile companies, they were Lutz and Reitzle. It's hard to imagine how much pain they must have felt when they were both passed over in 1992. No two individuals ever possessed so much raw talent, yet failed to parlay it into the CEO's office. "Sometimes now I think it happened all for the best," says Lutz. "The things I would have had to do to become CEO. It was not me." These two live wires had influence at the beginning and the end of von Kuenheim's career. What Lutz had helped to start under von Kuenheim in 1972, Reitzle helped put the finishing touches on 15 years later.

Early fast trackers in the auto industry burn out, not because their talent expires, but because they are so good so early and rise so fast that they don't acquire the requisite corporate political skills they need later on. There is something about great men that works against them in the social system that's part of a modern auto corporation. Both Lutz and Reitzle skipped through the early part of their careers so speedily that they didn't learn how to bend to anyone else's will. And both Lutz and Reitzle tended to intimidate their own immediate colleagues, including those who commanded them. Reitzle, like Lutz, attracted devoted followers and offended those who didn't like supreme stylishness and arrogance. Some critics felt he tried too hard to take too much credit—credit that belonged to von Kuenheim. Reitzle refused to work for Hans Hagen, a top engineer from the German truckmaker M.A.N., who von Kuenheim brought in to head product development in 1982.

Reitzle had the sense to ask von Kuenheim to send him instead to a graduate program at the Harvard Business School to tighten up his management skills for further progression up the BMW ladder. Hagen soon washed out, and Reitzle took complete command and control of the product program. His E-32, the 1986 7 series, was a landmark, immediately crowned the "world's greatest sedan" by the motoring press. The 7 series was so superior to the Mercedes-Benz S class that debuted a couple of years later that Mercedes was forced to rethink its entire philosophy—a self-examination that ultimately led to the merger that created DaimlerChrysler. Around the same time, Reitzle designed the physical layout of BMW's F.I.Z. (Forschungs- und Innovationszentrum) product-development center and imbued it with its own culture. The F.I.Z. became the industry standard and the model for the engineering temples later erected by Renault and Chrysler. It seemed inevitable that Reitzle eventually would replace von Kuenheim as BMW's chief executive. Reitzle was the quintessence of von Kuenheim. Had the great leader written on a piece of paper the attributes he wanted in a young engineer and manager he would have designed Reitzle. Reitzle was more than von Kuenheim's protégé, he was like a son.

In the early 1990s, Ferdinand Piëch's family's company was in serious trouble. The collapse of the dollar against the deutsche mark had dried up the company's lucrative U.S. export market. Porsche sales had collapsed from 50,000 a year to only 12,000 in 1992. The new chairman of the management board, Arno Bohn, had concocted a new-model development plan that Piëch regarded as unacceptable. Bohn was spending hundreds of millions of marks to develop a four-door Porsche sedan, a car that would never go into production.

There was only one man in Germany whom Piëch deemed good enough to rescue Porsche. Well, two. One was himself, but Piëch was busy positioning himself for the top job at Volkswagen. The other was Wolfgang Reitzle. Piëch never hesitated to go after what he wanted—and he wanted Reitzle. So after a month of discussions, Reitzle decided to go to Zuffenhausen, to Porsche. The small group of family friends and Porsche executives who showed up in Zell am See, Austria, for a birthday celebration of Piëch's mother, Louise, were shocked to see Reitzle there among the guests. It seemed a done deal. Reitzle would leave BMW, join Porsche—and grow rich with the stock in the company that would be given to him.

Piëch and his uncle Ferry Porsche knew that to extract Reitzle from BMW they would have to offer a big stock ownership package. After all, Reitzle would be giving up an almost certain appointment to the top job in Munich.

In effect, Reitzle would become president-for-life at the small company. He would be handed the keys to an operation that he could model in his own image, as von Kuenheim had done at BMW. That, more than the money, tempted Reitzle. It was the power of Piëch—the same persuasiveness that would cause Inaki Lopez to leave General Motors a year later. In a sense, it was just another example of Piëch's poisonous ways with people. As it turned out, crossing Eberhard von Kuenheim would be the great mistake of Reitzle's life. Von Kuenheim forced Reitzle to honor his contract at BMW. There would be no Porsche dream job and no top job at BMW, either. The prodigal son was punished and then passed over. In 1993, BMW's obscure 45-year-old manufacturing head, Bernd Pischetsrieder, replaced von Kuenheim as chairman of the management board. But Reitzle was irrepressible, and too talented to be hidden away. He became a strong second-in-command, one of BMW's twin pillars.

This twin-pillar configuration bore a strong resemblance to what was going on across the ocean at the same time. At Chrysler, Bob Eaton was the titular man in charge and Bob Lutz was the de facto boss. Reitzle was a kind of a combination of von Kuenheim, Piëch, and Lutz. He had von Kuenheim's manufacturing savvy, Piëch's technical vision, and Lutz's flair and instinctive understanding of cars customers craved. All three wanted him. Lutz many years later at General Motors tried to snag Reitzle. But in 1993, it was Piëch who tried and nearly succeeded. Piëch saw Reitzle as the only possible stand-in for himself. The two men got along well.

"Piëch and Reitzle spoke a common language," said an executive who worked for both of them. "They talked a lot about the future products of Porsche. Many ideas, for example the Boxster, came from Reitzle. Bohn had started the four-door sedan project. Reitzle and Piëch agreed it was a bad idea. Reitzle felt Porsche should build a cheaper car—what the Boxster became."

When von Kuenheim got the phone call from Piëch asking him to release Reitzle from his contract, the BMW chief remained calm and collected. "Astonishingly cool," said a man who was in the room. Von Kuenheim and Reitzle seemed to have a father-son relationship. But Reitzle broke the rules. He negotiated with Piëch for four weeks and then came to von Kuenheim. "It was the way Reitzle negotiated that bothered Kuenheim," said a BMW executive. "He negotiated through leaks in the media instead of going in at an early stage and talking to von Kuenheim and getting his permission to allow him to talk to Porsche. Reitzle never did that.

"Kuenheim simply thought about what was the best thing for BMW, and the best thing for BMW was for Reitzle to be head of research and development. Now I think it was a mistake not to release Reitzle because there would not have been the struggle between Reitzle and Pischetsrieder. Said another BMW executive, "I believe von Kuenheim felt instinctively what it would mean for the company to lose Reitzle. With his feeling for the brand, he felt that the loss of Reitzle was something he could not abide."

Those close to Reitzle say von Kuenheim promised to make Reitzle his successor. They also say Reitzle believes the biggest mistake of his professional life was not going to Porsche—the thing he most wanted to do. They quote him as saying: "I was sure about leaving for Porsche, and then they came and said there would be a hell of a lot of difficulty if I left. And they say von Kuenheim and the supervisory board promised Reitzle he would succeed von Kuenheim." Was Reitzle double-crossed? "I don't think von Kuenheim double-crossed him," said a

BMW executive. "It is hard to know. Maybe he wanted to choose Reitzle, but the Quandts wouldn't let him. The Quandts like a very low profile, and Reitzle had anything but a low profile."

Von Kuenheim once appeared to say that he didn't choose the best when he chose Pischetsrieder. The statement appeared in a newspaper article between the time that Pischetsrieder was named chairman of the management board in 1993 and the time he took over. "Von Kuenheim said we didn't choose the best one, we chose the most appropriate one," said a Reitzle colleague. A current BMW executive says von Kuenheim was misunderstood: "He said that a company at a certain time has two or three capable candidates. Sometimes you need the person capable for X, sometimes for Y. The idea that he was the best, but was not chosen, was a misinterpretation by Reitzle." Another BMW executive from that time period said: "Von Kuenheim felt Reitzle would be too polarizing. He made Reitzle so powerful. He was as powerful as von Kuenheim, maybe more powerful."

Some BMW insiders say it was a question of style. "Pischetsrieder was very down to earth," said one executive. "He enjoyed a good cigar. He was easy to talk to. Reitzle was BMW personified—young, fresh, dynamic and a great engineer," said a colleague. "But he wasn't the kind of traditional German executive von Kuenheim preferred. Pischetsrieder was nothing but a compromise." Another colleague said von Kuenheim wanted a "relaxed, reflective chairman, and he thought Reitzle was too emotional. A fast-running chairman would be dangerous in a critical period." Reitzle would have also demanded the full powers of the chief executive's job, said sources who worked closely with him. With the new man in place, they said von Kuenheim knew he would remain the real boss. At the June 1993 shareholders' meeting, where Pischetsrieder was officially installed, von Kuenheim told a colleague: "Ich trete nicht zurueck, ich trete zur Seite." ("I'm not stepping down, I'm just moving into the background.")

Not choosing Reitzle was von Kuenheim's one great mistake, said a former BMW official who remains a staunch admirer of von Kuenheim. Soon it would become clear that von Kuenheim might have indeed made a mistake. By the late 1990s, BMW had become a ghost of the great company that bought Rover for $1.3 billion in January 1994. And at the center of that deterioration was von Kuenheim, who had raised BMW from a minor player in the early 1970s to a powerhouse in the 1990s. Officially, von Kuenheim had retired before the Rover acquisition. But his choice of a successor and his own strategy brought BMW back to earth. It was the only stage of von Kuenheim's career that came under criticism—and he had retired. In 1992, BMW had surpassed Mercedes-Benz in sales for the first time and had defined the market for sporty luxury sedans. It had a lean, flexible management team, great products, excellent margins, and a crystal-clear brand identity. But by 1999, the company's two top executives, Pischetsrieder and Reitzle, were out because of Rover. And BMW briefly lost its mantle as the world's leading luxury-car maker. Executives had begun spending much of their time shuttling to England to put out fires rather than creating "the ultimate driving machine."

"Nobody has any time because of Rover, nobody has any money because of Rover," said a mid-level BMW executive. It was a humbled BMW that tried to reinvent itself. The new executive team led by former machine-tool professor Joachim Milberg was doing away with BMW's unique management style, with its emphasis on direct involvement by senior managers. The style was personified by the flamboyant Reitzle, who personally laid out the F.I.Z. engineering center and was largely responsible for BMW's highly successful hands-on management culture. Reitzle, while maintaining his BMW duties, served as Rover's chairman from September 1995 until March 1997, and departed BMW along with Pischetsrieder in February 1999. The Ford Motor Company hired him in March. BMW's new leaders claimed to know what went wrong. After Pischetsrieder pursued and acquired Rover, he set a doomed arms-length policy instead of attacking the English company's chaotic passenger-car operations. Rover had not developed a new car alone for 20 years, basing new models instead on cars from minority owner Honda.

Without BMW management support, Rover was dying—its weakness exposed when the British pound began to strengthen in 1997. Pischetsrieder's strategy of being a sensitive German owner of an old British company turned into a catastrophe. But there is another side to the story. BMW managers described Pischetsrieder as a chief executive who was dominated by his predecessor, von Kuenheim.

The man who ran BMW for 23 years couldn't bring himself to cede power when he retired in 1993, they said. He didn't have to, so long as the Quandt family that controlled BMW put its complete trust in him. After leaving the management board in May 1993, company sources said von Kuenheim stayed in control, operating from behind the scenes. He became the first BMW supervisory board chairman to occupy an office in the company's Four Cylinder Tower in Munich.

"He simply moved from the 22nd floor to the 21st floor," said an executive. "He came to work every day. Nothing changed." Some said he used Pischetsrieder as a tool and ultimately allowed him to take the blame for his own flawed strategy. "A lot of people thought that Pischetsrieder was the guy who bought Rover and had the wrong policy," said a source who worked with both men. "But that is not true. It was von Kuenheim's deal, never Pischetsrieder's." But Rover faltered under BMW. Its share of the U.K. market fell from 13.4 percent in 1993 to 8.9 percent in 1998. Under the weight of Rover's problems, BMW group profits plunged.

BMW finally got serious in the autumn of 1998. The arrival of former 3-series chief engineer Wolfgang Ziebart and a small team was the beginning of the end for Pischetsrieder. With help from the management consultancy McKinsey and Company, Ziebart was given complete freedom to fix what was broken. The Rover 75 that was due to be launched the following January was far below the quality standard Ziebart had demanded when he led the 3 Series project. He postponed the launch from January to June and ordered a long list of improvements. He expanded his turnaround team to about 100 specialists with technical, managerial, logistical, production, personnel, purchasing, and production backgrounds from BMW's Regensburg, Germany, plant. New synergies were found at once. Why didn't BMW seek them five years earlier?

"We owned the company, but we didn't manage the company," Ziebart said at the time. "I think we feared that by bringing in too much of the BMW philosophy we would end up with a second BMW instead of a company that builds distinctive cars." One of Ziebart's colleagues was more blunt. "Pischetsrieder and some of his people were too British-minded," he said. "He had a history in Rover because his great-uncle Alec Issigonis designed the Mini. He was really personally convinced that Rover would be able to pull itself up without external help."

Pischetsrieder believed that Rover needed BMW financial support, but little direct management support. "This wasn't the case," said Ziebart. "Rover didn't have the strength to really recover from inside." The explosive end to the Pischetsrieder era came at a marathon supervisory board meeting on February 5, 1999 at the BMW tower in Munich. Pischetsrieder was fired. Then Reitzle resigned when the supervisory board wouldn't give him Pischetsrieder's job.

Five years earlier in the same room, the young chairman—barely eight months into the job—had enthusiastically outlined the Rover strategy to the board, including Hans Graf von der Goltz and Herbert Quandt's widow, Johanna. The pair represented the Quandt family that owned more than 45.6 percent of BMW.

Pischetsrieder said Rover would allow BMW to become a volume producer without sacrificing brand exclusivity, and without the kind of shocking investment Mercedes-Benz planned for the smaller A class. Quandt and Graf von der Goltz supported Pischetsrieder because they supported von Kuenheim, who had anointed the bearded young man as his successor. But almost from the beginning Pischetsrieder made the wrong choices. The BMW machine that he inherited from von Kuenheim kept humming, but Rover continued losing money. Still, Pischetsrieder refused to get tough. He told an interviewer in July 1994 that two-thirds of all mergers or acquisitions failed because synergy effects were realized too soon.

"Mistakes made would be irreversible," he said. Pischetsrieder even considered giving Rover more freedom, floating the idea in 1996 of setting up a separate group headquarters outside Munich to further reduce German influence over the British subsidiary. The model was GM Europe's Zurich headquarters—set up 10 years earlier to make Germany's Adam Opel less dominant over the rest of GM Europe. Meanwhile, BMW executives began calling Pischetsrieder "zauderer," or "indecisive one." In 1993, the X5 sport utility vehicle and the Z3 roadster were shown simultaneously to marketing executives, who wanted both cars. The Z3 came out in 1994, and the X5 was planned for 1995. But after the Rover purchase, the X5 was reconsidered. Pischetsrieder eventually postponed the project out of fear that it would compete with Rover Group's Land Rover brand. The Reitzle-led project didn't hit the streets until several years later—and when it did, it was a huge success.

But Mercedes-Benz beat BMW to the luxury sport utility vehicle market with the U.S.–built M-class. Some BMW executives also fault Pischetsrieder for delaying management changes at the top of Rover. He also seemed distracted by his deep affection for Rover's roster of old brands. Pischetsrieder was a longtime admirer of the Riley marque, which came along with the MG, Triumph, Austin-Healey, and Wolseley names when BMW bought Rover. British Leyland had killed the Riley brand in 1969. But in July 1998, Pischetsrieder announced plans to reintroduce Riley at a celebration of the centenary of the brand. Rover design engineering director Nick Stephenson and marketing director Tom Purves heard the news only 24 hours before Pischetsrieder told delighted guests at the event, which was staged by the 1,000-member Riley Motor Club.

Von Kuenheim appeared to set the "hands off Rover" policy attributed to Pischetsrieder. A few weeks after the Rover takeover, a memo was sent to all top BMW executives with Rover contacts. Written by Hagen Luderitz, head of BMW corporate planning (and the man who over 20 years earlier traveled around Europe with Bob Lutz getting rid of BMW's independent distributors), the memo instructed BMW managers not to use "imperialistic tones" in its dealings with Rover counterparts and to "behave gentlemanly."

"Immediately this killed every constructive criticism," said one BMW executive. "Rover problems were no longer addressed. The BMW people who were sent to help out at Rover still saw the problems, but they no longer mentioned them to their Rover counterparts, and of course did nothing to fix them." Luderitz, BMW's former chief legal counsel, once lived in the U.K. He was the mastermind of the company's various legal agreements in Britain, including various Rolls-Royce aero engine deals as well as the complicated terms of sharing Rolls-Royce Motor Cars with Volkswagen. He was "a von Kuenheim guy for a long time," the source said. "He was much closer to him than Pischetsrieder was." The Luderitz memo was "a sign for us in Germany," said a former BMW man. "Rover had a lousy dealer network in Germany, and we had a lot of BMW dealers. We had the idea that a lot of BMW dealers could also be Rover dealers, with exclusive branding. But they didn't like this for political reasons. We lost a chance to integrate faster." Carl-Peter Forster, who was elevated to board member for production in February of 1999 and left a year later to run General Motors' Adam Opel division, denied at the time that von Kuenheim dominated the company and that he had used Pischetsrieder as an instrument of his will.

"Von Kuenheim is very disciplined and took the role he had very seriously," Forster said. But he was bound by *Aktienrecht* (German corporate law) from interfering too much. "In hindsight," he said, "von Kuenheim might have had sleepless nights, asking himself whether he maybe sometimes should have stepped over these borders of the *Aktienrecht* and taken a more active role to steer the group in a better direction than Pischetsrieder and the board did."

Richard Gaul, BMW's head of communications, said von Kuenheim's role had been overestimated. "He followed the German legal rules," Gaul said. "He didn't interfere." But Gaul conceded that after 23 years as boss, and given his close ties to the Quandt family, von Kuenheim was not the usual German boss moving up to the supervisory board. "The typical supervisory board chairman only meets with the management four times a year," said Gaul. "But von Kuenheim was much more involved than that. The thing about von Kuenheim is that you could not lie to him. He knew everything." Late in December 1998, Pischetsrieder made up his mind to resign. "He felt he was a symbol of the problems with Rover," said one cohort.

But he would have gone anyway. Von Kuenheim and the supervisory board were running out of patience. Pischetsrieder had not reacted quickly enough to correct the situation. Meanwhile, Reitzle said he had predicted the Rover calamity. "Every detail turned out the way I wrote it some years ago and tried to convince my colleagues," he said from his perch at Ford in 1999. "If you don't have your basics in place—product quality, attractiveness, loyalty rate, dealer-network image—you can't grow quicker than others. They invested for a growth rate at Rover that was higher than the growth of all car companies in history, and on the basis of such a weak foundation like Rover cars. I always said it couldn't work. Why should the miracle happen? Only because they were owned by BMW? It's not enough."

Reitzle had made clear to the board that if he didn't get Pischetsrieder's job he would quit.

After Pischetsrieder resigned under pressure at the February 5 board meeting, the supervisory board rejected Reitzle as his replacement. Some said Herbert's children—Stefan Quandt and Susanne Klatten, the two young Quandts who had recently joined the supervisory board—decided that Pischetsrieder had to go—and that Reitzle could not replace him. They didn't like Reitzle's public persona, his high style, and his frequent appearance in gossip columns. He violated the principles of the discreet BMW man. It was reminiscent of Lee Iacocca at Ford in the 1970s, when Iacocca's fame got under the Ford family's skin.

Another version of what happened is that the union members on the supervisory board rejected Reitzle. He had shown by his actions as Rover's chairman that he was too willing to cut jobs. Reitzle himself seemed to believe this. His friends said Reitzle thought he had made a grievous error by not cultivating the trade union representatives on the board. Years later Reitzle said, "One of my biggest mistakes was that I didn't take enough care about the workers council." But the real reason Reitzle was again passed over as CEO? Three months before the February 1999 bloodletting, there was a report in a German newspaper that Reitzle had visited von Kuenheim at this home to express his frustration about the way things were going at Rover.

Only three people knew of the visit—Reitzle, von Kuenheim, and von Kuenheim's wife. When von Kuenheim learned that Reitzle was leaking to the press it killed his chances to become chairman of the management board.

In March 1999, Reitzle joined Ford as head of the Premier Auto Group luxury marques—Jaguar, Volvo, Lincoln, Land Rover, and Aston Martin. He began to employ former BMW executives and hired BMW Great Britain marketing boss Dieter Laxy, BMW North America

President Victor Doolan, and Land Rover chief designer Gerry McGovern. Von Kuenheim retired from the supervisory board in June 1999 at age 71, turning over the job to his old ally Volker Doppelfeld, the longtime BMW finance chief.

The Rover ordeal was a sad final act in one of the most distinguished automotive careers of the century. And it began with the passing over of Reitzle. Those close to Reitzle say the former protégé still speaks of von Kuenheim with great respect. "He says von Kuenheim is a great guy, but you never know what Reitzle is really thinking," said one colleague. "Not even Reitzle knows exactly what happened to him in 1992. But they still speak to each other."

Reitzle's confidants say von Kuenheim told him in later years, "it should have been you," referring to the 1993 decision to pick Pischetsrieder. They say Reitzle says it with tears in his eyes. "Maybe it is true, but von Kuenheim never told me that," said a current BMW executive. "I have the impression Reitzle's heart is still with BMW. When he left Ford and joined Linde, he immediately bought BMWs."

Said one former BMW man, "All I know is that von Kuenheim exploited the best of Reitzle."

Reitzle, like Bob Lutz, suffered the destructive powers of the great industry leaders. Just as Lutz was beaten down for having been perceived as a threat to Henry Ford II and Iacocca, Reitzle was burned by his proximity to von Kuenheim and Piëch. Lutz survived, but he never became the boss. Reitzle fared less well. Like Lutz, Reitzle went to Ford. He was so highly regarded that Ford created an entire division for him, giving him leadership of all the European luxury brands that had been acquired by Ford over the years—the brands that Henry Ford II coveted.

But Reitzle ran into some of the same troubles that Lutz had faced a decade and a half earlier, wrestling with the remnants of the numerate culture that Henry Ford II's Whiz Kids had wrought—the bureaucracy, the meetings, the insistence on quantification, the lack of trust of men such as Lutz and Reitzle who operated on their golden instincts. Unable to stomach Ford, Reitzle left in 2002—not for another industry job, but for the comfort of running his own show, as CEO of Linde. In later years, Reitzle and Lutz would be friends, frequently dining together and sharing their enthusiasm for developing great cars.

CHAPTER SEVENTEEN

Piëch Today:
Looking Back

F ive-year-old Ferdinand Piëch would sometimes crawl beneath the dinner table when his grandfather, the immortal Ferdinand Porsche, entertained friends and colleagues at the family's summer home in Zell am See, Austria.

It was 1942, and World War II was raging. From under the table the inquisitive urchin would listen to the men as they sipped brandy, smoked cigars, and discussed great questions of engineering and world affairs. The well-connected technicians knew something of the inner workings of the Hitler regime.

On one occasion in 1942, the excited young "Burli," as the boy was called, had startling news for the other members of Anton Piëch's growing family.

The new bombs, he informed them at lunch one day, would not fall straight down from the sky, but would fly a great distance before reaching their target.

The other Piëchs didn't know what the child was talking about. Indeed, young Ferdinand was aware of the V2 rockets that would soon be fired at far-off England long before the great majority of citizens of the Third Reich. He had heard his grandfather's men discussing the new weapon while he scrunched under the heavy wooden table.

Soon little Ferdinand Piëch was designing his own rockets and attempting to build them.

The curious mind of the curious man had its beginnings listening to the brilliant men his grandfather surrounded himself with.

SIXTY-TWO YEARS and one extraordinary lifetime later, Ferdinand Piëch contemplated his former empire from an unremarkable office building in an alleyway alongside the Sulzach River behind Salzburg's Alpenstrasse.

He looked back on a career still smoldering with controversy—even in retirement, Piëch was at the center of a gathering storm at Volkswagen, the company Hitler had inaugurated, his grandfather had propelled, his father had managed during the war, and Piëch himself had led for 10 years, from 1992 until 2002.

The final decade of Ferdinand Piëch's professional career was the most contentious period of his life. History waits to pass judgment on his final performance.

The achievements during his decade in Wolfsburg were largely obscured by the weight of his personality. Even many of his successes were seen as blunders—the acquisition of Bentley Motors (because of the simultaneous loss of Rolls-Royce); the sharp reduction in VW's cost base (because he had hired purchasing hatchet man Inaki Lopez from GM); the improvement in VW quality and its price position (because of the dangerous venture into superluxury cars and companies).

He remained a misunderstood man right to the end of his career.

The now pervasive opinion was that Piëch had saddled Bernd Pischetsrieder, his successor as Volkswagen's CEO, with a mess, a confluence of upper-class cars and brands that had torn VW away from its commoner roots—much as Eberhard von Kuenheim had left the same man, Bernd Pischetsrieder, with a crisis that ended Pischetsrieder's career at BMW a few years before.

At BMW, Pischetsrieder's quandary was the opposite of what he faced at VW. Von Kuenheim had left the man with a distressed acquisition, Britain's fading Rover Group, a mid-market brand that did not fit with BMW's upmarket roots.

In RETIREMENT, von Kuenheim and Piëch, the two Olympian figures of the post-war European auto industry, still battled.

The very choice of Bernd Pischetsrieder, the out-of-favor former head of BMW as his successor, was Piëch's last jab at his great rival. Von Kuenheim had failed with Pischetsrieder, had allowed his handpicked successor to flounder in his handling of Rover in 1994, a year after von Kuenheim had moved to BMW's supervisory board.

Though von Kuenheim was no longer in day-to-day command, Piëch believed von Kuenheim had undercut the new man by meddling too much in the affairs of the company.

Piëch would choose Pischetsrieder as his own successor at Volkswagen and make it possible for the tall, lean Bavarian to reconstruct his reputation—under Piëch's auspices.

Bernd Pischetsrieder became a kind of competitive sport, a contest between Piëch and von Kuenheim where Piëch could prove his superiority. It would be Piëch's final triumph—his last reckoning with history.

It was the kind of bolstering he believed his life's reputation required.

Von Kuenheim was renowned as the great discoverer and nurturer of brilliant executives. Piëch was the super-technician, but was also regarded as a tyrant, an intimidator and even squanderer of talent.

Piëch would try to beat von Kuenheim at his own game by making a success of Bernd Pischetsrieder.

"Von Kuenheim destroyed in five years everything he built up," says Piëch. "I learned a lot from that about how I should do it. I never go to Wolfsburg and I never go into the company without Mr. Pischetsrieder, today's chairman. In two and a half years (since retiring as CEO) I only go there to official meetings with the supervisory board.

"I know Kuenheim spent all his time (after retiring) in the company running around and talking with the people. No, it's now Pischetsrieder who has to run Volkswagen, and he can only run it right if I disappear. Otherwise I would be doing the same as Kuenheim did.

"Until the end of his working career he was one of the best here in Europe, and after his retirement he destroyed in five years everything he built up.

"He destroyed Wolfgang Reitzle and Pischetsrieder. He didn't know how to follow his own career."

For his part, von Kuenheim disdains any comparison with his old rival.

"I hope Piëch and I are different," says von Kuenheim.

The long-time head of BMW never talked about the February 1999 dismissal of Pischetsrieder. His protégé had failed to bring the heavy losses at Rover under control. But in 2004, deep into his retirement, von Kuenheim looked back wistfully at the whole affair.

"I had to make a decision and he had to leave," he says. "I was happy that Pischetsrieder got another chance. But whether VW was the right company for him is another question."

PIËCH NEVER CONSIDERED another successor. He had to have the man von Kuenheim had tossed aside.

"I had the chance to get Pischetsrieder as my replacement if I did it at the right time," he says. "I was 65. If I waited one or two years longer I couldn't get him. I think he was the best solution I could find and I still agree 100 percent with what he is doing. I would say within the two and a half years I don't remember a single decision that I would have done differently from him.

"It's true, he can suffer more than I could sometimes in personnel decisions. I am faster to act. But he does it identically, only a little later. Maybe this is more human for the man who has to go."

VON KUENHEIM AND PIËCH had long stalked each other. And once they met to discuss Piëch joining BMW.

"I knew Kuenheim quite well because I had once talked with him for several hours about my career," says Piëch. "But my feeling was he didn't want me."

That was in 1988 as Piëch prepared, in a fit of temper, to resign from Audi, where he was vice chairman and head of product development.

"I had ups and down at Audi," he says.

He was deeply distraught when the contract of Audi President Wolfgang Habbel was extended by a year.

Piëch, who was 51, felt he was ready to take over as head of Audi's management board, and Habbel's extension meant a year's delay. It was more than Piëch could stomach. He believed that he was in fact running the company.

Piëch's wife agreed to move to Japan if he chose to do so. It was one of his options—to work as an engineer for a Japanese auto company, namely Honda.

But Ursula Piëch didn't want him to do anything until she gave birth to the baby she was carrying.

Piëch decided that in the time left on his Audi contract, which was less than a year, he would give up the extra responsibilities he had taken on—in effect, stop running the company. He would return to Audi's product development center and leave the rest of it alone. He'd turn the day-to-day operations back over to Habbel, who had all but abdicated as he neared his own retirement.

Piëch recalls the fateful year:

"In the spring of 1988, Habbel got a longer contract. I was told then they didn't trust that I was good enough. I was already vice chairman for a long time and I felt I was running the company. My president was out in the world, always with his golf bag.

"So when this prolonging of his contract was announced to me, I prepared on the same day the letter to the supervisory board. I was going to go immediately. But my wife was pregnant and would have the baby five months later. She stole the letter for one night and said she would take it to the post office. The next morning she told me she would go with me to Japan if I wanted to go or to any other company—but after the baby was born. So I agreed.

"I had a talk with Kuenheim, and I told my supervisory board that I would give back my responsibility to run the company. I told him I only wanted for the next nine months to run research and development. The president should run the company. Three months later, the company was in red figures."

So Piëch had his first chat with Carl Hahn, the head of the Volkswagen group and chairman of Audi's supervisory board.

Piëch says Hahn asked him to return to his more extensive role at Audi.

"'It's not my job,'" Piëch says he told Hahn.

"A month later, the labor representative on the supervisory board came to see me at a new-car presentation in California. He asked me what they had to do so that I would work again, so that the company wouldn't lose money. I said, 'It is very clear. At the time you want to send Dr. Habbel home—we do it from that day. When I have a contract that I am the successor I will work again.'

"The then head of the union and Dr. Hahn agreed that the timetable be put back to what is was."

STILL, PIËCH HAD BEEN dead serious about leaving Audi. He and von Kuenheim had a long chat in Munich. Piëch says he wasn't angling for a particular job or a guarantee that he would eventually become BMW's CEO.

"It was no issue at that time," Piëch says. "I just wanted to leave Audi."

But Piëch picked up strong vibes from the meeting. He felt pretty certain von Kuenheim, despite outward politeness and an apparent show of interest, didn't want Piëch to come to BMW.

He was right, according to BMW executives who were there at the time. They say von Kuenheim thought Piëch would bring the wrong chemistry to his BMW cocktail.

Piëch also thought long and hard about going to Japan to re-start his career.

It would have been an extraordinary career move—and today Piëch insists he would have done it had things not worked out for him in Ingolstadt.

"At that time Japan was moving the world. Europe was sleeping, and if you are not on the top it's hard to get a company to move faster."

Piëch had met Soichiro Honda during their racing days in Europe in the 1960s. He had a special regard for the great man and his company.

"When at Porsche we bought a small Honda—the S500, 8,500 rpm—to study. It was the one with the motorcycle chain. My motorcycle when I was working with [designer Giorgetto Giugiaro in Turin in 1971] was a Honda 1000."

Piëch was in awe of Soichiro Honda.

"Honda was for me the most interesting Japanese company because it was not typically Japanese. It was a mixture. American culture and Japanese technology.

"I never had a desire to work for somebody like Toyota. It is a very good company, but with a completely different mindset. It was very conservative, and Honda took risks."

PIËCH WOULD HAVE another go-round with von Kuenheim a few years later. This time it concerned Wolfgang Reitzle, von Kuenheim's protégé, his favorite, his youthful head of product development. Piëch wanted Reitzle at Porsche.

The question of which professional manager should run the Porsche sports car company after family members had been barred from management was always a matter of dispute.

"It was easy for the family members to agree on the idea of having a have a good outside manager, but it is hard to agree within the family about who is right for this job and who is not. Everyone always asks: 'Is he as good as my grandfather?'"

Peter Schutz, the American who was Porsche's CEO during most of the 1980s, pushed the company to new sales heights. Schutz got himself into trouble by suggesting to Ferry Porsche that he consider selling the company when it hit a rough patch in the late 1980s. The suggestion deeply annoyed Ferry and his nephew.

"Schutz wanted another big sum to invest for higher production for U.S. sales. My uncle asked Schutz what he would do if the market goes down again. He said 'sell the company' and from this time on Schutz and my uncle no longer had good relations. My uncle had expected an answer like 'We should make the engine cheaper.'

"Schutz had a good car feeling," says Piëch. "In good years he did a good job, but he was not a manager for a crisis."

After Schutz was forced out, he was replaced by a veteran finance man named Heinz Branitzki—a caretaker who was replaced in 1990 by a young computer company executive named Arno Bohn.

Meanwhile, Porsche's condition worsened. The October 1987 stock market crash cut into Porsche's buyer segment, and a strong deutsche mark caused the company's sales in the crucial U.S. market to plummet.

Bohn began to chart a new product strategy, but in Piëch's eyes he was getting it all wrong.

In 1991, Piëch decided that he wanted Reitzle to take charge of his family's flagging sports car company. Piëch thought he had an agreement with the young BMW product development wizard. And indeed, he did. Reitzle had made up his mind to leave Munich for Stuttgart in exchange for a stake in the Porsche company and complete control. But in the end Reitzle turned the Porsches and Piëchs down, informing Ferdinand Piëch that von Kuenheim would not let him out of his BMW contract.

Piëch said he never believed von Kuenheim was the real stumbling block—the verdict of most auto industry historians. Instead, he says it was Reitzle's belief that if he stayed at BMW he would be von Kuenheim's successor.

Piëch said Reitzle could have broken free of the BMW contract had he truly wanted to. But the talented young engineer seemed stunned by how word of his plans to leave had reverberated throughout BMW. The day he informed his legions at the FIZ, the vast technical development center in Munich, the men had tears in their eyes.

Says Piëch: "I always looked at my own contract, and his was not any different. You could get out of a contract—not in a very short time but within six months or so, and this was enough. I knew that under German law you could not keep a man for years, though he would have to get a lawyer and fight.

"Secondly, I was sure that in the end if somebody has very nearly moved out of a company, and then comes back, he will never be the president of that company. It is something that I feel. But Reitzle believed that if he remained at BMW he would become the chairman.

On the day Reitzle notified Piëch that he would stay in Munich, Piëch seethed.

"I told him 'today you are losing millions of deutsch marks, and you will also lose the top position at BMW.' I was right."

In 1993, Bernd Pischetsrieder got the job instead.

Von Kuenheim today says Reitzle's failure to become CEO was not a punishment for his Porsche dalliance.

"It had completely nothing to do with that," he says.

But as Reitzle made preparations to leave BMW, von Kuenheim says he asked the young superstar: "Is it worthwhile to give up everything you have at BMW?"

At Porsche, the alternative to Wolfgang Reitzle was Ferdinand Piëch himself.

Piëch had received the same offer the family had made to Reitzle. If he were to pull the company out of its nosedive he would receive 5 percent of the shares of Porsche AG.

In a time of crisis, company bylaws stated that the family could waive its 1971 rule against its members holding executive positions. Only Piëch was already committed to Volkswagen and his shot at becoming CEO of the giant group.

"When I had to decide to go to Volkswagen, Reitzle was 50-50," he says.

PIËCH HAD NEVER Expected to be in a position where he would turn the family down. Twenty years earlier, when Piëch went to work for Porsche AG as a young man, he understood that he was "in the wrong company." It meant, he believed, that he could never lead the family sports car business. He was from the side of the family that controlled Porsche Holdings, the Austrian car distributor and dealership group.

"There had been two companies from my grandfather—the one here in Austria, the importer, where my mother was ruling; and in Stuttgart where my uncle was ruling. It was the unwritten law that the Porsche family stayed in Stuttgart and my mother's family stayed in Salzburg. But I was the only engineer with a university degree, so I went to Stuttgart.

"That's part of the problem which led to all the family members being moved out. The eight family members always had more interest in Stuttgart than in Salzburg.

"My oldest brother, Ernst, was also an engineer and not very interested in doing this job in Salzburg. Everybody wanted to go to Stuttgart and make a career there."

The young Ferdinand Piëch also represented a threat to the four sons of Ferry Porsche.

"I was very young," says Piëch, "and my career was not to the pleasure of my uncle. But he accepted me. He accepted my technical work, but for his sons he didn't like very much that I made a very fast career in this company."

Still, Piëch insists there was no real competition between himself and his cousin Butzi, the oldest of Ferry's children and the designer of the 911.

"He was never in the race for the top because he was a designer and he was happy designing. He had no interest in running a company. I had to support him most of the time in the Porsche company. He was never ready with his design. He never wanted to release it so that you could build a prototype. He was an artist, and if you have a painter you have to take the paint away otherwise he never ends. This is the kind of person my cousin is."

But because he was a Piëch, not a Porsche, he believed he was never in the running to be CEO of the sports car company.

"As long the company worked fine I never could be that," he says.

But when Porsche AG lapsed into crisis—20 years after Piëch and his cousins were expelled—opinions changed. Now the family firm, the descendents of Ferdinand Porsche, would turn to Piëch.

Except that the vast Volkswagen group was many times as large as Porsche and gave Piëch the chance to prove himself on what he called "the free market."

"Within the family contract of 1971 there is a provision that with more than 75 percent of the family votes you can get any position in the company. I had 100 percent at that time. But to bring back Porsche in a good position and then have the same troubles with the family as before [was not what I wanted]."

Still, Piëch sacrificed something by his decision.

"If I had accepted the job, today I would be much richer," he says. "There was an offer of another 5 percent of the company to the person that saved Porsche. That was the offer to Reitzle. I had the same offer from the family as a backup if Reitzle didn't come. In the meantime the value of 5 percent now would be more than 100 million euro."

There was another consideration for Piëch—the protection of his mother's company in Salzburg, Porsche Holdings. The VW-Audi distributor depended on its good relations with the Volkswagen firm.

"Today it is a company that sells 300,000 new cars a year in the world, not just in Europe, all over the world. Choosing to go Volkswagen was also choosing to keep my mother's company safe.

"Volkswagen would have done wrong with the other half. The Porsche half in Salzburg would have died."

Thus Piëch was intent on winning the top job at VW and was unwilling to veer from that pre-destiny in order to run the family company.

WITH REITZLE UNAVAILABLE, Piëch determined that the right man to install as head of Porsche AG was 39-year-old Wendelin Wiedeking, the company's manufacturing chief.

Says Piëch: "Wiedeking was at that time very young, and it was a risky way to go. But there was no other choice, even though I had the whole family against me."

Wiedeking had left Porsche in 1987, then he returned to the sports car company to take a seat on the management board as production boss. In the meantime, he had led an impressive three-year turnaround at a German automotive bearings maker called Glyco.

"Then the owners of Glyco sold the company with him and Wiedeking didn't like it," Piëch recalls. "So he came back to Porsche as head of production. "That was a normal thing, agreed to by everyone in the family. But with [Arno] Bohn out, there was a competition between Wiedeking and finance chief Walter Gnauert for the job of chairman of the management board.

"Who should be the successor? The whole family, including my brother, was against Wiedeking. He was too young. It was too risky. I told them, 'if he could save Glyco, which was also a family company, he has to be really good. Let's take a risk and make him only the speaker [of the management board], and the family agreed.

"When I had convinced my brother we had to find a way to convince the other side of the family. So we asked the youngest Porsche (then 39-year-old Wolfgang Porsche) that he should try to get Wiedeking as the speaker for one year. Now he thinks he brought in Wiedeking. But he is no technician, so he didn't know what Wiedeking really did at Glyco."

BEFORE FERDINAND PIËCH left for his studies at Zurich Technical University in 1958, he needed six months of mechanical training. He spent the time working at the former technical center of his mother's car distribution company. The center was located on the Alpenstrasse in Salzburg—not far from his small office he occupies today as chairman of the VW supervisory board.

"There were machines, blacksmiths, everything you needed for prototype building," he recalls. "It had been moved here from Porsche's [pre-war headquarters in Gmund, Austria], and they still had all of the experts.

"Within four months I could repair a Beetle engine. After five months I learned that my older brother, who is eight years older, had a 'Fuhrmann' engine. It was the ultimate Porsche engine at that time with overhead camshafts. My brother broke the engine, and I found it. I asked him if I could have it and repair it. He said, 'Yes, I don't need it anymore.'

"So I repaired the engine. I polished everything inside, I increased the compression ratio and brought it to Stuttgart to see how much horsepower it had. There was no equipment here in Austria, so I tested it in Stuttgart and then I told my mother, 'now I need the body and the chassis.'" Soon after he started his studies he got the body.

"I have had in my life just one bad accident. It was a 911—90 horsepower, with Michelin tires and shock absorbers from Koni. The rear axle went sideways and I crashed the car—fully insured. It was my only crash. Myself and the man sitting beside me had belts, and we weren't hurt. But I got the money from the insurance, and with this I could buy a 356 with aluminum doors, aluminum hoods front and rear, plastic windows on the side. There was no heating. It was the race version from Stuttgart. I installed my engine and I took it to Zurich.

"In my first semester, I missed several hours in Zurich because with a vapor carburetor in winter the engine often didn't start. I had to screw off the eight sparkplugs, warm them on a cooking stove, and screw them in and start again."

HE GRADUATED IN late 1962, then began making waves soon after arriving at Porsche in 1963. He was quick to dislodge colleagues he didn't like or approve of.

Piëch started in the engine department. His first assignment was to work on the 901—Butzi Porsche's stunningly beautiful 356 successor that would soon be renamed the 911.

"I first had responsibility was for the 901 race engine—high power, six-cylinder, 180 horsepower, 2 liter. This engine was developed faster, with less breakdown than the normal production engine for the 911, so six months later I also got responsibility for the passenger car engine."

Piëch's race engine could run 24 hours without stopping. The 911 passenger car engine broke after six or eight hours.

"So the technical director fired all of the passenger car engine engineers. I got responsibility for both engines."

That was where Piëch built his first small team—the first of many.

Among the members were Hans Metzger, the engine designer. The chassis man was Helmut Bott.

"Those were the key persons," says Piëch.

Later, the young man took over the testing department for Porsche production cars and chopped away at more of what he considered deadwood in the company.

His job was to approve parts for production, and he used this power to the hilt.

"There was the problem of the release," recalls Piëch.

"The front shock absorbers were intended to be adjusted in production because of the tolerances. It was an expensive process. But Hans Tomola, the head of the technical department, including manufacturing, authorized a release to production for shock absorbers that could not be adjusted. The shocks broke in durability tests.

"I did not give a release, but he put it through anyway and for several months this kind of car was in production. There were three major releases that didn't pass my department—that went directly from design to production. That should not have been. So at that time I went to my uncle and said 'you have to fire one of the two—myself or the technical chief. You cannot give a release without testing the chassis part. That kills the company.' " A week of discussion followed before Ferry Porsche agreed to fire Tomola and give the job to Piëch. It was 1965.

THE RACING YEARS at Porsche were arduous ones for Piëch.

"During my studies in Zurich I went eight semesters, four years, and spent not a single hour skiing—and I liked skiing very much. My studies ended in the end of 1962. After that I went skiing for three months every day at Zell Am See. There were 1,000 meter cable cars there and I still have the record—19 times a day.

"But from that time until the end of my Porsche career, I was not once on skis. When I had my small consultant company in 1972, I had time for skiing again.

"But with the racing at Porsche, over winter you had to build the cars, so I had no time for skiing. Then for about 30 weekends a year we were out race or testing.

"From the middle of November it was testing. Daytona was around Christmas. I had to go to America for testing—testing for two weeks.

By 1968, Piëch was consumed with preparations for what many considered the greatest race machine of all time—the Porsche 917. The question is still asked today. How did he convince the board and his uncle to spend the money for the 12-cylinder Le Mans car?

"No problem," says Piëch today. "It was a technical fact, but later on when the whole thing was very expensive, my uncle had distanced himself more from the project.

"It was the riskiest program of my life. It was a 100 percent newly-designed car. No test and 25 cars built for homologation. You can say the 12-cylinder was basically putting two six-cylinders together, but it was not so easy. The crankshaft had a gear in the middle against torsion vibration, so it couldn't be made out of one piece, it had to be three pieces—the gear and the two sides.

"This was welded together out of a vacuum using a machine from aerospace industry in the United States. It was the only machine that could weld it. It was the first time such a thing was used, but it worked.

"Twenty-five crankshaft parts had been ordered. The whole thing was quite risky—engine, wheels, tires, brakes—was beyond what Porsche had ever done.

"Yes, it was my biggest risk," he says. "It was the only time in my life I couldn't sleep too well until it worked. But the Ford GT-40 had a five-liter engine. To have an equal car Porsche needed the V-12.

IN 1968, VOLKSWAGEN tried to buy Porsche.

"We knew how much Volkswagen paid for Audi-NSU, so in a business you should never say no if someone approaches you. So my uncle sent his son Ferdinand Alexander, my brother Michael, a lawyer, and myself to talk to VW. My uncle said he could not help us.

We said we wanted 10 times the price of the value of Porsche, otherwise it's not for sale. We were young, and we went to Wolfsburg and told them and we never heard a word from them."

PIËCH SAYS HE calmly accepted the decision of Ferry Porsche and his mother to ban family members from running the sports car company.

"At the end of 1971, all of the family members including my uncle and my mother decided that starting from 1972 all of us had to give up our jobs in the company. I had read a lot about family companies. The first builds up the company, the second generation keeps it, and the third destroys it. I am the third."

He didn't trust the abilities of his siblings and cousins, the children of Ferry and Louise.

"We are eight successors, seven boys, one girl. With the exception of my sister and my youngest cousin everybody was involved in the company in a higher position—not really in the position they would have been in on the free market, and this hurt the company. You could see this.

"Two of the eight worked on the free market later—my cousin, Ferdinand Alexander Porsche, who built up Porsche Design, and myself. The decision was better for the six others. We had to make a decision that everybody could live with and would allow the company to survive."

Piëch says personal choices in 1971 were limited—he could either continue to run the small consulting company he had set up or go to work for Audi or Mercedes-Benz.

"In 1971, I had a lot of fun with a very small group," said Piëch.

His little consultancy, with "one and a half employees," designed a five-cylinder diesel engine for Mercedes on contract.

But he was wary of living out his professional days as a freelancer.

"You had people that wanted you and people that didn't want you," he says.

He was working for "a very small sum of money," but delivered the five-cylinder to Mercedes a month ahead of schedule.

"But I knew that if at the top of the company they did not protect me I would die on this contract," he says.

"[But] I learned that with my one and one-half employees and myself I could work 16 hours in a day without getting tired. That was completely different from working in a company like Porsche and later a company like Audi, and a little later on Volkswagen. I learned that in a big organization the cost and the time exploded, but the outcome was not better."

PIËCH WAS WELL acquainted with Ludwig Kraus, Audi's head of research and development.

"I knew that he had to do much work for VW as well as Audi and it was a lot of work. There were a lot of interesting projects, and on the other hand the head of Daimler didn't trust really engineers. He thought engineers only spent money."

Piëch was told that the Daimler boss, Joachim Zahn, wanted someone heading research and development who "wouldn't spend too much money and wouldn't develop too many cars."

"So I told him I am the wrong man. I wanted to make new cars, and I wanted to have the money to do it. So I took a job at Audi. It was at a lower level, but it gave me a better chance."

After signing the Audi contract, but before joining the company, Piëch spent several weeks working at Giorgetto Giugiaro's new, independent styling studio in Turin.

"I wanted to learn about design because my whole career I never had to do anything with design. I also wanted to learn a little of the Italian language. I was there alone with only Italian people and very few could translate anything for me. In the evening there was no television, so I went to the cinema to learn the Italian language. I had only a Honda motorcycle with me at that time."

ONE OF HIS FIRST duties at Audi was to take charge of the Wankel engine operations. Audi owned the rights to the rotary engine designed by the legendary Felix Wankel.

"My (first) experience with Wankel was while I was still with Porsche. Porsche got the license to the technology, having paid a lot for it, and found out that fuel consumption was 5 to 15 percent higher than a normal combustion engine. Emissions were a lot more than with conventional gasoline engines, and having had this result at Porsche I went to Audi-NSU, which owned the technology and sold the license.

"When I showed Audi-NSU the results while still at Porsche they said, 'don't tell anyone—you'll get the license for free. With this knowledge I moved from Porsche to Audi."

Once installed at Audi, Piëch went to Japan four times to cancel Wankel contracts with Mazda, Honda, Toyota, and Nissan.

"All of them had paid a lot of money for the license. I had to explain that Audi would never put this engine into production. Later, I explained that the [NSU] RO-80 would be stopped."

The rotary engine–powered RO-80 was dropped in 1977.

"Inside Audi I was called the 'Wankel-killer.' Mr. Wankel was a genius in mechanical engineering, but he didn't learn thermodynamics. With the Wankel you lost too much energy on the cylinder walls.

"I saw that Audi would go to diesel engines and never to the Wankel."

As it turned out, Soichiro Honda was coming to the same conclusion in Japan.

A nervous Piëch went to see the Japanese men to give them the bad news about the Wankel. But he was surprised by the response he got. The Japanese respected Piëch's candor.

"They don't like to lose face. So to stop the whole development silently was a good job in Japan."

PIËCH HAD HIS sights mainly on Mercedes as he gradually took control of all product development at Audi. But in time the focus of his attention began to shift more to BMW.

Still, Piëch had a different approach than either company. Piëch was a mechanical engineer. His great advances at Audi were mechanical, while at BMW, von Kuenheim poured electronics into his cars.

It was the dual stimulus of Piëch and von Kuenheim that forged the modern Mercedes-Benz—while conversely Mercedes' build quality drove both Piëch and von Kuenheim to match it.

But Piëch felt the European auto industry had lost its way in the 1980s. Japan was No. 1 in automotive engineering, and he wanted to go with a winner. He fought hard to keep Europe in the technology race with the ideas and energy he brought to life in Ingolstadt.

"BMW got better and better, and our target moved a little more to BMW. It was the time when Daimler was a little bit for old people. So for us young engineers it was not the right target—for quality, yes, but for sportiness it was BMW."

Piëch was impressed by the way things were done at BMW—especially the marketing.

"One of the worst decisions VW ever made was to incorporate Audi sales at Volkswagen," he says. "It was soon after I came to Audi. Later, a vice president from Audi went directly to BMW and ran their sales and marketing."

The man was Hans-Erdmann Schoenbeck.

"He was the longest term sales and marketing boss at BMW," recalls Piëch. "He had around 16 people with him at Audi, and 15 of them went with him to BMW. It was about 1975. It was it was before Bob Lutz was at BMW."

Piëch's memory was faulty.

"Piëch is growing older, too," said a BMW man.

"Schoenbeck was head of sales and marketing *after* Bob Lutz—and stayed in that job from September 1974 till July 1984. As far as the 'management-flow' between BMW and Audi is concerned, it seems in the long run that Audi was substantially more on the take side."

Von Kuenheim also disputes Piëch's memory.

"There were more who went from BMW to Audi," he said.

Either way, Piëch's point was that Audi had blown an opportunity. He admired BMW's marketing approach and wanted the same for Audi. He now believes that BMW's great success had more to do with marketing excellence than engineering achievements.

"They used to make facelifts and sell it as new cars," he says. "Perfect marketing.

"When I took charge [of Volkswagen AG] on January 1, 1993, the first thing I did was give back sales to Audi. You did not need manufacturing by yourself, but you did need marketing and sales."

A SIGNIFICANT PORTION of Europe's automotive technical resurgence in the 1970s and 1980s came from Piëch's technical center at Audi.

The innovations streamed out.

In 1976, the first ever five-cylinder gasoline engine combined four-cylinder fuel economy with six-cylinder performance.

Later, Piëch launched a turbocharged, intercooled engine system.

He brought out the 1980 Quattro, the first major production car to spread the power across all wheels, improving handling, stability, traction, and safety.

The aerodynamic 1983 Audi 100 reduced drag 10 percent compared to similar-sized sedans, cutting fuel consumption.

In 1983, Audi was the first German carmaker to offer cars with catalytic converters to clean exhaust fumes.

By 1984, the Quattro won both the Manufacturers World Rally Championships and the Rally Drivers World Championships with Stig Blomqvist at the wheel.

In 1988, a Quattro won the USA Trans-Am Manufacturers and Drivers Championships.

Piëch's fully galvanized steel body shells were so rust-resistant that Audi guaranteed them against corrosion for 10 years.

In 1987, the Procon-Ten safety system put extra tension on the seatbelts and contracted the steering column, pulling it forward and away from the driver's head, all within a fraction of a second.

Piëch also led the industry in the introduction of lightweight materials. In 1991, two all-aluminum design studies—the low-slung Quattro Spyder and the Avus Quattro—turned heads at the Frankfurt and Tokyo auto shows.

A year later, Audi unveiled the Aluminum Space Frame (ASF) concept car with a 4.8-liter 12-cylinder 60-valve engine in a W configuration.

Daimler-Benz contributed much to the European technology explosion, but it often followed Audi.

"Mercedes' new four-wheel-drive is identical to Audi, but it took them 20 years," says Piëch. "They still have a higher belief in electronics. I am a mechanical engineer. A lot of things you cannot do mechanically—ABS, ASP, injection on diesel and gasoline engines, better environment conditions, its all electronic. But it needs a lot of backup learning. The 4matic (Mercedes' first all-wheel-drive system in the early 1980s) was just a cheap electronic solution that had to break. As mechanical engineers we looked at that and said it will not be good."

The Quattro helped launch the popularity of sport utility vehicles with passenger-car like appeal in the 1990s.

"The future Blazers, Grand Cherokee, and such vehicles will get more passenger-like, not as high, not as easy to drive off-road.

"Chrysler understood the Quattro concept. It is like man—if its slippery you fall on your hands and then you have 'all-wheel- drive.' It's better to be like a cat. Cats can go slowly, but can go straight up a tree too."

Among his catalogue of technical innovations in Ingolstadt, Piëch believed the fully galvanized body was the most important. In the early 1970s, rust was a huge problem in Europe, and Audi suffered in particular. The resulting lower residual value of its used cars was under-cutting the value of new Audis.

And while Audi was building a reputation for advanced technology, it was largely being offset by the corrosion problem.

The shift to fully galvanized bodies had actually began with Piëch in his Porsche days.

"I partly had the idea," he says. "The 911 torsion bar on the rear axle corroded in a short time. So in places such as Montreal and Garmisch-Partenkirchen, which had the most salt on the road of any place in the world, the housing for the torsion bar broke after three years. It cost 70 deutsch marks to galvanize the torsion bar, which was a lot of money at that time. I made the whole unit out of fully galvanized steel."

But when Piëch's new CEO, Ernst Fuhrmann, took over, he considered it too expensive.

"He stopped doing it. But after three months he had the same problem I had had a few years earlier. From that he got the idea of doing fully galvanized bodies."

FUHRMANN BROUGHT OUT a zinc-coated 911 body for the 1976 model year.

Piëch, meanwhile, had maintained close contact with Helmut Bott, and together they worked out a plan which brought the technology to Audi.

But Piëch had to do some creative thinking along the way.

Toni Schmucker had just arrived as chairman of Volkswagen in 1973. At his first auto show, the September 1973 Frankfurt show, the world's first energy crisis was roiling.

"He only had a sports car to present—the 924. He was going to be killed.

"He was laying off employees because we had no work for them and he was bringing out a sports car."

The 924 was a four-cylinder sports car that had been developed with Porsche's help. It was to be produced at Audi's plant in Neckarsulm, Germany.

"I had a private talk with Schmucker," says Piëch. "I said 'sell the car back to Porsche. They cannot pay for it immediately, but they can pay it car by car.'

"If Volkswagen just stopped the car, tooling and everything is lost. If you sell it back to Porsche—its a sports car, and I think they will agree.' VW tried and they did sell it back, and Neckersulm had better employment, and exactly at that time Porsche started the fully galvanized 911.

"I talked to Mr. Bott and said, 'How much could you pay if we also fully galvanized our 924 production. Help us with this and Audi will learn how to do fully galvanized cars.'

"We couldn't do everything at first, but we coated some parts with zinc, which was nearly as good as fully galvanized. There had been three or four parts coated, and you could give a 10-year warranty also on those parts."

Porsche had no problem with its small output of 911s, but Audi had to prove that it could build 150 fully-galvanized 924s a day. It was a learning process.

Early on, white smoke began appearing on the body assembly line where the zinc-coated body-in-whites were welded together.

"This white smoke was like alcohol," remembers Piëch. "The workers in the shop where like drunken people when they were welding. So immediately we had to put much more air in to get the white smoke out."

But the arrangement at Neckarsulm gave Audi the chance to learn how to mass produce rustproof bodies—and gave Audi another technical edge.

"The fully streamlined [1982 Audi 100] was the first fully galvanized car at Audi, so there was a big discussion: Can it be done by the entire Volkswagen group? Finally, Schmucker decided that we could not do it because, later on, the Golf and every car would have to have it, and that would be impossible."

Schmucker didn't want the VW cars to look bad in comparison.

Schmucker agreed to go along if Piëch could find a way to put on a 10-year warranty against rust without having fully galvanized the bodies.

Piëch knew the roof didn't need galvanizing, it just needed a better coating.

SOON SCHMUCKER BEGAN to understand the marketing value of "fully galvanized" and relented.

"Not having fully galvanized was idiotic," says Piëch.

Meanwhile, the mass production issues had been solved.

"Neckarsulm would build 150 fully galvanized 924s and 600 Audi 100s a day."

It was a triumph for Piëch, who later cleared out opponents in Ingolstadt who thought it couldn't be done.

A few years later, he spread the idea across the entire Audi lineup.

"After the Audi 100 was fully galvanized, I decided the Audi 80 and Audi 90 should be, too."

But Volvo also wanted to do it.

"I had enough influence on purchasing so that we reserved for three years the galvanized material from the Thyssen steel mills so Volvo couldn't get it. This was the end of the fully galvanized Volvo. They never did it. If it had, there would only be enough supply from all the steel mills in the world for the 924, 911 and Audi 100—but not enough for the Audi 80.

"We gave the steel mills a three-year contract."

Piëch often had to convince the men in Wolfsburg about his technical advances at Audi.

"It was 99.2 percent owned by VW, so in reality we couldn't decide at Audi. It would be as if Condor ran Lufthansa."

PIËCH WAS NOT a car designer, but he had an enormous effect on modern automobile styling with the streamlined 1983 Audi 100.

"The Audi 100 influenced all things," he says. "Up to that time no one was building flush windows. It was a way of showing the aerodynamics. In reality it doesn't do too much, but today nobody can have the windows set inside. It has been 100 percent flush windows since the Audi 100. It is the result high pressure from the customer. It *has* to look like this."

Piëch said the concept of the aerodynamic Audi came from studies at five wind tunnels.

The engineers at the various VW and independent wind tunnels Piëch had contracted only saw parts of the proposed car.

"They didn't know that this was one car," he says. "Only I had looked at them together. It was the Turin, Stuttgart, Hamburg, Wolfsburg, and Ingolstadt wind tunnels, and only I knew how it would be put together because what we didn't want was to have fast followers."

That included Volkswagen, Audi's parent company.

So Piëch—with Audi chief designer Hartmut Warkuss—assembled the design of the future from pieces.

"Only I knew how," Piëch says. "For instance, Turin had the front-end to see how the air flowed around the engine to minimize drag. The side was done in Wolfsburg. But Wolfsburg didn't know how to make the whole car. Only Audi had the key, so for a long time no Passat or Golf had any of its features."

Warkuss was the credited designer—"With high influence of these five wind tunnels," Piëch says.

"At the time, we thought that the wheels had to stand quite inside. That looked ugly and was not the wish of the designers. The designers wanted them out, but it was the first approach of this kind and we had to do it in a very short time. We had less than three years for the whole concept, and for normal designers such a big step usually took five years.

"I wanted to fire Warkuss at the time. He wanted shapes that had nothing to do with aerodynamics, though later on he always used aerodynamics. But I knew if designers thought about aerodynamics at an early stage the outcome would be good, the design good, and the drag coefficient low. I needed eight or nine years fighting with Warkuss until he agreed."

PIËCH SAYS HE ACHIEVED all that he had set out for himself during his decade as chairman of Volkswagen.

"I didn't think that you could achieve so much in 10 years at Volkswagen. I expected to do less. In the first years I could always double the profits. I say I couldn't do more in the 10 years."

He acquired Bentley, Lamborghini, and Bugatti for VW.

"There is so much written about luxury. I wanted one company. I had the bad luck of getting all three."

The one he wanted most was Bentley, which was twinned with Rolls-Royce under the ownership of Vickers, the British defense concern.

"The two others fell in at very low cost—we couldn't say 'No we won't take them.'"

Piëch says he never wanted to own Rolls-Royce, which he couldn't get because Rolls-Royce plc, the independent aero engine manufacturer, owned the rights to the name and wouldn't sell it to Volkswagen. Instead BMW got it, for a fraction of what VW paid for Bentley.

"It was too small a segment," Piëch now says. "There was no sportiness. You could have a limousine, a long wheelbase limousine, and a cabriolet, that's all. And in these times its better that people don't know how much your car costs.

"With Bentley, I could also have a four-door here in Salzburg and be able to park it, and one of my children doesn't have to stay with it to make sure it doesn't get scratched."

But Piëch's critics accused him of taking his eyes off the ball with his luxury pursuits.

"Why did we enter the luxury segment? Very easy. BMW and Daimler-Benz earn too much money in the luxury segment ,and if you did this in a platform system you can earn more."

And he had done it before.

"Audi's image in 1971 was lower than Opel's. We needed seven or eight years with Audi to be the same level as BMW and Daimler-Benz, and now Audi sells the highest number of 12-cylinder cars in the world. A few years it ago it was BMW, and in other years it was Daimler-Benz."

And there was another reason for VW's move into the prestige classes—perhaps the most important one to Ferdinand Piëch.

"An engineer can do more around expensive cars," he says.

The Volkswagen-branded Phaeton, which in some iterations cost more than $100,000, had become an industry joke. Not for its technology. No one criticized that. But because of the oversized VW emblem on the grille. It was the wrong brand for such an expensive car.

But it was the technology that mattered to Piëch.

"Volkswagen needs to bring it down from the top. An engineer never would have the chance without the Phaeton to do this.

Sixty-seven-year-old Ferdinand Piëch had just driven three new cars: the new 12-cylinder long-wheelbase Audi A8; the long-wheelbase Phaeton; and the next Bentley.

"Phaeton is still ahead of the two others, so I told Mr. Pischetsrieder when the Bentley goes into production it has to be better than Phaeton. By having the Phaeton chassis people engineer the car we can do that. It would be terrible if someone tests the Bentley and says they could get a better car for half the price—the Phaeton."

MEANWHILE, PIËCH INDIRECTLY influenced the wildly successful product plan that saved Porsche AG in the 1990s, thus making possible one of the most extraordinary auto industry turnarounds of the decade.

Arno Bohn had conceived of a plan for a four-door Porsche sedan, an idea Piëch and other Porsche purists despised.

Work proceeded on the car as Porsche groped for a model strategy that would allow it to weather the storms of the high-priced sports car market.

"Within three years costs doubled, and it was a product that you couldn't sell," says Piëch. "That was the end of Bohn."

Instead, Porsche and Wendelin Wiedeking decided to base a new 911 and the less expensive Boxster sports car on the same platform. The sharing of one platform was a fundamental Piëch idea, one he was about to impose on Volkswagen when he took control of the monolith in January 1993.

"What was done at Porsche with the platform was part of what Volkswagen did," Piëch says.

But he claims only indirect influence on the Porsche plan.

"The 911 and Boxster were different, but they combined in a different way the basic idea of Audi's common platform and engine and gearbox. Porsche uses different front and the rear ends to create different types of cars."

In 1991, Piëch showed the Audi Quattro Spyder concept at the autumn Frankfurt and Tokyo shows.

"The Quattro Spyder made Porsche very, very nervous because this was built out of mass production parts and it was a nice sports car. This idea drove Porsche to the idea of Boxster. I never dictated that they should do this, but I did an interesting model as a show car that made them think about what they were doing was wrong.

"They showed me the Boxster very late because they feared the Quattro Spyder. In the end, the Spyder never came out, which was the wrong decision by Audi."

Ferdinand Piëch transformed Volkswagen in the 1990s. The first all-new VW car completed under the new leader was the 1997 Passat. It was a landmark model, with quality and style that drove up the price VW cars could command. It set a new standard for Europe's so-called upper-medium segment.

Piëch chose the design—an alternative to the proposal picked for a new generation of the Audi 100.

"I liked the shape better than the Audi that was decided on, so I took the second choice and modified it."

The designer was again Warkuss, by now head of Volkswagen design.

Making something of the Passat was critical to VW.

"The whole company had really not been a car company, it was a Golf company. All the good people worked on the Golf, which had 10 times as many people as you needed to make a new car. The Passat and Polo were stepsisters. The front of the Golf was important. The front of the Passat was not supposed to be as good as a Golf. The front of a Polo could not be as good as a Golf. People didn't want to work on the Polo."

Piëch changed the Passat from a transverse-mounted engine to longitudinal—"again because we had seen the positive outcome of putting the Audi 100 and Audi 80 into one model system; one front axle with different widths; then one rear axle with different widths."

Piëch's common platform strategy generated immediate cost savings for VW. The Passat meant another 700,000 units in volume for the platform on which the Audis were built.

"It was a minimum 10 percent cheaper because the suppliers got the higher numbers out of the same equipment they had for the two Audi lines, and they could do it by working extra shifts and some weekends."

The VW platform strategy had its critics.

"Some competitors said, 'Its bad because the more expensive car takes the cheap parts from the cheaper car. In reality, BMW had done this with the 5 Series and 7 Series for generations and nobody said it was bad. But they did it from the top down. The big dimensions and the heavy weight was brought from the 7 Series into the 5 Series so the 5 got heavier.

"My idea was to get the parts from the lighter car and make them strong enough so that they would work in the upper car. This brings savings, reduced weight, and higher quality because you test many more cars."

PIËCH MET HENRY FORD II for the first time at Le Mans in the 1960s.

Porsche and Ford were not yet competitors. Porsche was still in the 2-liter class.

He remembers Henry Ford II being surrounded by a great number of people.

"My grandfather had something to do with his grandfather. Henry Ford I allowed my grandfather to hire 11 engineers of German origin out of his company. It is partly why Volkswagen could continue to work after the Second World War, because these 11 had been German, and after the Second World War they had been more Americans. They were all production men who knew production methods."

Piëch believes Henry Ford I was the most influential industry leader of the first half of the twentieth century. But he says Soichiro Honda had the greatest influence on the modern auto industry.

"Eiji Toyoda influenced a lot, but he was never my target. It's different. As for my contemporary competitors—I never thought about them. I was too much involved to judge them."

"I met Iacocca several times. He was different. He was a marketing guy. He was very impressive. When they were still in one company, I met Bob Lutz and Iacocca in Paris. A cousin of mine ran the Chrysler importer in France and he always gave a dinner party during the Paris motor show.

"Iacocca saved Chrysler by his marketing ideas, but it is a very small time in life where he was really at the top. And he outsourced all research and development. This was the reason for the high price Daimler had to pay for the company in 1998, because there had been nothing prepared for the future. If you stop research and development one day and put all the money you saved there to the earnings, you have the best company in the world, but only for a short time. This I didn't like so much."

OF ALL OF THE GREAT LEADERS of the modern automotive industry, Piëch was the most difficult to work for.

"It's not so good if a person comes twice telling me they couldn't do a job. One time it could happen, second time . . ."

Piëch says his own style came mainly from his mother, Louise Piëch.

"She always looked after the money. I could not have worked for her. She had a typically feminine decision making style—waiting, because half of the problem disappeared by itself. She never fired any person, but she found a way for the man or woman to be hired by somebody else.

"If I see that somebody is not right in his place in the company, I get nervous because the money you lose in a company with the wrong man in the wrong position is much more than if you give him a good handshake and money and a good recommendation for the competition. A big company takes a long time to find out if somebody is good or bad.

"If internally I decide to do something I do it—straight. I learned in a small company like Porsche, then in Audi, that people want clear orders, they want better pay; they want better conditions, higher rank if they are successful."

Piëch said he never set out to emulate his grandfather.

"When I reached the top of Audi, I already had a bigger responsibility than my grandfather ever had in his life. It was enough for me."

But the men Ferdinand Porsche surrounded himself with had an enormous influence on Piëch.

"He had about five people: chief officer Karl Rabe, Josef Mickl, his theoretical man, who influenced me most. He was a genius in the First World War. He built airplanes, he designed the turbine in the air-cooled Beetle, he designed wind turbines, a kind of water turbine for farmers here in Austria after the Second World War. When he died, I got all his personal technical books. From these people around my grandfather I learned all about his philosophy."

Besides Mickl and Rabe, there was Franz Xaver Reimspiess, the man who designed the Beetle engine, not to mention the VW logo. Erwin Komenda designed the exterior shape of the Beetle and, after the war, the Porsche 356. Some of the men were still at the Porsche company when Piëch joined in 1963.

These were the men who sat at his grandfather's table in Austria, where the men visited during the summer vacations of 1942 and 1943. Young Piëch learned their secrets and absorbed their passion.

"I was sitting under the table, five years old," he recalls. "I explained how the bombs would fly to Great Britain [he traces a parabolic line with his hand] from the next months on. I explained to the family because I was hearing the talk of the engineers. I was told I should forget it because what I have heard is terrible."

But the child was fascinated. Mickl gave the boy materials to help him make his rocket designs. Young 'Burli' grasped the principles the engineers at the table above him were discussing.

"Otherwise I couldn't explain it to the family," he says.

Mickl later stayed on at Ferdinand Porsche's house, where he kept his archives and developed new ideas. Fifteen years later, when Piëch was studying in Zurich, he went back to his old mentor, Mickl.

"He explained to me the theory of gas turbines. I didn't want to do car design. Not at all. I wanted to be an aeronautical engineer."

That dream ended when the head of aerodynamics at Piëch's university designed two Swiss jet fighter prototypes that crashed into Lake Konstanz.

"My career in airplanes was over suddenly. I couldn't go to study in England or France, and I didn't want to go to Russia, and America didn't accept Austrians at that time, so I had to make cars. But during my education I learned how to build airplanes mechanically, and therefore I learned my love for aluminum, for magnesium, for carbon fiber. All these light materials I learned in Zurich."

Piëch did follow his grandfather's credo of surrounding himself with talented colleagues.

"My grandfather had five important people around him. At Audi I had about 60 people, important people. I made sure they never had to come to me to ask for more money or for a better position. I thought that if somebody deserved to be in a better position or receive better pay they should get it without asking. This is how to do it.

"When it came to running a big company like Volkswagen, I had 1,200 key people. But you could learn only about 120 of them well enough to really get to know them. Four to six times a year you meet with the key people about products—testing them, talking about them. You learn how they think, how they work."

Piëch relied mainly on technical people. He was never completely comfortable with finance types and marketing specialists.

"My key team was very unconventional. Yes, there were financial people and marketing, but I would say 80 percent were engineers—and of course the designers. I think that is partly why I could run more than 60 models and know the advantages and disadvantage of each."

Bob Lutz, five years Piëch's senior, remained active in the corridors of power at General Motors, while Piëch was squirreled away in a Salzburg office a fraction the size of Lutz's in Detroit. Piëch said he doesn't miss the day-to-day scramble of the industry. Seated behind his desk, the noise of traffic outside drowning out his quiet voice, he knows he is through. It's over, controversy or not. There is only his place in history to ponder.

"I think you have to know when you should finish. I would say it is the most difficult decision in everybody's life—when to retire— because at the top of your power you can be an egoist. You can stay until everybody sees that you are tired. So I would say it is better you make the decision when you only see it yourself."

CHAPTER EIGHTEEN

Art and Science

C ool Hand Lutz returned to General Motors in September 2001, but he had nearly been hauled back to his first employer in the car industry once before—27 years earlier.

The man Henry Ford II sent to hire Bob Lutz away from BMW in 1974 was Bill Bourke, then head of Ford of Europe, which was having huge problems in Germany at the time. The idea of hiring Lutz was planted with the Deuce by his friend and trusted confidant Walter Hayes.

Hayes, Ford's personal public relations man, was one of the members of the Ford imperial court. Being British, he spent a lot of time in Europe. He knew dozens of journalists and read all of the enthusiast books. He was hearing a lot about Lutz, who was having problems with von Kuenheim and was ready to leave Munich.

But Lutz had an agreement with GM President Elliott "Pete" Estes. When Lutz left for BMW in 1971, Estes made the young Opel executive promise that if things didn't work out at BMW he would call GM. Lutz told Bourke that his former employer had the right of first refusal and called Estes. Estes was excited about the prospect of the prodigal son returning and promised to find a place for him at GM. But Lutz heard nothing for weeks.

With Bourke growing impatient, Lutz started intense discussions with Ford. He came to the United States over the Fourth of July weekend in 1974 and met with Phil Caldwell, Lee Iacocca, and Henry Ford II. During those interviews, he met Iacocca and Ford for the first time. Lutz sat down with Iacocca and Caldwell and Bourke in Iacocca's office in Dearborn.

"Here, Lutz, have a Montecristo," the Ford president told him. The two men began puffing away on cigars as the interview proceeded.

Iacocca was his usual absolutely direct self.

"Look," he told Lutz, "we've got a problem in Germany, and I've been telling Bourke here he's got to solve that goddamn problem. I'm not gonna sit still and watch our market share continue to decline in Germany. Now he tells me you are a pretty good guy and you'll be interested.

"You know that I do due diligence on stuff like this, and I know you used to be at GM four years ago. So I picked up the phone and called Pete Estes. . . . Your former employer says good things about you, so I figure you're pretty good, but you're going to have to perform."

That was the kind of interview it was—straightforward.

Caldwell's interview was very stiff. He asked Lutz, "So, did you serve in the military?"

"Yes, I did."

"Why did you leave the military?"

"Because I wanted to go to college."

"You did not go to college before going in the military?"

"No, sir."

"Why was that?" It was all 20 questions.

Caldwell asked, "Why did you choose to leave General Motors?"

Lutz told him the whole story.

"I see. So you went to BMW?"

"Yes, sir."

"And now you'd like to leave BMW."

"Yes, sir."

Caldwell had a piercing stare. There was no warmth, no humor.

Then came the final interview with Henry Ford II, who kept Lutz waiting for about five minutes, then came out of his office and introduced himself. He was wearing gray slacks and a light-blue shirt, and on that very hot July weekend, Ford's shirt was soaked in huge crescents of sweat.

Ford was very courtly. "Thank you very much for taking the time away from a weekend where you probably would have preferred to be with your family. I hear you have a very good reputation, and your resumé looks great. We need you badly, especially in Germany."

It was a short interview and at the end, Ford said to Lutz, "You know, there is only one thing that worries me. We just haven't been too lucky with outside hires."

Lutz then went back to Europe and told Bourke "give me a little more time with GM."

Lutz called Estes, who said, "I haven't forgotten it. I'm working on the goddamn thing. It's tough here. Don't do anything rash. Where are you with Ford? Well, hold them off as long as you can. We're going to get this thing done." In the end, Estes couldn't make it happen.

"It was just the way GM was organized at the time," said Lutz. "I don't think it was political, there were just so many competing and conflicting cultures and organizations at GM that not even the president could figure out where to re-enter a guy.

"Nowadays, we could do it in a heartbeat, Gary Cowger and Rick Wagoner and John Devine would get together over lunch and say, 'Hey, we've got an opportunity to get this guy,' and we'd decide where to put him, and that would be all done in 24 hours. But back then it was like running a federation rather than running a company."

So Lutz was hired as managing director of Ford of Germany. In the years to come, Lutz and Ford got along very well. "Lutz liked Henry Ford II, and Henry Ford II liked Lutz," recalls one veteran Ford executive who worked closely with both men. When the Deuce was in Europe, he'd often go out to dinner with Lutz. He'd ask his man in Europe all manner of questions about strategy and the Ford Motor Company—what did Lutz think of this, what did he think of that.

"They were excellent questions," said Lutz, "and sometimes you were a little cautious about answering because it would be questions about other senior executives, so you had to be a little circumspect in the replies."

But Lutz always answered the Deuce's questions with as much brutal honesty as he felt he could get away with. Sometimes Ford would say, "Well, gee, that's not what everybody else tells me. Why do you say that? Why does everybody else tell me something different?" and Lutz would say, "For this, that, and the other reason people think that it's what you want to hear."

Bourke once cautioned Lutz about Ford's drinking: "Jesus, try to avoid going out with him in the evening because he will be nice, nice, nice, nice, nice, then all of the sudden one glass and he turns really nasty."

But Lutz said he never saw this other side. "I think he liked me because, number one, I had a European background, and he was partly raised and schooled in Europe. He had kind of a respect for Americans who had had a European education, and he kind of identified with that, and I think he liked the fact that he saw me as a relatively cultured person compared to some others in the company that he didn't consider to be adequately cultured."

The two aristocrats, Henry Ford II and Bob Lutz, understood each other. They weren't engineers or cost analysts or production experts, but they each grasped the art and science of their industry. And managing an auto company in the second half of the twentieth century was both—an art and a science.

Henry Ford II had fathered both approaches within the Ford Motor Company, and for the remainder of the twentieth century, car companies seemed to swing from one extreme to the other. At the end of the century, the art/science tension remained the great philosophical divide in auto-industry management.

The auto business was too large and complex and mysterious to be managed from a ledger book. But neither could it be managed by pure intuition and gut-level impulse. The greatest companies and the greatest executives had found ways to combine the emotion of cars with cold-blooded operational efficiency. Without Henry Ford II's vision of modern management, the industry might have suffered the kind of trauma that went on in the airline business and countless other American industries.

The Ford Motor Company would exist as a brand name somewhere inside the General Motors orbit. Henry II created energy in the American auto industry by trying so hard to catch Chevrolet. There were hard consequences. The price war he started in 1952 all but killed Studebaker, Packard, Nash, and Hudson.

Henry II started several lava flows. His Whiz Kids turned corporate finance into high art. The senior General Motors executives hired after the war spread the organizational thinking of mighty Alfred Sloan to Ford. And there was the second generation of post-war Ford executives—the product and marketing dynamos who lived to defeat Chevrolet. This was a group of executives born in the 1920s—typified and symbolized by Lee Iacocca. It was the generation that would save Chrysler in the 1980s.

The Whiz Kids craved facts and figures that provided insight into the mysterious inner workings of the company. The U.S. Army Air Force Stat Control had begun as gathering place of data and only later in the war evolved into a place where statistics were analyzed and acted upon. The evolution would be the same at Ford. After the logistical miracles they had worked during the war, the Whiz Kids believed that data could be used to classify, understand, and tame large and complex companies.

Data would eliminate guesswork. Decisions on new cars and new plants and new investments could be made by the numbers, not by the gut. All of the Whiz Kids and their disciples—who held sway at Ford through the mid-1990s—believed in this principle. But none believed it more than Robert McNamara.

In the fall of 1960 Henry Ford II elevated McNamara to Ford's presidency—the first of the 10 original Whiz Kids to rise to that level. But the former Harvard Business School instructor had made his mark at Ford long before then. Throughout the 1950s, McNamara had conceived and then implemented a corporate culture that spread across the divisions and through the ranks, ultimately touching just about every remote corner of the company. Ford became almost as much a reflection of McNamara's personal style as Henry Ford II's.

And McNamara had made mistakes along the way. Iacocca's famous adage "you can't sell safety" was the result of McNamara's unsuccessful attempt to do so in 1956, while head of the Ford Division. He had used a series of safety features to promote the new model year's cars. McNamara, the ascetic, the unemotional businessman, believed that American car buyers should desire an automobile because it offered "Lifeguard Design," padded dashes, and double-grip door locks. They should want it simply because it was good for them.

It was not the last time McNamara would try to appeal to the rationalism of his customers, but it was a setback in his career and nearly got him fired.

McNamara thought the auto industry had a social responsibility, something few other car executives of his day believed. In some ways, McNamara's personality resembled that of consumer crusader Ralph Nader, the great scourge of the auto industry a decade later. Both were abstemious men. Some of McNamara's critics would claim the two men had approximately the same appreciation of automobiles.

McNamara was turning the internal operations of the company into an extension of his own logical, numerate mind. Numbers became the currency of the Ford Motor Company. Any manager who could marshal statistics could win an argument—could push through a car project or get one killed—and advance his own career in either case.

McNamara and Lee Iacocca represented the two wings of Henry Ford II's company—the numerate and the instinctive. But Iacocca's intuitive product guys relied on the financial structure that McNamara and the Whiz Kids had built.

McNamara constructed a huge labyrinth of data that sales executives and product planners could draw upon. Iacocca's generation at Ford never knew any different. The numbers were always there. Everything was measured. Iacocca used the McNamara systems as a mechanism for accountability, for evaluating his people.

"If our stockholders had a quarterly review system, why shouldn't our executives?" Iacocca asked.

In the 1950s, Iacocca began asking his managers, "What are your objectives for the next ninety days?" and would then hold them accountable. He'd reward them if they made their targets and punish them if they didn't.

McNamara also tried to use cold-blooded rationalism in the sales and marketing side of the business. He had mastered the numbers that held the secrets of production, distribution, logistics, and profit and loss. In the late 1950s, he tried to use them to render the irrational part of the auto industry logical and predictable. He suspected that data crunchers could churn out answers to eternal questions about public taste, and he was the first auto executive who sought to measure the effectiveness of advertising.

It was as if McNamara were trying to expunge talent from the automotive industry. He wanted a business that didn't need the raw bootstrap ability of a Henry Ford I or a Walter Chrysler or a Lee Iacocca. He wanted a company that ran like a Univac computer.

To a degree, McNamara succeeded. When he left the industry, just one month after he became president of Ford, he was at the vanguard of a movement that would continue to build momentum for many years. Japanese carmakers began to adopt ideas that McNamara first put into play at Ford.

The common belief among auto industry historians is that McNamara's theory of rational management failed in the auto industry. In 1975, a management consultant named Dave Power began surveying new-car customers about the quality of their vehicles and their experiences with the dealerships. These McNamara-inspired J.D. Power customer-satisfaction rankings would become a tremendous force in the industry by the 1990s.

J. D. "Dave" Power III graduated from the Wharton School in the early 1960s and became a financial analyst at Ford. There he absorbed the lessons of McNamara. But the pure numbers work at Ford bored him, and Power moved to General Motors, where he did customer research. He found that less than satisfactory as well and soon opened his own consulting firm in Los Angeles.

Power had left Ford, but some of the Whiz-Kid culture stayed with him. Like McNamara, he studied the data to derive insights into the company that were not available through mere observation. In his way, Power helped bring the Ford Motor Company to Toyota.

In 1968, he got a contract to advise the Japanese company, which was re-entering the American market after failing in the U.S. in the 1950s. Ford and the other Big Three wouldn't give Power the time of day, but Toyota asked him to suggest ways to impress American customers. He came up with the ideas of better braking and improved rust protection.

Years later, when Power began publishing his customer-satisfaction ratings, Toyota did extremely well. Soon the Japanese company was advertising its Power scores, which helped it make its first inroads in the American market.

Other forms of rationalism descended from McNamara too. Statistical process controls, for instance. Toyota latched onto American controls-theorist J. Edwards Deming, who applied numbers to the production process in the way that McNamara had applied them to financial discipline. By the mid-1980s, Ford was benchmarking Toyota's statistical process controls. Once again, Toyota benefited most from an idea that had been tried at Ford many years earlier. In the 1950s, the Whiz Kids had attempted to put statistical controls in place at Ford, but it did not take. Why hadn't it happened at Ford?

"It was the same old story," wrote former Ford CEO Donald Petersen years later. "The effort was initiated by the people at the top; the employees in the plants didn't buy it and they didn't use it. They just papered their bulletin boards and office walls with graphs and charts of statistics that they could show to any management people who might stop by."

When Petersen became Ford's president and chief operating officer in 1980, he rediscovered statistical process controls, and they became a mantra inside Ford.

McNamara was also the first to dream of a scientific understanding of customer brainwaves. By the early 1980s, U.S. auto companies were relying heavily on the results of customer focus groups. Ford was the most sophisticated consumer researcher. But General Motors went for it in a big way in 1993, after the engineers who had briefly taken control of the company were swept out.

The GM board brought in a finance specialist to head the company, Jack Smith, and made John Smale, the former head of Proctor & Gamble, one of the largest consumer-products companies in the world, its non-executive chairman. For years, GM's product plans were made through statistical analysis of consumer test groups in a way that McNamara had envisioned.

But the equilibrium was missing. In 2001, it would take Lutz to redress the imbalance at GM. At Toyota, the influence of Henry Ford II's Whiz Kids was stabilized by another great influence—Soichiro Honda and Honda's own brand of Whiz Kids.

The entire Japanese auto industry was made in the image of Soichiro Honda. The mechanic from Hamamatsu blazed a trail for all of his country's vehicle manufacturers. The CVCC engine proved that with cutting-edge technology small Japanese firms could compete with General Motors, Ford, Volkswagen, and Mercedes-Benz. It didn't require genius, merely the innovative application of existing knowledge.

Honda inspired his employees, who powered his company. The company stirred the other Japanese carmakers, which drove all auto manufacturers everywhere else to improve. It was a beautiful marriage of art and science.

Among industry experts at the end of the twentieth century, the consensus choice for "world's best all-around automaker" was Toyota. But without the challenge and stimulus of the unorthodox genius Soichiro Honda, Toyota would have been a different company—a very good one, to be sure, but possibly not a great one. It would have evolved differently, more methodical, less magical.

"He had run businesses before and had learned by trial and error how to motivate people," said Dave Nelson, who served as Honda of America Manufacturing's head of purchasing from 1987 to 1997. "He was the first in so many things. He was the first to build cars in America, now everyone does."

Toyota's success is often attributed to its lean manufacturing ethos— the Toyota Production System. But it was prodding from the Honda company that drove Toyota to the summit. "If somebody whips around you, you are all of the sudden energized to do better than that competitor," said Nelson. For decades, Toyota had benchmarked America's Big Three auto manufacturers, but the company it learned most from was Soichiro Honda's eager, egalitarian little carmaker in Japan.

Likewise, the men of Mercedes-Benz would have been much more complacent in the 1970s, 1980s, and 1990s without BMW buzzing in their ears. Mercedes-Benz and Toyota were large companies with proud histories, but the competitive spark of BMW and Honda forced the two giants to improve. In the following decades, the smaller companies proved faster, nimbler, more creative, and more determined than the older ones.

Statistical process controls could govern quality in the factory, but consumer-research statistics could not tell Toyota what cars to develop or how to develop them. In this area, Toyota turned to the example of Honda, not McNamara.

The developers of Honda's motorcycles, and later its cars, had a freedom that Ford's engineers and product planners did not have. McNamara's numbers culture tended to restrict creativity and innovation. There was no American Soichiro Honda after World War II to set the pace for Ford. There was merely the giant General Motors to chase.

So it was Honda's early success in America that led Toyota to take the United States so seriously. It was Honda that spurred Toyota to create its enormously successful Lexus luxury brand. It was the Honda Accord that prompted Toyota to respond with its Camry.

But even though Honda's and Toyota's executives became aware of the importance of measurable customer satisfaction before their American competitors, it ultimately led to a kind of complacency, an overdependence on the data. Toyota and Honda had become so focused on pure quality and efficiency and the abstraction of customer-satisfaction polling that it led to a creative lull in Japanese products.

In the early 1990s, Bob Lutz and Lee Iacocca at Chrysler took advantage of this. Chrysler's lack of dependence on focus groups—its willingness to tackle new product concepts—helped it become the most robust American company of the era.

Lutz had tied the strands of genius together—the Zen-like teamwork of Honda, von Kuenheim's linkage of product and brand, the market instincts of Iacocca, and the systems approach to business begat by Henry Ford II. From a most unlikely place, Chrysler became the model for the melding of art and science in the auto industry.

CHAPTER NINETEEN

Iacocca: The Lion in Winter

Lee Iacocca's passage from Ford to Chrysler in 1978 was an event as meaningful to the modern auto industry as any giant merger. The effects continue to the present day.

"It caused ripples, but it was more than a ripple in my household, it was an earthquake," Iacocca said in a late 2004 interview. He had recently turned 80—a lion in winter—but his mind still raced, firing away on all cylinders.

At the time of his ascension, he had been the perfectly tuned American businessman, precisely the right age to grasp the essence of post-war American commerce. Iacocca led a whole class of young executives on the make in 1950s America; he was their king.

He was a perfect combination of Depression-era child (he'd watched his entrepreneur father get hammered by economic catastrophe) and the dynamic post-war American man, young enough to feel the energy and yearning of the country.

Over the next 40 years, he would strive like no other corporate executive before. There was fire in every action, drama in every anecdote. Iacocca was a visionary, but also intensely practical. He made people work their heads off for him. His language was salty, punchy, and profane, but it had its own beauty.

At 80, sitting in his den in Los Angeles, he looked back at a life and career studded with achievement, controversy, deep admirers, and second-guessers. While he talked he often stared at the cloisonné vase that Soichiro Honda had given him in 1975 in Tokyo. He looked back further, to the day he visualized the car that would become the Mustang. And he recalled a recruiter from the Ford Motor Company who had driven to Lehigh University in Bethlehem, Pennsylvania, in a Continental Mark I.

"I got crazy about a long hood and short deck," Iacocca said.

He has eased off the throttle some. His last attempted power grab came in 2001, at age 77. He tried convincing DaimlerChrysler Chairman Juergen Schrempp to appoint him as Chrysler's U.S. front man—again. He could have been an advisor or spokesman—or even just a morale builder. He was looking for a role to play.

Iacocca had said he would do almost anything to help Chrysler. Schrempp seemed interested, strung him along for a while, and then froze him out.

He still keeps busy. He has business interests, and his pride and joy, the Iacocca Foundation, established to fight diabetes, the disease that took his beloved wife, Mary.

WHEREAS FERDINAND PIËCH talks slowly, choosing his words carefully, Iacocca still fires them off like a machine gunner, punctuating his most important points with a cigar.

He sifts through the past like he is going through an old photo album, stopping at this or that remembrance. Things happened so fast for so long that it's amazing he can remember anything at all. And his memory is not selective; he recalls the good with the bad.

He is less angry at Henry Ford II than he once was. Iacocca understood the Deuce's point of view all along, but Iacocca was too fiery, too much a scrapper, to let Ford fire and humiliate him without landing a few counterpunches. He hit back with his success at Chrysler, his minivan, and his autobiography, which was a direct blow to the solar plexus.

"THE MAN WHO saved Chrysler" believes the company would have survived without him; the company he inherited in 1978 was very underrated.

"It was just going through a bad patch because it was being run by a bunch of accountants," he said. Lynn Townsend and his successor, John Riccardo, were good people, "but they didn't like product," says the man who—for a time—was America's best-known pitchman. "They didn't like cars. They had come out of a big accounting firm—Touche Ross. John Riccardo was a good guy. Frankly, though, he was in over his head. Chrysler was a mess financially."

Iacocca discovered that the beleaguered company had a fantastic powertrain engineering department.

"When it came to combustion, hemi heads, whatever, it was really their strong suit. The engineers at Chrysler had had a lot of firsts in the industry. The company just didn't have any money. It couldn't build on what the engineers were capable of designing."

Deep in the bowels of Chrysler, he said, engineers were working on emissions controls not unlike what Soichiro Honda and his boys in Japan had come up with—a combustion system that didn't require the catalyst being promoted at GM by Iacocca's friend Ed Cole, GM president and engineering honcho.

"Chrysler would have changed the world if it had had enough money," Iacocca said. "Those guys were doing what Honda was doing. Chrysler's facilities had gone to hell, the plants were lousy, the quality was bad. But they did have that core of engineering that allowed me, when I got there, to do the only thing I could do at the time. Warranties.

"We believed in warranties. We went from one year to three years to five years and 50,000 miles to [60,000] and 70,000. Now some manufacturers are at 100,000 miles at 10 years. We could never have warranted the body or the air conditioning systems, but they were fantastic in the engine department and in the axle and transmission department. That allowed us to say, 'We have a car that will last five years.'

"But that was all we had to sell. Marketing-wise, what I spent my time doing when I got to Chrysler was extending warranties. I couldn't do it at Ford—the stuff wasn't good enough to warrant the powertrain for that long."

Before Iacocca arrived, Chrysler was selling cars by handing out rebates to customers.

"Joe Garagiola would say, 'Buy a car get a check for $300; for the custom model $500.' Now I sit out here I look at rebates that are $5,000 to $7,000 and I think we've all lost our goddam minds."

Yet it was the young Lee Iacocca who started it all in the 1950s.

"56 for 56" was the precursor to the rebate and warranty tactics that Chrysler used to squeak by in the early 1980s and that drive the entire auto industry today.

"Monthly payments. People forget that during the Korean War you were restricted by something called 'Regulation W.' You could not finance anything over 24 months."

When that rule came off, Iacocca figured out that with a 20-percent discount and a three-year payback, a man could buy a 1956 Ford for $56 a month.

The 1956 Fords hadn't sold well because Robert McNamara, who ran the Ford Division, had decided to market safety attributes rather than power and roominess. Iacocca, a young field sales staffer in Pennsylvania, got around that by emphasizing the payments.

"The whole thing was evolving in the mid-fifties. I joined Ford in the second half of the century when the fantastic change in the auto business depended on two things that people ignore in history: the Eisenhower 42,000-mile turnpike system—you could go across the country without a stoplight—and the GI Bill. Now what did *that* mean? Well, guys got educated, then they got married after the war, they moved to the suburbs, and—eureka!—here comes the two- and three-car family market.

"Those two things were public programs that revolutionized the auto industry from 1950 to the year 2000. From 1900 to 1950 there were a lot of great guys, like Henry Ford and so forth and there was the Model T and the Model A and the assembly line. But the industry didn't become so much of the gross national product—I think at one point it was over 20 percent—until the turnpike system and the GI Bill. Those were the significant milestones.

"Now later on you think of the good products you did, you think of research centers you built. You rolled with the punches. But really the transformation was how could a guy afford a car? How much a month can you get it for?"

In Philadelphia, where Iacocca was a sales trainee in the late 1940s, a couple of veteran Ford guys taught him the leasing business. One was Charlie Beacham, his first mentor. He learned that payments were everything.

"I didn't invent this stuff. I just figured out that there was a market for that kind of thing. Monthly payments. Think of marketing as monthly payments. The rebates that came later were just a phenomenon of how we spread it out. The guys need a down payment, so the factory says, 'Let's give them cash for the down payment on top of it.' That was the fillip added to it. And then we extended warranties."

Just about everything Iacocca would need to know he learned in the backroads and dealer lots of Pennsylvania as a young man working for Charlie Beacham.

"Charlie Beacham rubbed my nose in it. He said, 'You've got to learn the retail trade. You've got to go on the used car lots, you've got to become a used truck salesman.' Christ. Used truck salesman? Think of it! In the coal regions of Pennsylvania after 17 years of schooling. What the hell am I doing here?"

A few years later Iacocca started something called the pony car craze with the Mustang.

"Forget that it was a hot car, it became a whole new class! Then 20 years later came the minivan, which was really not the Volkswagen bus as some say. It had nothing to do with that. We were just going again with the market."

Iacocca did both the Ford Mustang and the Chrysler minivan with his friend, ally, and underling Harold Sperlich. There was also Don DeLaRossa, who was one of the main Mustang designers. He later joined Iacocca at Chrysler to help young stylist Tom Gale do the minivan.

"We started with what we called the miniMax concept car at Ford," Iacocca recalled. "That was going to be the minivan. But we didn't have a front-wheel-drive car and we couldn't do it without a flat floor. We just couldn't do it. That was the revolution, and that's when I went to see Mr. Honda."

Iacocca wanted to buy engines and transmissions to put in what would have been the first front-drive car in America, the so-called "blown Fiesta."

"Mr. Honda said, 'I'll give you 300,000 powertrains.' Then Henry Ford said, 'Are you out of your goddam mind, Lee? If you think there is going to be a car with a Ford name with a Jap engine under the hood you *are* out of your goddam mind.'

"Tom Gale did the final styling of the minivan, but you know it was a box. It depended on low height for garaging and step-up low height. And it was walk-through. That was one thing I didn't even consider when I did it. The soccer moms years later wanted to walk to the back of the bus without getting out to slap the kids around if they were making noise. Those were the things. It was a phenomenon."

346

Would the minivan have happened if Iacocca had not gone to Chrysler?

"That's called fate. Harold Sperlich was the genius in our company in product planning. He was always doing concepts. Flat floor. World car program. He wanted to do a small car, we wanted a minivan, but we didn't have front-wheel drive at Ford.

"He got fired and went to Chrysler. He's the guy who talked to me and said, 'Hey, now you can do the damn minivan at Chrysler. We've got the Simca in France. We brought that powerpack front-wheel drive over here in the Omni/Horizon.' They were the first front-wheel-drive cars in the U.S. It just happened."

Sperlich had gotten under Henry Ford II's skin in the mid-1970s and the chairman ordered Iacocca to get rid of the cheeky young car guy.

"Henry didn't like Harold. But he was my right arm for product. He was a genius, really. I mean we all liked product, me and Lutz and a lot of guys. Carroll Shelby. But Harold was the real catalyst—so damn much he'd drive you nuts. Harold was a sort of a genius in saying, 'Here's how the market is going. Here are the pieces we can cobble off. Shit, we've got all of these Falcon pieces. Let's do this new car called *Mustang*.'

"Looking back on it, I guess if Harold hadn't gotten fired first he wouldn't haven't come to my house on a foggy night with the K-car concept car and said, 'Here's the car. First prototype. Now come over and do it.' And that's what talked me into coming over to Chrysler."

Iacocca is immensely proud of his two grand product successes.

"They were 1964 and 1984, 20 years apart. It's fortuitous. Some things fell into your lap. If I hadn't been fired—that's a whole other story of course."

IACOCCA JOINED THE Ford Motor Company in Dearborn on September 26, 1946. Harry Bennett was gone, but his spirit still permeated the place.

"Everyone was scared shitless," Iacocca remembered. "His name was around. I think I saw him once. He holed up in an office in the Rouge plant. They had been a bunch of hoods. Henry brought in John Bugas from the FBI to clean up the joint. Henry depended on John Bugas for everything. Then came the Whiz Kids. They were a very good group; financial guys led by Tex Thornton, McNamara, Lundy, Arjay Miller. They were geniuses with numbers.

"But think of whenever a company got taken over by the bean counters alone—like General Motors under Roger Smith in the 1980s. Once those guys took over from the car guys, it was over. I would always watch GM. When the car guys were running it, they were pretty goddam good. They had 60 percent of the car market—that's because they had people like Ed Cole and Pete Estes and great stylists.

"They had John De Lorean. He went south after a while, but he was a helluva product guy. He was tough competition. And they ran a good railroad. But they were car people first and the profits would follow.

"The Whiz Kids were all geniuses, no question about it. I got to be great friends in later years with Ed Lundy. I still talk to him. He was pretty damn good. But he was all about financial control."

Lundy's young men and Iacocca's even younger men staged many boardroom battles in the 1950s and 1960s over the costs of new models and marketing programs. But Iacocca grew to respect them.

Ed Blanch was one of Lundy's best financial executives.

"I ran into Ed Blanch three months ago," Iacocca said. "He was a controller under McNamara. He was driving along and he sees me walking along and, God, he went crazy. He said he couldn't believe it. There I was walking down the street. He just wrote me a letter for my 80th birthday. Ed Blanch. Those guys are still around."

Iacocca also grew friendly with Arjay Miller. But it was McNamara he got to know best among the original Whiz Kids.

"McNamara liked me early on, after '56 for 56.'"

Iacocca had put the whole plan together, and it saved the company's bacon in the year when McNamara's safety campaign was flopping badly.

"When '56 for 56' came along, McNamara said, 'What was *that*?'

"I had just got the job I always wanted—I was district manager in Washington DC, the nation's capital. I loved it. McNamara said, 'Yeah, well that job is over already.' I was only there about three months. He said, 'Your next paycheck is in Dearborn.' So I met McNamara and he took a liking to me.

"My two mentors really were Charlie Beacham and Bob McNamara, who were completely different temperaments. Each was a genius, but one was a savvy Georgia cracker marketing guy and McNamara was the ultimate computer mind. A real whiz kid. I learned from both of them. I was lucky. It was one of those things that happen in life—to run into mentors early and have them change your head.

"My father got to be friends with Beacham, like bosom buddies. He was similar to my father. They both had the knack of knowing how to talk to people and how to sell."

IACOCCA WON'T GO along with what many say—that he saved McNamara's job with "56 for 56."

"Not at all. McNamara was safe over at the Ford Division. He was never involved with the Edsel fiasco. That was Lewis Crusoe. With safety, he was just ahead of his time. They quote me saying 'safety doesn't sell.' But what I said was: '*I* can't sell it.' You don't talk about accidents and getting killed.

"McNamara was a terrific guy. He wanted small cars way back then. He wanted pollution controls. I didn't know what he meant when he talked about emissions in the 1950s. He said we had to start worrying about pollutants. People didn't know what the hell the ecology was."

You'd never find two guys less alike.

Iacocca was a young corporate centurion who knew in his gut how to sell cars and motivate people and vault himself up one of the most complex and treacherous terrains in corporate America. McNamara was completely cerebral, the rational thinker, the bloodless brainy leader. Yet they connected.

In 2004, Iacocca saw Errol Morris' film *The Fog of War: Eleven Lessons from the Life of Robert S. McNamara*. The portrait of McNamara, which won the 2004 Academy Award for best documentary, is based on interviews in which McNamara discusses the complexities and moral ambiguities he confronted while secretary of defense under presidents Kennedy and Johnson and as an aide to General Curtis LeMay during World War II.

The film had a powerful affect on Iacocca, who sent copies of it to presidential candidates George W. Bush and John Kerry.

"The 11 principles to avoid screwing up in war—that was typical McNamara. He would never change. He was always numbering everything."

"I saw him not long after I had seen the film and I congratulated him on the Oscar. I told him 'You've had a pretty good career, President of Ford, Secretary of Defense, President of the World Bank, and now you win an Academy Award.' He said 'Wow' and I laughed with him. He invited me to dinner and he said, 'We should do it pretty quickly because I'm 88.'"

No sooner had McNamara left Ford in autumn 1960 to become the secretary of defense than Iacocca began undoing some of his legacy.

"Since he was big on small cars and safety, he did the Cardinal, a small car in Europe," Iacocca recalled. "He was going to bring it to America. After he left I had to go cancel it. It was front-wheel drive and way ahead of its time. But it was an ugly little son of a bitch and they sunk—I'll never forget—$35 million into it.

"Arjay Miller asked me, 'What are you going to do with it?' and I said 'I'm going to go to Europe and cancel it.'

"He said, 'We can't, we'll look like fools.'

"But we had just come out of the goddam Edsel fiasco. That's why the Mustang was a hard sell, by the way. The Edsel had a terrible effect on the company, though now I look at the Edsel and I think that the grille doesn't look too bad compared to some of the things out there now."

As remarkable as it may seem today, Iacocca had to convince Henry Ford to do the Mustang. But if anyone could do it, it was Iacocca.

"I could appeal to Henry," he said. "He thought he was a really hip guy and he was. He loved the youth market and he pushed me like a son of a bitch in racing. He said, 'Spend whatever you want to win all races.' We went to NASCAR, we went to Le Mans, we went to Indianapolis. Shit, we won everything.

"But he was reluctant about the Mustang. He said, 'We don't need another Edsel.'"

IACOCCA SAID THE INSPIRATION for a long hood and short deck came in 1946.

"I got crazy about [it] based on the original Continental Mark I. . . . Leander Hamilton McCormick-Goodheart, the Ford recruiter, came to pick me up at Lehigh driving [one] and I got stuck with the idea. I had a book called the *Auto Universum*, which had all the cars. I looked at all the cars that had those proportions and I said, 'Wow. If we could get that particular look they'd think they'd died and went to heaven.'

"I told [Ford designer Gene] Bordinet, 'Let's get a long hood and a short deck and make it look like a two-seater, but for four passengers— with enough room in the back so it's not a joke.'

"Then once we got the styling going, I used to take Henry over to the studio. I made sure I got him involved and he put his imprint on the car in a hurry. He got in the back and said, 'Well, shit, I thought this was a four-passenger [car] but there's not enough room for me. Add an inch or two.'

"We had a deadline to meet to introduce the car at the World's Fair in 1964. We had a bunch of young Turks led by Sperlich and Don Petersen [and] Don Frey, and we had a good agency, J. Walter Thompson, which got in early."

The decision to do the Mustang was part instinct and part analysis of the emerging American youth market—the baby boomers coming of age.

"You can't rely on gut too much, but we had a great bunch of guys and they all had a gut feel," Iacocca recalled. "Like all the young Turks [at Ford] they couldn't wait to get to work in the morning. We had to go off campus to work on the project. It was all overtime.

"Finally, the financial guys said, 'We'll give you $75 million to do the car.' But we already had all the powertrains. And you know, the Mustang was barebones stuff."

What's more, the bean counters had made a mistake when they did the business plan for the car.

"They forgot that they had allocated the fixed costs on a total company basis in the financial plan. They based the financial planning money on 75,000 units a year so it didn't carry the fixed cost load the way they accounted for it. So all of a sudden no fixed costs we sold 500,000 the first year. They couldn't count the money fast enough.

"The bean counters were scratching their heads. 'How can they make that much on that product?' Well, they never allocated fixed costs. The fixed costs were all paid for. The Falcon paid for it all."

"Mr. Honda and I got to be good friends," Iacocca recalled. "He was out to my house for dinner a couple of times and I went to his house in Japan a couple of times."

The 1975 visit, the deal for the engines and transmissions, could have changed everything. It was a magical evening. Honda gave Iacocca that beautiful vase. Iacocca gave Honda the first automatic transmission Mustang.

"I tried to get 300,000 engines and he was willing to do it. He was ready and the price was right, but Henry said 'no.'"

Ford would have had the front-wheel drive layout it needed to do the first minivan.

"When I got fired, I even asked to take all the research we had done," Iacocca remembered. "I had to go to Bill Ford. We had come pretty far along on the miniMax project. But we didn't have the engine and transmission to do it so that's why I went to see Honda. Well, you know that's life—what if, what if—you never know.

"But Honda was a great guy who disrupted a lot of the conventional thinking in Japan. He was a real entrepreneur. That company got big and they do good work, I'll tell ya."

WHEN MCNAMARA resigned as Ford's president in 1960, Iacocca was caught in the updraft. He was promoted to the top job at the Ford Division. Iacocca had lost his chief sponsor in the company, but he didn't see it that way at the time.

"My first thought was 'What happens now?' I knew I could not be president as long as he was there. I thought, 'He's out of the way. Now I can get that job.' I was so ambitious."

Iacocca's years of partnership with Henry Ford II were about to begin. In the 1960s, Iacocca would accompany the Deuce on many of his joyous sojourns to Europe, trips that were part business and part pleasure.

"In Europe he was like a king—and I followed him. He'd be up until 2 or 3 in the morning while I wanted to go to bed.

"But Henry did his homework. He was the first guy to walk into the meeting the next morning. And he asked the right questions.

"He paid me a lot of money, and I admired him because whatever he took in pay and bonus, I got the same. It was never a dollar less or a dollar more. That was his way of telling me I was equal."

Still, Beacham told Iacocca not to get too close to Henry.

"I told Charlie, 'If he asks me to go hunting, I'm not going to turn him down. What am I supposed to do?'"

Beacham said, "Well, be careful with your press."

In the late 1960s, Iacocca wound up on the cover of the *New York Times Sunday Magazine*.

"It was a knockout story and Henry had called and congratulated me on it. But a couple of these guys said, 'Yeah, that's bullshit. You're getting more press than Henry Ford.'"

Franklin Murphy, the chancellor at UCLA and a Ford board member, gave Iacocca some advice.

"Frank Murphy said, 'Henry hates Asia and the Japanese, so do what you want there. But stay out of Europe. That's his baby.'

"I said, 'When I go to Europe, shit, I go with him. I can't upstage Henry Ford.'"

Yet Iacocca managed to overstep his bounds.

"I think Henry decided he was mortal," Iacocca said. "He had heart problems and he got scared. I think deep down he reached the point where he said, 'Son of a bitch, what do I do now?' And in fact Bill Ford told me that he had gotten pretty sick.

"Then his mother died [in October 1976] and she was one of my great proponents. She called him 'Henny.' Bill Ford was also in my corner, but he wasn't strong enough, and he didn't want to ever contradict Henny. Bill said, 'He turned the company around, and I have to be in his shadow.'

"I told Bill, 'Why, you're the smartest son of a bitch of all.'

"But you've got to remember Henry was going through the trauma of divorce with Christina [Vettore], the Italian girl, and he was sort of mixed up and his great fear was that his family was too weak to keep the company running and therefore he diffused power. He brought in McKinsey. The company spent, Christ, a lot of money on that."

At the consulting firm's recommendation, Henry created the power-sharing office of the chairman, which included Henry, Bill, Iacocca, and eventually a newcomer to the power circle, Phil Caldwell.

"It seemed like five guys were running the company at one time," Iacocca said.

Henry had been slowly maneuvering for years, nudging Iacocca out of the picture. His very deliberateness was a sign of respect—of fear of his underling.

"I don't know what happened, to be honest," Iacocca said. "You look back and say, 'Well, God dealt ya a pretty good hand.' But those days were tough. I don't like the way he did it. Every quarter he found something to change. And then Caldwell came in. For five years he kept giving the message that he wanted to make sure the power was spread. Henry was concerned that his family was so weak, and I was too strong and he wanted to decentralize."

The final meeting was on July 13, 1978, in Henry Ford II's office. It lasted 45 minutes. Bill Ford was in the room.

"He knew he had to fire me, but he just couldn't get around to doing it without Bill there," Iacocca recalled.

"I said, 'Jesus Christ it's awful. It's not fair, it's not right. And Bill starts crying. By the way we are still good friends with Martha and Bill. They never missed a year of sending me a Christmas card. They're good people.

"But it was one of those things where Henry made up his mind and nobody wanted to go against Henry. Henry had told Frank Murphy, 'It's either him or me,' and the board had to knuckle under.

"Well, I could understand that, but it shouldn't have gone that far. But he wanted to diffuse the power of the company.

"Henry said to me, 'My family will fuck it up. Look at them. They all drink too much. They're all getting fat. What the hell is going on? I'm working my ass off and they're having a free ride.'

"And then he told me: 'You'll run over them.'

"I said, 'No, Jesus, I'm a loyalist, Henry. In my 32 years with the company, why would I want all that bullshit? I came here as a trainee. You had confidence in me. We've had a good eight-year run as president. What the hell did I do wrong?'

"'Well,' he said, 'sometimes I don't like somebody.'"

That was the end of the meeting. Henry Ford II and Lee Iacocca never spoke again, although they did cross paths.

"He saw me once. It was with Katherine Graham at a *Newsweek* affair. He saw me and my wife, Mary, all dressed up. Here comes Henry. He sees me. I always wondered what would happen, and guess what? I just sat there and he ran away from me. He didn't want any contact.

"Listen, I wasn't much for carrying a grudge. We had a bad moment. That's past. First of all, I don't think about the past. We did a lot of stuff. We had a lot of good days.

"I never expected to be chairman. They have a [Ford family] chairman to this day, Bill Ford Jr. I was happy. We were making close to a billion dollars a year. We made $800 million that year. My mother said, 'What would they have done to you if the company had been doing poorly?'

"I wouldn't want to do it again—put my family through it. But it came over time. It came as an insidious wind. You knew that something was up. But I was made president in 1970 and I always said, 'Well, I lasted two terms, eight years. That was a pretty good tenure to be president.'"

"WHAT IF I HADN'T gotten fired? I wonder about my life. I wonder where I would have gone. I guess there were a lot of companies I talked to. I had a lot of friends, a lot of offers, but my heart was in the auto industry. I guess the big one was Lockheed. They wanted me, and International Paper wanted me. Airplanes and paper.

"Bill Hewlett of Hewlett and Packard nearly hired me."

Iacocca in the Chrysler financial crisis of the late 1970s and early 1980s is a compelling picture. It was a period of enormous tension in Highland Park. Both groups of crisis managers adopted the thinking and jargon that McNamara had created at Ford. Discussions always revolved around "the options." At Chrysler, the options for Iacocca were pretty grim.

"When I got to Chrysler, I asked Sperlich, 'Why aren't things better than they are? Jesus Christ, the place is bankrupt. Where's the money you talked about?'

"Those Chrysler guys had been good accountants. They weren't cooking the books, but lets say they weren't that far from it. They couldn't let it out in public how sick they were. The company was virtually bankrupt."

McNamara-style financial controls were nowhere to be found. It reminded Iacocca of the mess Henry II had found at Ford Motor Company when he took over in 1946.

"At Ford in the 1940s, Henry said everything was in bad shape. There were no controls. Purchasing was done in a hundred places. He said, 'We'd weigh the bills. There was too much detail to count.'

"When I went to Chrysler, everybody was doing his own thing. It wasn't coordinated. My wife said I went from the frying pan into the fire. I wondered how I got into this mess. Glenn White, who is still with me on the board at my foundation, was the general manager at Chrysler-Plymouth. He was the only survivor among the vice presidents I inherited.

"Holy shit, I had to get rid of everybody. A lot of them quit. They were in over their heads. They were scared. It was a mess. But we had Harold there. Dick Dauch, the manufacturing guy, turned out great.

He and Lutz fought at lot. I used to tell a story: 'I've been so lucky. God, you sent me Lutz, Dick Dauch, and Harold Sperlich, three Germans, all at one time. But boy are they tough to control.'

"Lutz would always say 'Don't say that. I'm not German, I'm Swiss.'

"They were all terrific guys."

In 1974, Ford Vice President Bill Bourke had asked Iacocca to meet Bob Lutz and talk to him about running Ford of Germany.

"Lutz was a guy from BMW, the motorcycle world. And he was a breath of fresh air. We got to be good friends. Then, of course, we went through a cycle and he got sideways at Ford. His wife called me one night when I was at Chrysler and said, 'Bob is unhappy—would you be willing to talk to him?' and I said 'Sure.'"

It was 1985. By then, Don Petersen was CEO at Ford.

"Don Petersen said, 'We didn't know what to do with Lutz anyway.' He said, 'In fact, you took him off my hands.'

"I said, 'Well, I still think he's a good car guy and I'm not trying to shake up the joint, but we need to get somebody in. Sperlich is running everything, and he's entrenched with the old Chrysler guys, and I need some help.'

"Sperlich was great with trucks. He did the Ram pickup and he did the minivan. We bought Jeep. The truck side was great, although I didn't know it would be 60 percent of the market.

"But Harold and Lutz were always at odds with each other. They thought one was better than the other. Then Harold quit on me. I still talk to him. Harold wrote me a really personal, sweet letter recently. Beautiful letter. We went through some rough times but all in all it was a helluva ride."

The early days at Chrysler were almost too much for Iacocca.

"I thought I was dying. Those were tough times, like getting ready for the Battle of Britain. It was pretty bad."

He brought over Gerry Greenwald from Ford to serve as his top financial officer.

"One day I said to Gerry, 'I don't know how we're doing, but I never see any money. Will I ever see any money? If I asked today for you to give me some cash where would you get it?'

"Gerry said, 'I could put together, lets see—I could scrape together a million dollars.'

"I said, 'You mean that's all we have?'

"'Right.'

"'Holy shit.'"

"'Suppliers are trying to get concessions and we don't have any money. Why do you ask?'"

"I said, 'I want to know how close we are to bankruptcy.'"

"I need $250 million every Friday," Greenwald told him. "Every week that's what we've got to do to cover what we owe suppliers and the payroll itself."

"I said, 'Shit, we *are* bankrupt. We just haven't told anybody.'

"I'll always remember that. It was a Friday afternoon and I said, 'God, I think I'm in over my head.' I said, 'Where am I going to get relief?'

"Riccardo started wondering what the government would say. Would it give us some tax credits, [or] whatever. We tried to blame it on the government. Then I heard about loan guarantees.

"I said, 'Do you guys in Congress know how many loan guarantees you have out there right now? Don't stop now. We've got 600,000 jobs on the line.'

"I did my homework. Once I told them, 'You senators who live over in Virginia, you put in the monorail with a $1 billion loan guarantee.'

"Someone advised me, 'Don't go there, that's a sacred cow.'

"In the end, we only won the Senate by four votes. I learned how representative government works—with Tip O'Neill at my side."

The Democratic Speaker of the House and Iacocca created a war room, with a map of every congressional district in America. The map listed the number of jobs that would be affected by a Chrysler collapse in each district.

"We covered everything, including dealers and mechanics. In Michigan, we had 100,000 jobs. And we had a lot of jobs in big states like New York and California. We got their attention in a hurry."

But Iacocca was able to gain support in the House of Representatives by winning over districts in places such as Idaho and Utah. Those states didn't have big manufacturing plants, but they had plenty of dealers and mechanics that depended on Chrysler's continued existence.

"We won the house. That was an experience. It taught me one thing—I never wanted to go into politics. I wouldn't touch it. When people talked about me running for president, my mother said, 'You gotta be nuts. Don't even get near it.'"

LEE IACOCCA WAS always a general manager, not a specialist. Marketing, engineering, finance, he did it all. It seemed only natural that he would introduce cross functionality at Chrysler toward the end of his career. It was essentially Soichiro Honda's concept and it had come to the American auto industry—to Chrysler—via Bob Lutz and Lee Iacocca.

"It was what we had to do at that time—cross function," Iacocca said. "Lutz and François Castaing came to us with the idea. So we quit the sequential-stuff bullshit. Before, we'd take a product and hand it off. The engineers would hand it off to manufacturing. Manufacturing would hand it off to marketing. Lutz and Castaing asked, 'Why aren't we doing cross function?'

"So we cross-functioned the minivan, our bread and butter. And guess who became head of the team? Tom Gale. He had responsibility not only for the styling, but for everything. He had to run that team. He not only did the planning, but the engineering and the manufacturing.

"They had the ad agency in for the cycle plan three years ahead. Under the old system they called the ad guys and said, 'We've got a great car, now name it and tell us how are you going to market it.' But with cross functioning those guys went to all the meetings for three or four years. They got to know each other. So we were breeding good general managers and they turned out to be our best guys. Tom Stallkamp, Gale. I said when I left Chrysler, 'What am I leaving behind here?' . . . On the design side, Gale, he was number one in the world. Stallkamp in procurement. Best in the world. And marketing? Number one in the world with Jim Holden.

"Manufacturing, we had Steve Scharf, an old-timer who got along with Dauch. Dauch was so brilliant in manufacturing. There is a lot of hype about him, but he's brilliant. That's why he is making $100 million a year today [as head of American Axle & Manufacturing Inc.]

"I met Dick Dauch through Roger Penske. Penske had a program training manufacturing people in dealerships. They would have them work for a year in sales and marketing and Roger Penske—who owned dealerships—was one of Dick Dauch's teachers. Penske sent Dick Dauch to me and I said, 'Holy shit, I need manufacturing help, to hell with your marketing training. We'll get to that later, Dick.'

"Dauch did a helluva job. He's such a tough guy, a former Purdue fullback. But he was great with people. I would walk through a plant with that son-of-a-bitch Dauch, and they'd say, 'Hi ya Dick,' and he'd say, 'How are the kids?' and he'd name the kids—and I'd ask, 'How do you remember all this shit?'

"He'd say, 'It's my management team and I get to know them.'"

"IT WAS A REAL TOUGH DECISION" not to appoint Bob Lutz as his successor at Chrysler, Iacocca said. "The board was all split up. I had a fractured board. I'm not blaming them, but it almost got to be Lutz. . . . Actually, I wanted to bring Greenwald back. I thought, 'Those are the guys who brought me here—Greenwald, Steve Miller, and Sperlich.'"

Greenwald, the former vice chairman, had left to lead an unsuccessful buyout of United Airlines.

"One of our board members said of Greenwald, 'When a guy is disloyal, you don't make him CEO.' I said, 'What would you have done?' It was a function of timing in his career. So we said, 'Lets look and see what is available.'

"I don't get into this anymore, but I think the biggest mistake of my life was hiring Bob Eaton. I didn't know at the time that he was that much a weakling. GM sent him to Europe to be trained. The other guy that headed Europe, [Opel Chairman Lou] Hughes. That's the guy we were supposed to get.

"Anyway I couldn't sell Lutz to the board. We had a couple of guys who said, 'He's not right for the job.' I won't get into why they said that."

Iacocca did have his own issues with Lutz—especially when Iacocca tried to negotiate a broad cooperation with Fiat in the early 1990s.

"Lutz had said publicly one time 'Why in the hell is Lee talking about doing a joint venture with Fiat? Why would we do that? We must be crap. Fiat makes some of the worst cars in the world.'"

Fiat chairman and patriarch Gianni Agnelli was enraged.

"Gianni Agnelli called and said, 'Lee, does Bob Lutz work for you?'

"'Yeah.'

"'Well, if we're talking about a joint venture why would he bring Fiat's name up publicly like that?'

"I said, 'I'll talk to him.' Now I had done a lot of press conferences, and there were things I was sorry I had said, . . . [but] there were a lot of things like that. Lutz was a candidate, no question about that. But the board said Lutz was the wrong person."

Then Iacocca recruited Eaton.

"I made the mistake of taking lots of people's word on how good Eaton was. But he had no experience. He wasn't an operating-type person. He was a staff guy all his life. That was the problem. But those were the candidates.

"Ben Bidwell. You gotta remember Bidwell was a candidate to take my job. But he got a bad report on his heart, and it was bad. He said, 'I'm getting out before I die.'

"The guy I really talked to at length was Roger Penske. He was interested, but he had bought Detroit Diesel, and he said, 'If I come in I want to bring my guys. I want to bring 15 executives in.'

"I said, 'Holy shit, Roger, our executives are pretty good.' So the very top candidates were gone. That's why we had to open the book on outside, and I don't think we did our homework on Eaton."

"I THINK LUTZ would tell you this—I gave him a lot of room. I had him on a long leash. He's the guy who wanted to do the Viper and he had to sell me on it—he and Shelby. And after I left they did the Prowler.

"I said, 'Hey guys, that's play period time. You got to get your quality on your bread-and-butter cars straightened out.' But there was nothing wrong with those image cars. Vipers helped put Dodge dealers on the map.

"But Bob Lutz is a pretty impressive guy. I had the two Bobs there and little Bob got eaten up by big Bob. De facto, Lutz was the guy running the company, not Bob Eaton. Jesus Christ, it turned out fine. It gave Lutz the chance to run the place really."

IACOCCA AND SPERLICH dreamed up "Global Motors" while Iacocca was between jobs in 1978 and had time to muse. The idea was to combine American, Japanese, and European manufacturers and thus have an entity capable of standing up to General Motors and Ford.

"I always wanted to try to merge with a couple of people . . . to get ready for the next cyclical downturn. I think about how prophetic Gianni Agnelli was 25 years ago. He said there would be 10 companies because of high capital investment, the world so big, emerging markets, China. He said, 'I don't think there will be 10 left and I'd like the one in Europe to be Fiat because we own diddly.'" Iacocca agreed with the Fiat patriarch.

"You didn't need two French companies; you didn't need two Swedish companies, Volvo and Saab. You didn't need them. But you've got to have somebody to back you up. You need a bank. I used to say to the Japanese guys, 'Jesus Christ, Mitsubishi, you own the Mitsubishi Bank.' Deutsche Bank practically runs Mercedes and I always said, 'If I only had Citibank.' Maybe I should have bought a goddam bank, but its not allowed in the U.S. You can't own a bank and be a big corporation."

Daimler-Benz in effect perpetrated Iacocca's vision of Global Motors by acquiring Chrysler in 1998 and then taking control of Mitsubishi Motors in 2000.

"Juergen Schrempp was still working on it, though I think he's given up on Mitsubishi. But our idea, Harold Sperlich's and mine, was that we've got a big market in Europe and that is where the upscale cars are. Then we could get a Japanese partner to teach us more about quality, assembly line quality.

"I always had my eyes on the Japanese. You couldn't get into Toyota—it was too big. So was Nissan. But I got close to Honda over the years. I got to know Soichiro Honda well, but whether we could have merged there, I don't know.

"At Ford, about 1965, Sidney Weinberg of Goldman Sachs set up a meeting with Henry. They said they had a client called Honda and maybe we'd be interested in buying them and getting them on the cheap.

"I said, 'Well, shit, that's an interesting idea. And I remember Will Scott, one of our product planners said, 'It's a good buy, but why are we getting into motorcycles? They aren't safe. Why take on the liability of motorcycles?'

"I said, 'Yeah, but young kids start with motorcycles.'"

Iacocca had become head of Ford's global car business by then, biding his time until he became president of the company.

"We were studying the youth market—get them young, get them when they start with a bicycle and go up. Honda Motor was doing all kinds of things. But it was about that time that I asked, 'Is it worth trying to buy them?'

"They had a little car and it was so bad. Now Honda makes some of the best cars in the world. But their first car was such a piece of shit that I said, 'We don't have to worry about this guy. They should have stuck to motorcycles.' Still, buying them was a way to gain additional business—to get to the youth market when they buy their first pumpkin.

"Soichiro Honda and I hit it off well. He liked me and I liked him and every time I went to Tokyo I made sure I went to see him. I got to know him. He was always in a white coat, was always in the shop and doing something, like the first Henry Ford. He was a tinkerer. He was like an upstart."

"I used to think of all of Tokyo as a big Ginzalike area. But Honda had this beautiful estate with a lot of foliage right in the middle of Tokyo. He had us there to celebrate the deal we never did, the deal for the front-wheel-drive powerpacks. His house was pretty elaborate and he threw a big party. I remember there were stations set up for the different kinds of Japanese food, one stop for the tempura and another for the sushi and so on. The fish were caught that morning.

"He gave me the cloisonné vase and I gave him the first automatic-transmission Mustang II. We went out to the front of his house and a big van pulled up with the car, a white car, with an automatic transmission built in Japan."

Iacocca would return the favor, eventually inviting Honda to his house in Michigan.

"I remember once we had seven or eight tables set up in my house in Bloomfield Hills. I had a wonderful time with him."

THE OTHER JAPANESE COMPANIES were different, including Chrysler's long-time partner, Mitsubishi Motors.

"Mitsubishi was always pissed off. They helped wreck us in the war. Tomio Kubu, the former head of Mitsubishi, was a designer on the Zero, and they weren't at the head table on cars. The powerhouse was Toyota and Nissan, of course, and Honda came out of left field and taught them all a lot about cars."

NOT LONG AFTER he joined Chrysler, Iacocca tried to merge the company with Volkswagen. Toni Schmucker, a former Ford executive in Europe, was running Volkswagen.

"Toni said, 'We'll have to merge, Lee. Volkswagen and Chrysler.' And then we looked at the fact that he's going broke and I'm going broke and we decided maybe we're putting two losers together and we should break off the negotiations right here."

The company that Iacocca wanted for Chrysler was von Kuenheim's BMW.

"I once tried to merge with him," Iacocca recalled. "I admired him. He was a tough son of a bitch, but he was a great guy. He made BMW, no question about it."

Iacocca once accompanied Henry Ford II on a trip to visit Herbert Quandt, whereupon the Deuce made one of his efforts to persuade the family to sell its crown jewel.

"Henry could open the doors of all the jet-setters like the Quandt family. But they weren't selling."

"THE SUV REVOLUTION was started when I bought the Cherokee [with Chrysler's 1987 acquisition of American Motors and Jeep] and spent a billion dollars to build the Jefferson Avenue plant in Detroit. But I don't claim credit for SUVs.

"If you'd told me that from 1987, when we bought it, until now, in 17 years, that instead of just our Grand Cherokee four-wheel-drive off-road [vehicle] the industry would be selling 4 1/2 to 5 million [SUVs a year] I'd tell you that you are out of your goddam mind.

"There is no justification for this kind of popularity. The minivan has all the attributes. But now people just want iron. They want safety. They believe the bigger Hummer you get, the longer you are going to live. Other than a woman having a command position, like the minivan, what's an SUV for? It pollutes. It has a big engine. It can't get fuel economy.

"You say, 'Well people like it.' But if you had told me everybody was going to have an SUV including Porsche and now Volvo I'd say, 'You gotta be nuts.'

"We were the catalyst, but do I want to claim credit for that? No. I don't mind taking credit for the minivan team because we started with nothing. We took a million dollars and an idea and a little bit of research. But SUVs took on a life of their own and I don't understand it.

"Catalysts. That's all we were. The Cherokee and American Motors."

IACOCCA SAYS HE DOESN'T spend much time reflecting on his career.

"But I often count my blessings. Financially, things turned out terrific. I'm well-off and stuff. But when people, say, 'What's your legacy?' I say, 'My legacy is my two daughters and seven grandchildren.' And the research center."

The Chrysler Technology Center was dedicated in 1991.

"When I retired *Forbes* magazine said this is what you will be remembered for. The rest doesn't matter. The cars come and go. But we built the center at a time when we didn't have anything under one roof. I think the most sensational part was putting a little mini–pilot plant right there in the same place with all the engineers.

"At the opening, Bob Galvan, Motorola's chairman, came and said, 'You don't even know what you've done here. You won't know where it's coming from, but this place alone, all under one roof, will make you 10 percent more profits in total forever. The guys won't figure out how to account for it. But having all these guys under one roof, manufacturing, purchasing, engineering, is a remarkable thing.'

"And he was right. We got efficiency that we never knew we had. We were so scattered. Ford has a pretty good engineering center in Dearborn and, of course, there is the tech center at General Motors. But we had nothing like that. If a guy was on a car program—we actually tracked this—the efficiency depended on how much snow was on the freeway because they had to travel. Some engineering guys had to go to 15 or 16 different locations to get organized on a program. I said, 'Shit, this has got to stop.'

"It was a crapshoot, but if you asked, 'What did you do at Chrysler?', I'd say probably more than anything the research center."

"MY HEROES WERE Harry Truman, Churchill, Joe DiMaggio, Leonardo da Vinci, Ben Franklin. I read so much about them. I tried to emulate them even without knowing it. I learned more reading how scared Winston Churchill was to make a speech, and how nervous he got, and why he wrote down his ad libs. I thought that was sort of redundant, but you've got to do that. I got a lot of tips from him—a great communicator in dark times. He had a turn of phrase. People respond to language that they understand.

"People asked, 'How did you get such good press?' Well, first of all, I talked to the press. I never turned down any kind of interview. I never got up there and said, 'I can't see them,' or 'No comment.'

"I never said, 'I want to see them only when I got good reports. Bad reports, I wish the bastards would go away.'"

Iacocca may be by far the most famous student the Dale Carnegie public-speaking course had ever had. Many thousands of businesspeople took the Carnegie course because of Iacocca's unsolicited endorsements.

"I told our guys that. I said, 'Tom Gale, you've got to be able to express yourself. You're a terrific stylist, but you never could communicate how well you're doing. Go to a Carnegie class. Have an outline, make sure you're well-prepared. Make a speech. Tell people what you've done. They taught me to get out of my shell.'

"Believe it or not, when I first started, being an engineer all my life, it was not easy for me to talk to strangers. It was tough when they put me on the phone to sell fleet cars in Philadelphia. But you learn from the guys around you. Those guys were old veterans that went back with the Ford Motor Company to the time when Henry Ford was running it. Neat old guys. You learn from them and what I learned more than anything else was communication."

Iacocca turned out to be a man who could deliver a message.

"Everybody told me that. McNamara told me, 'You communicate so well, Lido, that I can't depend on the sweetness of your voice any more. You want to ask me for $100 million for something? I want you to write in 25 words or less why the hell you want that. And if you can't put it I writing, you haven't thought it out.'

"He'd keep his word on that, by the way. You had to write it down and then when you asked for the $100 million, you not only had to write down what you wanted it for, you had to give him two options.

"He always did that. He'd say, 'Okay, there are five things I'd like to get across.' He'd go: 'Number one' and then go right down the list. He'd say, 'I'm going to give you five good reasons why you don't know what in the hell you're talking about' and then he'd tick them off. When I tried that, I couldn't remember what the hell my fourth point was."

But it was Charlie Beacham, not McNamara, who sent Iacocca to Dale Carnegie.

"McNamara and those guys, they weren't very good at charisma and talking themselves. They never got on their feet much. They were uncomfortable. But Charlie Beacham talked with the guys who buy and sell our cars, the dealers. For McNamara and his guys, going to a dealer convention was like getting a root canal. They didn't like it. They didn't grow up that way. They were typical control officers and that's what they knew."

Iacocca was different. He was interested in people as much as cars or financial numbers.

"I studied engineering at Lehigh University, but when it came to my electives I took abnormal psychology for four years. I dealt with deranged people at the state hospital. I went to school all those years to learn about nuts and bolts. You've got to get into human relations, industrial relations, customer relations."

Iacocca's public personae ultimately led to the TV commercials.

"People ask me all the time about that, but I didn't want to do the commercials. But the ad agency, Kenyon and Eckhardt, said, 'You're stuck. You've got to give the message out there. People will look at you and say 'Well, this guy has got to go back and make sure those goddam lousy Chrysler cars don't leak and rattle so we'll believe him.' And they sold me on it. I was uncomfortable at first.

"I have 61 of them on one tape, 61 commercials I made through thick and thin. I thought later it probably helped the company to be out there. People said, 'We'll try his car, just give it a test drive.' That was all we were asking. But you know, I gave up my privacy and it was a pain in the ass."

The immense fame made it a harder for Iacocca to run Chrysler.

"But I like to believe it was the right thing to do. I didn't want to be before the cameras. My job was to make sure the cars were right; get the quality problem straightened out; make the dealers happy and take care of the servicing. But I didn't enjoy that much being recognized in restaurants. People bother the shit out of you for a picture or a signature while you're eating. But I think it turned out okay."

INDEED, IACOCCA INVENTED the kind of talk that now runs rampant in American business. He didn't dream up all of the clichés and catch-phrases, though he is responsible for his share of them.

"Level playing field" was his handiwork. And if he did not invent the term "bean counters" to bedevil corporate accountants, he certainly popularized it.

His manner of expression changed the way business talked to itself. He worked with rich, visceral metaphors. His plain-talking style was among the reasons he struck such a chord with the American public in the 1980s. Business people began to imitate him.

Today, vivid Iacocca-style imagery is heard wherever managers gather, though even the most compelling metaphors quickly congeal into cliché. Today, businesspeople talk about what you "bring to the table" and having "a full plate."

Difficult tasks are "like nailing Jell-O to the wall" or "drinking from a fire hydrant." Something easy "isn't rocket science" or "isn't brain surgery." Breaking new ground is "pushing the envelope" or "thinking outside the box." Going to market is "skating where the puck's going to be." Studying an issue in detail is "drilling down to the granular level."

It's all Iacoccaspeak. It's complex issues conveyed with striking clarity, and it became the way to communicate in business.

It was far different from how McNamara talked. The other constituency at Ford invented a whole other kind of business incantation: the technocrat verbiage from which sprang such modern chestnuts as "customer-centric proactive solutions" and "value propositions."

IACOCCA COINED THE PHRASE "level playing field" to describe the built-in advantage he and others felt Japanese carmakers had in the 1980s and 1990s.

"Level playing field, 1982. It was simply a way to make a speech. It was because of our income tax and their value-added tax. Taxation was different, and the rate of the Bank of Japan, and they get money for 0 to 1 percent, and they control the yen. I wasn't bashing the Japanese people, I was bashing MITI [Japan's Ministry of Trade and Industry].

"By the way, it turned out to be true. They had a 10-year recession because it was run by the bureaucrats and the financial institutions had trouble. When you have an agency like that, an arm of the government running the thing, it will eventually catch up with you.

"They respected me in Japan. My book sold 600,000 copies in Japan. They liked me. I talked to the U.S. Chamber of Commerce here and they want to talk about my Japan bashing. I go to the Tokyo Chamber of Commerce and they give me a standing ovation because they learn from us.

"Steve Scharf once went there, and as he sat in the lobby of the Osaka Hotel he saw some people reading my book. He asked them why and they said, 'Because we go through life and we can never speak up the way he does. It's not in our culture. But we respect and admire that you can take anybody on in the United States, anybody, and say 'We've got to clean up this mess.'"

IACOCCA WAS PROBABLY the greatest product packager the industry had ever seen, grabbing parts off the shelf, fitting them onto an existing vehicle platform, then performing some wonder with the sheet metal to make it all seem fresh.

"I had to do it with the K-car platform at Chrysler," he said. "The K-car became the platform for the minivan and for the LeBaron. We had LeBarons up the kazoo. We kept stretching it. We tried to build big luxury cars on the one type of platform and we had a big run of that.

"But without the front-wheel-drive package we couldn't have done the minivan. The fact that the Chrysler minivan would still be getting 30, 40 percent of the world market 20 years later—and everybody's got one—is unbelievable."

Chrysler was first with the garageable van in 1984, but the Japanese had been widely expected to overtake Chrysler in minivans within a few years. They never did, though.

"The Japanese didn't know about American values in the late '80s. But the other guys in Detroit did. That's what amazes me. General Motors and Ford came out at the same time with a minivan and they've had about six generations over the years. Now Ford, more than anybody, is catching up. GM hasn't done it yet. Ford finally copied the goddam Chrysler almost across the board.

"It took them 20 years to do it, mind you. It was a case of 'not invented here. Therefore, little Chrysler can't tell us how to do a car.' And they sat it out. They conceded the market.

"The upscale Chrysler Town and Country was designed in my driveway in Italy. I'll never forget it. Joe Campana, our marketing guy, said 'I think we can sell 1,000 a year, 1,000 planning volume.' That was what he thought the market was for the Town and Country. They sold at their peak 100,000 at $10,000 gross per unit. And that saved the company. It also made us vulnerable." The huge profits made Chrysler an irresistible target.

"Remember that when the Germans came and bought us they only showed $10 billion cash. Twelve billion was to be floated for the damn company. They bought the company. They *stole* the company. Would I have done the merger? Yes. But we should have bought them! The other guy ended up owning it! We had this market here.

"Mercedes? How much synergy can there be? Some, but there can't be a helluva lot."

Daimler-Benz's takeover of Chrysler in 1998 pissed off Lee Iacocca.

"I fought so hard to keep a Big 3 and all of a sudden it was gone," he said. "I couldn't predict we'd have this culture clash heard around the world between the Germans and the Americans.

"I like Dieter (Zetsche). I just got a letter from him yesterday, in fact. He's done a helluva good job in a short time. But the rest of them . . . well. I said, 'It would be nice, Dieter, to get an American or two and keep 'em and put 'em. . . . and he says, 'Well, that's for other people to decide.'"

Iacocca believes the feeling inside DaimlerChrysler today is that if you are American you are lousy.

"You can't do that. You should look at everybody. And, by the way, they suffered for it. Look how long it has been—the merger and takeover—whatever it's called. But, yeah, I was upset. Jesus.

"It's a good company, no question about it. But they should have kept it an American imprint. It's not in the S&P 500. It's a foreign company controlled by foreigners. It's a German company."

Iacocca had been deeply criticized a couple of years before the merger. He had tried to take over Chrysler in league with Kirk Kerkorian.

He is not apologetic.

"Eaton, the bastard, said 'This company is not for sale.'

"Well, I wanted to do it. Kerkorian had the money. But they didn't come up with the financing. They didn't have it ready. There should have been a management buyout. But Daimler-Benz bought them out.

"What got me mad was that they in effect bought out Eaton and the top guys. They made them rich. Those guys got $50 million? It was penny ante to the Germans. And off the top Eaton got $100 million. So why wouldn't he sell, the son of a bitch. There was no loyalty to the employees or anything. We should have been at the head table at that merger."

In September 1946, Lee Iacocca was a 21-year-old trainee working at Ford's body-engineering building in Dearborn. He was sitting at his desk one day detailing the design of a clutch spring when out of the corner of his eye he saw two men approach. One was Henry Ford— The First. The other was Charles Lindbergh. Henry Ford and Lucky

Lindy . . . and Lee Iacocca. The two men stopped at Iacocca's table and hovered over the young engineer for a moment.

"Henry Ford was escorting Colonel Lindbergh around. I was scared shitless. I was wearing a student engineer badge and everyone knew that Henry Ford didn't like students."

The old man asked what Iacocca was doing.

"Nothing," replied the young man.

"What's that?" Mr. Ford asked, pointing to the mechanical drawing Iacocca was laboring over.

"I told them what I was working on. They just nodded and went on to the next desk. I only saw him that one time."

Henry Ford died the following March.

No one spanned the history of the auto industry like Lee Iacocca. He was surely the only man to have worked in the same auto company at the same time as both the original Henry Ford and the young man who designed the 2004 Car of the Year in the United States, the Chrysler 300.

Gilles had joined Chrysler as a 22-year-old stylist in 1992, the year Iacocca retired as chairman. One day in his final year Iacocca passed through the Chrysler styling studio with Bob Lutz to see what the designers were up to. The young Gilles was among them. Iacocca paused briefly over Gilles' desk to catch his own glimpse of the future. He nodded, then moved on.

The torch had been passed.

Epilogue

G reatness doesn't roll up neatly, like a carpet. The six men who dominated the automotive industry after World War II had trouble letting go of their formal positions as heads of auto companies. They meddled, even when they promised not to—even when they fully intended not to. They sat on boards of directors or supervisory boards where their presence cowed and frightened successors.

Soichiro Honda set the best example. He didn't have to retire in 1973, but he did—in part because he had begun to agrue with the young engineers he so valued perhaps to the detriment of the company.

As one of his last acts, Henry Ford II had killed plans for a front-wheel-drive minivan that could have benefited Ford for two decades.

Lee Iacocca had too much pent-up ambition to drift gracefully into his golden years. He delayed his retirement several times so that his name really did come to stand for "I am chairman of Chrysler Corporation always."

In 1995, Iacocca had become party to billionaire Kirk Kerkorian's misguided attempt to buy control of Chrysler, seeing it as a chance to strap on the guns once again. Kerkorian was Chrysler's largest shareholder and was angered that the stock price had languished while the company sat on a huge cash pile.

In April 1995, Kerkorian's Tracinda Corporation announced plans to acquire the 90 percent of Chrysler's stock it did not already own. The shocking part of the announcement was that Iacocca would join

Tracinda as a substantial investor. As the viability of Kerkorian's bid faded, so did Iacocca's reputation in Detroit. He was viewed as a traitor and a scoundrel who was trying to destroy the company he had saved 15 years earlier. His standing in Motown only began to recover when it became plain that the 1998 "merger of equals" between Daimler-Benz and Chrysler had in fact been nothing other than a German takeover.

In 1993, BMW manufacturing boss Bernd Pischetsrieder replaced Eberhard von Kuenheim as BMW's management board chairman, but some BMW executives saw Pischetsrieder as a CEO dominated by his predecessor.

They felt that von Kuenheim, who ran BMW for 23 years, simply couldn't bring himself to cede power when he retired in May 1993. Indeed, he didn't have to as long as the Quandt family, which controlled BMW, put its complete trust in him.

As head of Volkswagen, Piëch tended to overreach. He was surrounded by too many yes men who could not prevent his Rolls-Royce blunder and his controversial 1993 hiring of General Motors purchasing boss Jose Ignacio Lopez. The hard-charging Lopez was later indicted by German authorities for taking secret GM documents with him to VW.

The mistakes were pure Piëch. His genius was not in his short-term cunning, but his long-term vision—his refusal to be swayed by the usual forces. Certainly Piëch had the longest-range vision of any of the six men who created the modern auto industry. He thought in terms of decades. He saw his work as a continuation of his grandfather's. As a boy, he had watched the family's sports-car company rise from the ashes of World War II, and he saw no reason why the Volkswagen name could not strike at the heart of Mercedes-Benz. Piëch could not be embarrassed in the pursuit of great goals.

The late life miscalculations were natural phenomena—excess energy being discharged, like blue sparks off the dynamo of their careers. These were proud, driven men, constitutionally unable; they could return to obscurity, but could not switch off their intellects or their enthusiasm. To expect them to go quietly was asking too much.

Their influence and ideas lived on well into the new century. Soichiro Honda is the model for China's Young Tigers—the scrappy start-ups led by boisterous Honda-like entrepreneurs trying to be the first since Honda to launch a successful auto company from scratch.

Henry Ford II's influence carried on in the new millennium. His nephew Bill Ford's decision in 2001 to take matters of a fumbling Ford Motor Company into his own hands was inspired by his uncle's brave actions in the 1940s. No third-generation scion of an industrial family had achieved what Henry II had. Without his example, the fourth generation of Fords would have lacked the verve to step in so forcefully.

Von Kuenheim's BMW never really lost momentum, even in the worst of the Rover times. And the great man survived his role in the affair of "The English Patient." The new Mini that came from the Rover experiment was wildly successful, from the start and ensured BMW's Rover losses would be wiped out within a few years.

Towering BMW was a monument to von Kuenheim. What he had constructed over 23 years had been built to last. But this was also reflected, in a bittersweet way, by the many leaders of auto companies in 2005 whom had been discovered and promoted by von Kuenheim at BMW.

"They all came from my school," he said. "On one hand I am very proud and on the other very sad. BMW lost capacity and very capable men."

Iacocca fought on in his own way, still lusting for power, yet secure in his standing, especially considering the way things were turning out for DaimlerChrysler. By 2005, the Chrysler he saved a quarter-century earlier was out-performing its two great rivals once again. It had been given new life by the Germans, but his intrepid leadership still seemed to hover over the place—like a revisiting spirit.

And Lido's legacy endured in other ways. Carlos Ghosn's Nissan recovery was modeled on the miracle Iacocca performed at Chrysler.

Iacocca himself acknowledged his disciple: "The guy from France, I didn't know him, but he did a hell of a job with Nissan and that environment you play in with the keiretsu."

The eighty-year-old Iacocca didn't approve of everything he saw in the modern industry, even some of the things he was responsible for. He thought the sport-utility vehicle vogue was ridiculous. And he didn't care much for the 2005 Mustang.

"The new Mustang that's coming out now—I don't like it. I'm hung up on the long hood and short deck and they're hung up on the fastback."

But the Chrysler minivan still dominated the segment it created. And the engineering culture Iacocca and Lutz assembled at the No. 3 U.S. automaker kept pouring out products that put GM and Ford on the defensive.

Iacocca believed with all his heart, though, that selling out to Daimler-Benz was utterly wrong, the worst mistake Chrysler could have made. Still, he admired Dieter Zetsche, the German Daimler sent to do Iacocca's old job. He called Zetsche often, congratulating him, for instance, on the new 300.

At 72, Lutz labors at General Motors, longing for his last great box office success—a Chrysler 300–like success of his own. Three years after being hired by Rick Wagoner the question was being asked around Detroit: Where is the Lutz magic?

Yet there was no way to measure it in one new model or another. The answer was not in the Buick LaCrosse or Chevy Cobalt or Pontiac G6; it was in the successors to those cars, the Lutz-inspired young engineers and designers who would develop those cars, and the systems and procedures he was setting up at GM.

In 2005, Piëch was under assault for the luxury-car strategy he left behind at Volkswagen in 2002 and for the group's financial trouble. Yet his acquisition of Bentley—his supposed lesson in humility—was doing far better than the Rolls-Royce brand that eluded him in 1998.

And 25 years after he had introduced all-wheel-drive on passenger cars, Americans were turning to all-wheel-drive sedans in record numbers. It was a final vindication of Piëch's long-ago Quattro vision. It was classic Piëch—a man who looked deeper into the future than his contemporaries. He was undaunted by disappointing sales of the Phaeton. VW's day would come. Sooner or later it would become a luxury-car producer in good standing. He was sure of his redemption and he calmly offered evidence: "Audi's image in 1971 was less than Opel," he said.

Time had ground down some of the differences between the men. Iacocca's feelings for Henry Ford II had even softened some over the years. And he seemed to regret—without quite saying so—his role in preventing Lutz from becoming the CEO of Chrysler in 1992.

Von Kuenheim, too, was wistful about Lutz. "It was a pity he left," he said.

But when Lutz was at BMW he felt von Kuenheim "was constantly looking over my shoulder and wondering if I was getting too big for my britches."

"I viewed myself as a member of his team, but maybe he didn't," Lutz said. "In terms of his behavior toward me, it was the polar opposite of Rick Wagoner's. It was a little rocky back then, but Von Kuenheim and I get along extremely well now."

The six were contradictory in disposition. They were a blend of faults and virtues. Letting go of leadership was hard to do. It was not just the intoxication of power they missed, it was a deep-rooted sense of duty they still felt—the obligation to meddle, to fix what was broken and leave be what was not. What had begun as a simple matter of personal success had become a greater cause, a grander purpose.

That controversy followed them into retirement was no real surprise. The six men would always have their reviewers and their detractors. Although great communicators, yet they were often misunderstood. But if they had been faultless they would not have been great. The dust they raised during their careers could not be expected to settle for years.

381

Careers

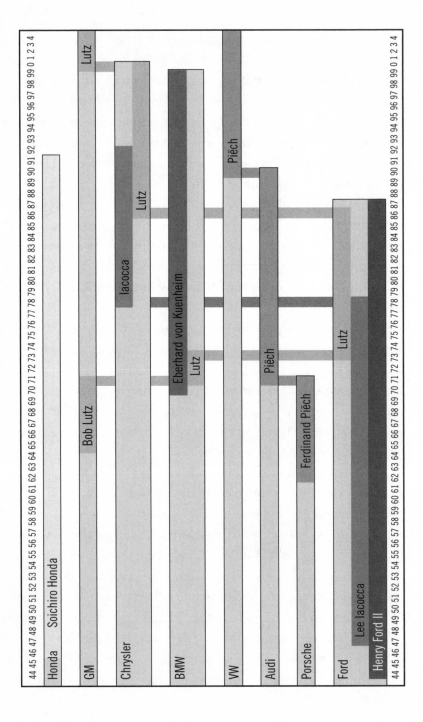

Index

384